Twentieth Century Mystics and Sages

Anne Bancroft spent the early part of her life in the Quaker village of Jordans. While her four children were growing up she became a lecturer in comparative religion and at the same time began her own quest for spiritual understanding. Over the years she has found strength and inspiration in Buddhism and a deepening understanding of western mysticism. She is the author of several other books on religion and mysticism including *Origins of the Sacred* (Arkana 1987) and *Weavers of Wisdom: Women Mystics of the Twentieth Century* (Arkana 1989).

TWENTIETH CENTURY
MYSTICS AND SAGES

ANNE BANCROFT

ARKANA

ARKANA

Published by the Penguin Group
27 Wrights Lane, London W8 5TZ, England
Viking Penguin Inc., 40 West 23rd Street, New York, New York 10010, USA
Penguin Books Australia Ltd, Ringwood, Victoria, Australia
Penguin Books Canada Ltd, 2801 John Street, Markham, Ontario, Canada L3R 1B4
Penguin Books (NZ) Ltd, 182–190 Wairau Road, Auckland 10, New Zealand

Penguin Books Ltd, Registered Offices: Harmondsworth, Middlesex, England

First published by William Heinemann Ltd 1976
Published in Arkana Books 1989
1 3 5 7 9 10 8 6 4 2

Printed and bound in Great Britain by
Cox & Wyman Ltd, Reading

Contents

Bibliographical references and "further reading" will be found at the end of each section.

Preface

"Whoever *knows* that he knows must be amazed," says Alan Watts. And it is just this sense of existential wonder that forms the background to this book. "Who am I?" and "What is this world that I am in?" are the questions that arise from the awareness that I am. To find the answers, people feel a need to go beyond words and to *experience* the truth about themselves. It is this longing for real meaning that has led many to look for guidance from the mystics and sages who, consequently, have leaped into prominence.

It is the purpose of this book to present a number of such modern spiritual leaders from all religions and from none —representatives of new paths to religious truth. Those chosen are all full-time exponents of the spiritual life. They are not philosophers or poets who have a mystical streak, but are people who have devoted their lives to imparting inspired knowledge or to living a holy life. They have not always succeeded. Sometimes they have been given too much publicity and adulation and have succumbed to it, or sometimes they have set themselves too far apart from humanity. But what they have to say and how they have lived their lives is the concern of this book. It seeks to convey the teachings of some of the best-known mystics and sages, and it is less concerned with the groups of disciples who have formed themselves around those masters. Care has also been taken not to include the mini-mystics who like to scramble about on the periphery of experience. There is a form of intellectual insight that moves many theologians to take up their pens, and which provides a background of discussion for all sorts of conferences and weekend schools. This pleasant skirmishing often produces good talk, but has little to do with real insight and has its rightful place in other books.

Three criteria have governed the choice of subjects for this book. One criterion has been integrity of approach; another has been the international reputation of the sage; the third has been the originality of his teaching. Not all subjects have all three qualifications—some, for instance, are considerably better known than others. But all have a certain quality of intensity about them that makes them at least worth reading. There is not a great deal of difference between a mystic and a sage, but enough to call them by different names. A mystic seeks direct experience of, and communion with, the divine; his whole life centers around this purpose. He tends to be solitary and to communicate his understanding through books. A sage, on the other hand, is a wise man who is perceptive, discerning, and thoughtful about life in general. He, too, pivots himself on the wish to experience the truth of existence and he, too, may write a lot of books. But he tends to be more outward-turned than the mystic and more taken up with teaching and advising; he originates methods and attracts disciples.

The selection of the subjects in this book is a personal one and several other selections, equally representative, could have been made; they might have included such mystics as Simone Weil, Aurobindo, Evelyn Underhill, and Sai Baba. It was with regret that a halt had to be made, and the present selection is not intended to be definitive.

The mystery of man's own internal identity—who and what he is when he apprehends himself as "I"—has turned out to be the central concern of most of the mystics and sages, and the biggest snag to placing all these highly different personal teachings and philosophies within the covers of one book has been the many interpretations of this central word "I." They range from Ramana Maharshi's, in which he points out that the feeling of "I," when detached from body and mind, is itself the supreme Consciousness; to Alan Watts's "I" which, he believes, cannot be found apart from experience ("you don't think thoughts any more than you hear hearing or smell smelling"). Because the nature of "I" is regarded in so many different ways, the subjects have been grouped. Cross-references can then be followed easily and the discoveries of one mystic can amplify another. Consequently, a short preface to each group precedes it (except for Mother Theresa, who needs no introduction), so that the reader can have some idea of the seas into which he is about to plunge.

Photographs are included of all the mystics and sages with the exception of two who prefer not to be photographed.

Anne Bancroft

Acknowledgments

The following sources are gratefully acknowledged:
Those Barren Leaves, Aldous Huxley, Chatto and Windus, Harper and Row, Publishers, Inc.; *Eyeless in Gaza,* Aldous Huxley, Chatto and Windus, Harper and Row, Publishers, Inc.; *The Perennial Philosophy,* Aldous Huxley, Chatto and Windus, Harper and Row, Publishers, Inc.; *Doors of Perception and Heaven and Hell.* Aldous Huxley, Chatto and Windus, Harper and Row, Publishers, Inc.; *Aldous Huxley 1894-1963—A Memorial Tribute* edited by Julian Huxley, Chatto and Windus, Harper and Row, Publishers, Inc.; *This Timeless Moment,* Aldous Huxley, Chatto and Windus, Farrar Straus & Giroux, Inc.; *Aldous Huxley: A Biographical Introduction,* Philip Thody, Studio Vista Ltd., Van Nostrand Reinhold, Inc.

This Is It and Other Essays on Zen and Spiritual Experience, Alan Watts, John Murray (Publishers) Ltd., copyright U.S. and Canada by Pantheon Books, a Division of Random House, Inc.; *Beyond Theology,* Alan Watts, Hodder and Stoughton, copyright U.S., Canada, and the Open Market by Pantheon Books, a Division of Random House, Inc.; *In My Own Way,* Alan Watts, Jonathan Cape, copyright U.S., Canada, and the Open Market by Pantheon Books, a Division of

lishers, Harper and Row, Publishers, Inc.

Candles in the Wind, Lady Emily Lutyens, Granada Publishing Ltd., *The Impossible Question*, Krishnamurti, Victor Gollancz Ltd., Harper and Row, Publishers, Inc.; *Talks in Europe 1956*, Krishnamurti, copyright and reprinted by permission of Krishnamurti Writings, Inc., Ojai, California.

In Search of the Miraculous, P. D. Ouspensky, Routledge and Kegan Paul Ltd., Harcourt Brace Jovanovitch, Inc., *Teachings of Gurdjieff*, C.S. Nott, Routledge and Kegan Paul Ltd., Samuel Weiser, Inc.; *Gurdjieff*, Louis Pauwels, Times Press Ltd., Samuel Weiser, Inc.; *Boyhood With Gurdjieff*, Fritz Peters, George Allen and Unwin Ltd., Penguin Books, New York; *A Study of Gurdjieff's Teaching*, Kenneth Walker, the Executors of the Estate of Kenneth Walker, Jonathan Cape Ltd.

Zen Poems, Prayers, Sermons, Anecdotes, Interviews, Lucien Stryk and Takashi Ikemoto, Doubleday and Company, Inc.

The Meaning of Subud, Muhammad Subuh, Subud Publications International; *Susila Buddhi Dharma*, Muhammad Subuh, Subud Publications International; *Subud In The World*, Muhammad Subuh, Subud Publications International; *What Is Subud?*, Gordon van Hien, Rider and Company.

Ramana Maharshi and His Philosophy of Existence, Dr. T.M.P. Mahadevan, T.N. Venkataraman, India; *Talks With Sri Ramana Maharshi, Vols. I to III*, T.N. Venkataraman, India, *The Teachings of Ramana Maharshi*, Arthur Osborne, Rider and Company; *The Collected Works of Ramana Maharshi*, Athur Osborne, Rider and Company; *Ramana Maharshi and the Path of Self-Knowledge*, Arthur Osborne, Rider and Company.

Treatise of Human Nature, David Hume, J.M. Dent and Sons.

The Ashtavakra Gita, Hari Prasad Shastri, Shanti Sadan; *The Bhagavad Gita As It Is*, Swami A.C. Bhaktivedanta, copyright 1968 by A.C. Bhaktivedanta Swami, The Macmillan Publishing Company, Inc.

The Thousand Petalled Lotus, The Venerable Sangharakshita, William Heinemann Ltd.

Transcendental Meditation, Maharishi Mahesh Yogi, The New American Library, Inc., *The Everything and the Nothing*, Meher Baba, copyright 1963 by Meher House Publications, 12 Kalianna Crescent, Beacon Hill, N.S.W., Australia, and by permission of the Beguine Library, California; *Listen Humanity*, Meher Baba, Harper

Colophon Books, Harper and Row, Publishers, Inc.

The Wayfarers, Dr. Donkin, Adi K. Irani, India.

Satguru Has Come, Shri Hans Publications, by permission of the *Divine Times; Farewell! Satsang of Shri Guru Maharaj Ji., 15th July 1973 Alexandra Palace; Divine Light Mission Magazine, Vol. 3, No. 4,* Shri Hans Productions, by permission of the *Divine Times.*

Born in Tibet, Chogyam Trungpa, George Allen and Unwin Ltd., Penguin Books, New York, Harcourt Brace Jovanovitch, Inc.

Cutting Through Spiritual Materialism, Chogyam Trungpa, Robinson and Watkins Books Ltd., Shambala Publications Inc.

Garuda II, Shambala Publications Inc.

The Real Way to Awakening, Dhiravamsa, Vipassana Centre; *The Middle Path of Life*, Dhiravamsa.

I and Thou, Martin Buber, translated by Walter Kaufmann, T. and T. Clark Ltd., Edinburgh, Charles Scribner's Sons.

Mysticism, Evelyn Underhill, Methuen and Co. Ltd., London, 1930.

The Esoteric Orders and Their Work, Dion Fortune, Aquarian Press, 1930; *Psychic Self-Defense*, Dion Fortune, Aquarian Press, 1930; *The Mystical Qabalah*, Dion Fortune, Ernest Benn Ltd., 1935; *Applied Magic*, Dion Fortune, Aquarian Press, 1962.

The Magical Revival, Kenneth Grant, Frederick Muller Ltd., London.

The Course of My Life, Rudolf Steiner, Rudolf Steiner Press, London and New York, 1951; *Theosophy. An Introduction to the Supersensible Knowledge of the World and the Destination of Man*, Rudolf Steiner, Rudolf Steiner Press, London and New York, 1973; *Agriculture*, Rudolf Steiner, Bio-Dynamic Agricultural Association, London, 1974; *Fundamentals of Therapy. An Extension of the Art of Healing through Spiritual Knowledge*, Rudolf Steiner and Ita Wegman, Rudolf Steiner Press, London and New York, 1967.

Supernature, Lyall Watson, Coronet Books, Hodder Paperbacks Ltd., London, 1974.

A Separate Reality, Carlos Castaneda, The Bodley Head, Simon and Schuster.

My Brother, My Sister, by Sister Sue Mosteller, Griffin House Toronto, 1972, revised 1974.

Photographs
Aldous Huxley: Chatto and Windus, London
Alan Watts: Richard Borst, Pantheon Books, a Division of Random House, Inc.

Thomas Merton: Sheldon Press, London
Teilhard de Chardin: Editions du Seuil, Paris
Krishnamurti: Mark Edwards, London
Gurdjieff: Routledge and Kegan Paul Ltd., London
Maharaj Ji: The Divine Times, Shri Hans Productions
Ramana Maharshi: Rider and Company, London
The Maharishi: Transcendental Meditation, London
Trungpa: The Movement, California
Dhiravamsa: himself
Martin Buber: T. and T. Clark Ltd., Edinburgh, and Charles Scribner's Sons, U.S.A.
Rudolf Steiner: Philosophisch-Anthroposophischer Verlag, Switzerland
Douglas Harding: Michael Scott, London
Mother Theresa: Times Newspapers Ltd., London

1

The Bridge Builders

The bridge builders come from sharply varied backgrounds, but the first three hold at least one thing in common—their understanding that aspects of the truth are found in both Eastern and Western religion. In the case of Aldous Huxley, the belief that there was any truth to find at all took some time to mature. All his later years were spent in a search for the mystical experience, and he remained, to the end of his life, preponderantly an intellectual man with moments of real insight rather than a true mystic. His brilliant command of language, however, makes him easy to understand, and his descriptions of his experiences are wonderfully direct and uncomplicated. Wherever he saw the truth expressed, he *knew* it. Thus his *Perennial Philosophy*, a book in which he links many spiritual writings and sayings from all of the religions, is not merely a collection of excellent quotations; it is a deeply spiritual book which has helped many people gain a clearer understanding of what they are looking for. This book, perhaps more than any of his others, is the firmest bridge for people to cross between their person-hood and the mystical experience.

Alan Watts, also English in origin and also domiciled in California, became adept at comparing the central truths of Christianity (for some years he was an Episcopalian minister) with those of Hinduism, Buddhism, and Taoism—religions which he deeply loved. He was very moved by his own experience of egolessness, and he evolved a personal philosophy from this experience which he linked with both Eastern and Western religion, thus becoming one of the most stimulating mystical philosophers of our time. His own beliefs centered around the crucial problem of human identity and his greatest attacks were on the common feeling of being an "I" di-vorced from everything else, even from its own experi-ence. The "I" does not feel feelings or think thoughts, he said, any more than it smells smelling. He, too, is an easy writer to read and an entertaining builder of bridges, with a love of language and an especial fondness for puns.

Thomas Merton, an American Cistercian monk, gradu-ally moved away from a rather over intense in-Christianity to an illumined understanding of Eastern religions, particularly Zen Buddhism and Taoism. His insights came through his own contemplative life and mystical realization, and, to some extent, he was able to isolate the contemplative experience and write about it clearly and freely. His overwhelming interest in every-thing to do with contemplation made him entirely at home in Zen and Taoism, and his friendship with D. T. Suzuki, a great Japanese exponent of Zen, gave him such an insight into its practices that he seemed able, shortly before his untimely death, to reach right through the outer trappings of both Christianity and Buddhism to the ground of pure, direct experience from which they have both sprung.

Teilhard de Chardin's bridges were built to span a different gulf. A French Jesuit priest, he was not interested in other religions at all, but only in going deeper and deeper into his own. To him, belief in Christ meant that mankind must and would evolve in certain directions, evidence for this being shown by a study of the past. So convinced was he that the human race was becoming more conscious, more sensitive, more communally minded, and nearer to the Parousia when all men would be merged in Christ, that he gave up his life to discovering scientific proof for this theory. He was trained as a paleontologist, and this discipline engendered in him a great reverence for the material world which, as a mystic, he saw as Christ-consciousness expressed in more and more diversified forms. God's presence, he believed, is felt throughout the created world, and the whole of evolution is a continuous movement towards him. In his own highly poetic language, he linked the spirit with matter, and for many people throughout the world this particular bridge is one of the most valuable.

Aldous Huxley
1894–1963

But the greatest tragedy of the spirit is that sooner or later it succumbs to the flesh. Sooner or later every soul is stifled by the sick body; sooner or later there are no more thoughts, but only pain and vomiting and stupor. The tragedies of the spirit are mere struttings and posturings on the margin of life, and the spirit itself only an accidental exuberance, the product of spare vital energy, like the feathers on the head of a hoopoe or the innumerable populations of useless and foredoomed spermatozoa. . . .

Those Barren Leaves[1]

The horror of ultimate meaninglessness, expressed in one of Huxley's first novels, underlay most of his thoughts in the early part of his life. The seeming conflict between spirit and matter provided a constant whip which spurred him on to a search for further and yet further inner experience. The apparently terrible injustice of life—the tortures people endured in concentration camps (of which the sensitive and socially concerned Huxley was painfully aware), the plight of the poverty-stricken, and the build-up of arms in the thirties for certain use in an appalling war—not only turned him into a convinced pacifist,

but also made him seriously wonder if this world could be the hell of some other planet.

He himself was not the victim of any modern horror for he was fortunate enough to be a descendant of two comfortably secure and notable families. His grandfather was the scientist T. H. Huxley, and his mother's grandfather was the famous Arnold, headmaster of Rugby. Matthew Arnold, the poet, was his great-uncle, and his mother's elder sister Mary Augusta became Mrs. Humphrey Ward, the novelist. As a child, Aldous was much attached to his Aunt Mary, and perhaps her influence turned him towards his own, very different, novel writing.

His sheltered background did not, however, prevent a series of three tragic misfortunes overtaking him when he was in his teens. First, his mother died of cancer when he was fourteen, and he missed her sadly. His father married again quite soon afterwards, but Aldous never took to his stepmother. Secondly, he developed an eye infection when he was sixteen, which was not looked after by his masters at Eton, with the consequence that he lost the use of one eye altogether and was nearly blind in the other for several years. He could distinguish night from day but not much else, although he eventually regained a fair amount of sight in one eye. Thirdly, when he was nineteen, his beloved elder brother Trevenen hanged himself.

The flesh must have seemed extremely frail to the young Aldous. His blindness cut him off from most activities and developed an aloofness in him, and he was overconscious of his exceptionally tall, thin body. He was six foot four and had immensely long legs, which he was never quite sure what to do with when he was sitting down. His self-isolation and physical vulnerability gave him the impetus, however, to develop the powers of his mind. He learned braille, and made a joke of the fact that he could secretly read in bed after lights out. He started to memorize a great quantity of facts. He learned to follow music in braille. His first (unpublished) novel of 80,000 words was typed by touch. He never read it; it was lost before he regained his sight. He took a First at Oxford, having studied mostly by braille, although by then his sight was beginning to return. By 1919 he was sufficiently confident in himself to marry Maria Nys, a young Belgian girl, a protégé of Philip and Lady Ottoline Morrell. Maria was a loving companion, and their marriage a very happy one.

His questing, roving, fact-finding intelligence became exceptionally keen. Leonard Woolf says of him, ". . . his mind was of the finest tempered steel, his arguments always had the sharpest cutting edge; his intellectual honesty was perfect; but what reconciled one to having these steely weapons turned against one, what made exasperation or irritation impossible, was Aldous's character, his temperament, his essential gentleness and sweetness."[2] Yet pessimism underlined his novels for all the early years of his life. He was particularly aware of the feeling of separation from existence, of the uniquely human consciousness of being a lonely and isolated entity.

In *Eyeless in Gaza*, Huxley wrote:

> Separation, diversity—conditions of our existence. Conditions upon which we possess life and consciousness, know right from wrong and have the power to choose between them, recognize truth, have experience of beauty. But separation is evil. Evil, then, is the condition of life, the condition of being aware, of knowing what is good and beautiful . . . even with the best will in the world, the separate, evil universe of a person or a physical pattern can never unite itself completely with other lives and beings, or the totality of life and being. Even for the highest goodness the struggle is

without end; for never in the nature of present things can the shut become the wholly open; goodness can never free itself from evil. It is a test, an education, searching, difficult, drawn out through a lifetime, perhaps through a series of lifetimes. Lifetimes passed in an attempt to open up further and a little further the closed universe that perpetually tends to spring shut the moment that effort is relaxed. Passed in overcoming the separate passions of hate and malice and pride. Passed in making still the self-emphasizing cravings. Passed in constant efforts to realise unity with other lives and other modes of being. To experience it in the act of love and compassion. To experience it on another plane through meditation, in the insight of direct intuition. Unity beyond the turmoils of separateness and divisions. Goodness beyond the possibility of evil. But always the fact of separation persists, always evil remains the very condition of life and being. There must be no relaxation of the opening pressure. But even for the best of us, the consummation is still immeasurably remote.[3]

Huxley's struggle to see with his physical eyes is curiously reflected in his battle with the darkness of his own pessimistic conclusions. It was a fight against a metaphysically black and hostile world (he later noted that schizophrenics live in an exaggerated form of this arid world), and although his philosophy was constantly shot through with humor and gladness, yet it was not until he took mescaline in 1952 that he really shook off his despondent conviction that the world was inherently divided and bad.

Mescaline gave him the actual experience of a condition in which duality was transcended ("no subject, no object," he kept repeating happily), for which he had been searching so long. Religions had helped him to approach this state intellectually but had never taken him there, and, in fact, during the early part of his life, he had discarded dogmatic religion altogether and had developed a cynical agnosticism, especially when he visited India in 1925: "One is all for religion," he wrote, "until one visits a really religious country. Then, one is all for drains, machinery and the minimum wage."[4]

His attitude toward religion began to change—and eventually reversed itself completely—after 1937 when, because of a mixture of bad health and pacifist convictions, he went to live in California. He was accompanied by one of his closest friends, broadcaster Gerald Heard, a convinced Vedantist who was brilliant at making his philosophy comprehensible. When Heard founded Trabusco College in California, which was devoted to the study of mystical religion and Vedantism, Huxley took part in the project. He became an ardent advocate of Hinduism—although he later found that a more complete answer to his spiritual questions lay in Buddhism, particularly the compassionate Mahayana of Tibet.

It was while he was associated with Trabusco College that he wrote *The Perennial Philosophy*, his own "eternity-philosophy," a book which has stimulated many people. It is a book about mystical experience and is based, he said, "on direct experience, as the arguments of the physical scientists are based on direct sense impressions." Using quotations from Eastern and Western mystics, he writes about the great themes of existence —suffering, contemplation, charity, self-knowledge, grace, and others. It is a beautifully compiled book, but Huxley was still trapped in his intellect—the mystics themselves seem to glow with wisdom, and it is they who make the book memorable. Huxley, like a clever spider, weaves a finely worded web which holds his captured jewels together, but he himself is not one of them.

Intellectually, he was convinced that the "ultimate Ground simply 'is,'" that all problems can be seen in the light of the "fundamental all-rightness of the world." And yet there is an uneasiness about these conclusions which

shows itself in a clearly defined separation of human
sheep and goats:

> ... It is a fact, confirmed and re-confirmed during two or
> three thousand years of religious history, that the ultimate
> Reality is not clearly and immediately apprehended, except
> by those who have made themselves loving, pure in heart
> and poor in spirit. This being so, it is hardly surprising that
> theology based upon the experience of nice, ordinary, unre-
> generate people should carry so little conviction. . . . The
> self-validating certainty of direct awareness cannot in the
> very nature of things be achieved except by those equipped
> with the moral 'astrolabe of God's mysteries.'[5]

Huxley saw part of the truth but knew that he did not
feel it. He lacked personal experience, barred from it by
his own whirling intellect which could see all the view-
points but commit itself to none, and by the exciting
panorama of the world, which continually provided him
with new food for thought. "Glimpses . . . glimpses . . .
sick or well, Aldous was always catching glimpses," said
his wife, Laura, "that ability of glimpsing, and expressing
in part what he saw, made living fascinating. Aldous
could experience immediate facts, moment by moment.
Then—outside and inside the present facts—he could
simultaneously perceive innumerable other, actual or potential, facts."[6]

Rejecting his own theory that to know the ultimate
Reality one must be "poor in spirit"—empty of ideas
—Huxley, like a grasshopper, leapt from one mystical
path to another. Hypnosis and psychic phenomena took
their turn with straight meditation, the Alexander
method, and automatic writing. He was a positive collec-
tor of ideas, but always retained a scientific attitude to this
medley, and never gave way to any sort of woolly acceptance. " 'The heart,' he once quoted from Pascal, 'has its
reasons.' Still more cogent and much harder to unravel

are the reasons of the lungs, the blood, and the enzymes, of neurones and synapses."

And then, in 1952, he first took a dose of mescaline under controlled conditions, and everything became real for him.

This first experience was, above all, radiant with light—and one remembers Huxley's desperate lack of light during his boyhood blindness. Under mescaline,

> . . . I became aware of a slow dance of golden lights. A little later there were sumptuous red surfaces swelling and expanding from bright nodes of energy that vibrated with a continuously changing, patterned life. . . . The books, for example, with which my study walls were lined . . . glowed, when I looked at them, with brighter colours, a profounder significance. Red books, like rubies; emerald books; books bound in white jade; books of agate, of aquamarine, of yellow topaz; lapis lazuli books whose colour was so intense, so intrinsically meaningful, that they seemed to be on the point of leaving the shelves to thrust themselves more insistently on my attention.[7]

As well as light and color, this experience brought him a whiff of real nonduality. His "doors of perception were cleansed" and he found "the percept had swallowed up the concept":

> I took my pill at eleven. An hour and a half later I was sitting in my study, looking intently at a small glass vase. The vase contained only three flowers—a full-blown Belle of Portugal rose; shell pink with a hint at every petal's base of a hotter, flamier hue; a large magenta and cream-coloured carnation; and, pale purple at the end of its broken stalk, the bold heraldic blossom of an iris . . . the little nosegay broke all the rules of traditional good taste. At breakfast that morning I had been struck by the lively dissonance of its colours. But that was no longer the point. I was not looking now at an unusual flower arrangement. I was seeing what Adam had

seen on the morning of his creation—the miracle, moment by moment, of naked existence. . . .

I continued to look at the flowers, and in their living light I seemed to detect the qualitative equivalent of breathing —but of a breathing without return to a starting-point, with no recurrent ebbs but only a repeated flow from beauty to heightened beauty, from deeper to ever deeper meaning. . . . Being-Awareness-Bliss—for the first time I understood, not on the verbal level, not by inchoate hints or at a distance, but precisely and completely what those prodigious syllables referred to. . . .[8]

But still there was some separation. In the middle of bliss, Huxley found that he was deliberately avoiding the eyes of the two people in the room with him, that he did not want to be aware of them, for "both belonged to the world from which, for the moment, mescaline had delivered me—the world of selves, of time, of moral judgments and utilitarian considerations, the world (and it was this aspect of human life which I wished, above all else, to forget) of self-assertion, of cocksureness, of overvalued words, and idolatrously worshipped notions."[9]

The fly had appeared in the ointment. Mescaline took him to an isolated island of contemplation where objects shone with meaning and significance; but, to someone with Huxley's intense concern for the world's suffering, the drug posed as great a problem as it solved:

. . . How was this cleansed perception to be reconciled with a proper concern with human relations, with the necessary chores and duties, to say nothing of charity and practical compassion? The old-age debate between the actives and the contemplatives was being renewed—renewed, so far as I was concerned, with an unprecedented poignancy. For until this morning I had known contemplation only in its humbler, more ordinary forms—as discursive thinking; as a rapt absorption in poetry or painting or music . . . but now I knew contemplation at its height. At its height, but not yet in its fullness. For in its fullness the way of Mary includes the way of Martha and raises it, so to speak, to its own higher power. Mescaline opens up the way of Mary, but shuts the door on that of Martha. It gives access to contemplation—but to a contemplation that is incompatible with action and even with the will to action, the very thought of action. . . .[10]

It was not until three years later, after his first wife Maria had died of cancer and he had remarried, that this great conflict seemed to have a solution. Again, it was after taking mescaline:

There was absolutely no recall. Instead there was something of incomparably greater importance; for what came through the opened door was the realisation—not the knowledge, for this wasn't verbal or abstract—but the direct, total awareness, from the inside, so to say, of Love as the primary and fundamental cosmic fact. The words, of course, have a kind of indecency and must necessarily ring false, seem like twaddle. But the fact remains . . . I was this fact; or perhaps it would be more accurate to say that this fact occupied the place where I had been. The result was that I did not, as in the first experience, feel cut off from the human world. I was intensely aware of it, but from the standpoint of the living primordial cosmic fact of Love. And the things which had entirely filled my attention on that first occasion, I now perceived to be temptations—temptations to escape from the central reality into false, or at least imperfect and partial Nirvanas of beauty and mere knowledge.[11]

Because both mescaline and lysergic acid (LSD) had played such a remarkable part in Huxley's "enlightenment," he regarded them as entirely beneficial, a means of saving the human race. He argued that because most believers regard God as entirely spirit, only to be approached by spiritual means, they would not believe that a divine experience could be brought about by chemical conditioning. But, he said, "In one way or another, *all* our experiences are chemically conditioned, and if we imagine that some of them are purely 'spiritual,' purely 'intellectual,' purely 'aesthetic,' it is merely because we have never troubled to investigate the internal chemical environment at the moment of their occurrence."[12]

He emphasized that the methods used by all religions, from yogic breathing to hymn singing, are really devised to create a chemical change in the body—extra carbon dioxide in the blood stream. One wonders if his defensive fervor is inclined to protest too much. Now that we have discovered the chemical conditions for self-transcendence, he said—and he writes persuasively on how LSD inhibits the dualistic action of the brain, so that there is no more sensation of separation between subject and object—it is pointless to go in for years of meditation or spiritual exercises when everything can be obtained in half an hour by the use of a drug. In what sounds rather like an advertisement for a businesslike enlightenment, he says: "For an aspiring mystic to revert, in the present state of knowledge, to prolonged fasting and violent self-flagellation would be as senseless as it would be for an aspiring cook to behave like Charles Lamb's Chinaman, who burned down the house in order to roast a pig. Knowing as he does (or at least as he can know, if he so desires) what are the chemical conditions of transcendental experience, the aspiring mystic should turn for technical help to the specialists—in pharmacology, in biochemistry, in physiology and neurology, in psychology and psychiatry and parapsychology."[13] Almost as much a labor for the aspiring mystic, one would think, as if he went in for years of meditation.

But who knows, perhaps he was right. Even though the action of LSD does not always bring "gratuitous Grace," a whole new generation of "aspiring mystics" has emerged who are demanding transcendental experience

—an unheard of situation before the wide use of LSD.

Huxley died of cancer, as did his mother and his first wife. The nine or so years before his death brought him contentment and happiness, and many people remarked on his softer, mellower outlook. He grew out of the rather undergraduate, intellectual humor which, at a psychiatrist's conference, caused him to cross himself every time Freud was mentioned, and which made him think that it would be "amusing" to marry Laura in a drive-in wedding chapel. His astonishing fund of knowledge, observation, and real wit always provided him with many good friends from all walks of life. An astonishing picnic was once given by the Huxleys in the desert, to which were invited Krishnamurti, Greta Garbo, Anita Loos, Charlie Chaplin, Bertrand Russell, Paulette Goddard, and Christopher Isherwood, as well as some Theosophists who came to cook Krishnamurti's vegetarian meal—the high point of the picnic occurring when a sheriff arrived to tell them that they were desecrating the Los Angeles riverbed and demanded their names. When given, he refused to believe them, called them a lot of tramps and, pointing to a notice, asked if any of them could read!

Perhaps, with all his gifts, what attracted people most to Aldous was his gentleness, kindness, and sincerity. He was humble enough to say, near the end of his life, that the only real advice he could give was that people should be nicer to each other. His own nature was basically tender and compassionate and, as he became more able to detach himself from the power of his intellect, his compassionate aspect was able to fulfill itself.

When Maria was dying of a particularly painful form of cancer, she was put under hypnosis and Aldous sat beside her, holding her hands and reminding her of the lights of the desert that she had loved. He urged her to give herself up to those lights, "to open herself to joy, peace, love and being, to permit herself to be irradiated by them and to become one with them. I urged her to become what in fact she had always been, what all of us have always been, a part of the divine substance, a manifestation of love, joy and peace, a being identical with the One Reality. And I kept on repeating this, urging her to go deeper and deeper into the light, ever deeper and deeper."[14]

When Aldous himself died, he was lovingly helped to a peaceful end by Laura, who gave him LSD when he asked for it, and sat beside him reminding him of the Clear Light of the Void from the *Tibetan Book of the Dead*.

An article on *Shakespeare and Religion,* written during his last weeks and published posthumously, contains perhaps his simplest and yet most profound statement about life:

The world is an illusion, but it is an illusion which we must take seriously, because it is real as far as it goes, and in those aspects of the reality which we are capable of apprehending. Our business is to wake up. We have to find ways in which to detect the whole of reality in the one illusory part which our self-centered consciousness permits us to see. We must not live thoughtlessly, taking our illusion for the complete reality, but at the same time we must not live too thoughtfully in the sense of trying to escape from the dream state. We must continually be on our watch for ways in which we may enlarge our consciousness. We must not attempt to live outside the world, which is given us, but we must somehow learn how to transform it and transfigure it. Too much "wisdom" is as bad as too little wisdom, and there must be no magic tricks. We must learn to come to reality without the enchanter's wand and his book of the words. One must find a way of being in the world while not being of it. A way of living in time without being completely swallowed up in time.[15]

Alan Watts
1915–1973

. . . I had been attempting to practice what Buddhists call 'recollection' (*smriti*) or constant awareness of the immediate present as distinct from the usual distracted rambling of reminiscence and anticipation. But, in discussing it one evening, someone said to me, 'But why *try* to live in the present? Surely we are always completely *in* the present even when we're thinking about the past or the future?' This, actually quite obvious, remark again brought on the sudden sensation of having no weight. At the same time, the present seemed to become a kind of moving stillness, an eternal stream from which neither I nor anything could deviate. I saw that everything, just as it is now, is IT—is the whole point of there being life and a universe. I saw that when the *Upanishads* said, 'That art thou!' or 'All this world is Brahman,' they meant just exactly what they said. Each thing, each event, each experience in its inescapable nowness and in all its own particular individuality was precisely what it should be, and so much so that it acquired a divine authority and originality. It struck me with the fullest clarity that none of this depended on my seeing it to be so; that was the way things were, whether I understood it or not, and if I did not understand, that was IT too. Furthermore, I felt that I now understood what Christianity might mean by the love of

17

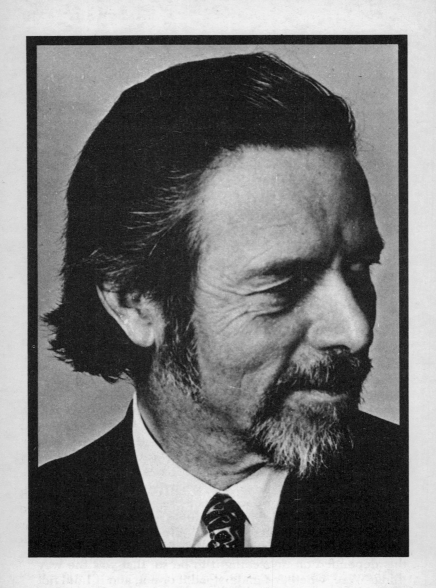

God—namely, that despite the commonsensical imperfection of things, they were nonetheless loved by God just as they are, and that this loving of them was at the same time the godding of them. . . .

This Is It[1]

Living in IT and by IT, altogether allowing IT to be himself, was the great theme of Alan Watts's life. But he was certainly not a mystic in the traditional sense. He loved sensual life and lived with enormous gusto. He drank a good deal, took LSD many times, married three times, and had seven children. He died in 1973, at the age of fifty-eight. His vocation in life, he said, was to wonder about the nature of the universe, and this feeling of awe and fascination led him into philosophy, psychology, religion, and mysticism—not just in ideas but also in experience. He refused to talk about anything he had not actually discovered. He was not afraid to call himself a mystic but saw with amusement how the people who hoped he would be their guru, or spiritual guide, were shaken when they saw his "element of irreducible rascality." He knew what they wanted—an idealized incarnation of radiant tranquility, love, and compassion—but he was too honest to confess to anything but "a quaking and palpitating mess of anxiety which lusts and loathes, needs love and attention, and lives in terror of death putting an end to its misery"[2] when he looked inside himself. This insight led him to see that to try to control the "quaking mess," to deny it and despise it in favor of what a mystic was *supposed to feel,* was to miss reality altogether, for the very attempt to do so was simply one more desire of the quaking mess. The quaking mess itself was as much a part of the universe as the rain, or flies, or disease. To see it as divine did not abolish it but allowed one the peace of mind of acceptance and delivered one from schizophrenic dichotomy of good against bad.

Watts's vigorous philosophical-spiritual life began in early youth when, while still in King's School, Canterbury, he started to read Hindu and Buddhist scriptures. By the age of seventeen he had already published a booklet on Zen. He failed to get a scholarship to Cambridge, left school at seventeen, and launched himself on the world. He decided to design his own "higher education" and was helped to do this by his very understanding father; by Christmas Humphreys, president of the then Buddhist Lodge; by Nigel Watkins, owner of a "mystical" bookshop in the Charing Cross Road; by Dr. Eric Graham Howe, a psychiatrist; and by Mitrinovic, a "rascal-guru" Slav.

Watts steadfastly refused a conventional career. He loathed the idea of being made to play any business or professional role and although he took jobs to keep himself going, he was an original dropout, not letting anything get in the way of his intense living of life. However, after he had married Eleanor Fuller, daughter of Ruth Fuller Sasaki and stepdaughter of Zen roshi Sokei-an Sasaki, and had gone to America with her, he was forced to find a means to support a family. The ideal way seemed to be to become a minister in the Episcopalian Church, and this he did, deciding that as a priest he would be sincere and natural, although not at all heavy. He felt that Protestantism lacked a light touch, with regard to both religion and sex, because of a sense of guilt. He wanted to help people enjoy ritual for its own sake without looking for any wordy meaning in it.

At this time, he also began to write and to expound an unconventional and mystical approach to some of the aspects of Christianity which perplex many people. For instance, in what sense is Jesus Christ an answer to the problems of the world?

Does it help by guaranteeing that every word he said was the solemn, literal, and absolute truth, which we are therefore bound to believe? That 1900-odd years ago, he somehow settled a mysterious debt for me which I don't remember incurring? That everything he did was the perfect and finally authoritative example of conduct and morals—which we are expected to follow without the aforesaid advantage of being God the Son in person?[3]

He felt that on these sorts of points the Christian doctrines were bewilderingly complex and unhelpful. They had developed into a sort of symbology which "fails absolutely to make any direct connection between the crucified and risen Son of God, on the one hand, and the daily life of a family in the suburbs of Los Angeles or London, on the other."[4]

To Watts, the answer to it all was to drop the image of Christ and thus to understand the Crucifixion and the Resurrection properly, "for we are spiritually paralysed by the fetish of Jesus. . . . His literary image in the Gospels has, through centuries of homage, become far more of an idol than anything graven in wood or stone, so that today the most genuinely reverent act of worship is to destroy that image."[5] He felt that the real meaning of the Crucifixion was that the imagined, conceptualized Jesus, the historical image, should be relinquished because while Jesus remained an object of possession, of knowledge, and of safety, there could be no spiritual growth or eternal life.

He saw the style of Christianity as artificial and inorganic because of the idea of God "as the *maker* of the world, and thus of the world itself as an artifact which has been constructed in accordance with a plan, and which has, therefore, a purpose and an explanation."[6] He compared this idea with the Taoist *wu-wei*, which is the way of "nonstriving" and "nonmaking," where things grow from within and are not made, shaping themselves from within outwards spontaneously. He felt that the Christian image of God was that of an architect or a mechanic, standing outside the world as a mechanic will stand outside an assemblage of separate parts and that this belief had led to Western minds thinking of man himself as a separate bit, brought in from outside instead of emerging from within the universe as a leaf emerges from a tree. Thinking of God as outside creation had led to conceptualizing him as a set of principles rather than the living reality and inwardness of all things.

For, he pointed out, what is truly inward can never become an object. Life itself and our living of it is truly inward and this was why, Watts felt, the atmosphere of Christianity seemed cut off from all that lay outside it:

> . . . When I leave the Church and the city behind and go out under the sky, when I am with the birds, for all their voraciousness, with the clouds, for all their thunders, and with the oceans, for all their tempests and submerged monsters—I cannot feel Christianly because I am in a world which grows from within. I am simply incapable of feeling its life as coming from above, from beyond the stars, even recognising this to be a figure of speech. More exactly, I cannot feel that its life comes from Another, from one who is qualitatively and spiritually external to all that lives and grows. On the contrary, I feel this whole world to be moved from the inside, and from an inside so deep that it is my inside as well, more truly I than my surface consciousness.[7]

After some years as chaplain to Northwestern University, Watts formally resigned from both the post and the ministry. His old love of Vedanta, Buddhism, and Taoism had never taken second place in his life. Meetings with Dr. D. T. Suzuki, the great translator of the Zen scriptures, gave Watts an illuminated understanding of Zen and he became one of the first popularizers of Zen in America, with such books as *The Way of Zen* and *The Spirit of Zen*. He moved to San Francisco and became a lecturer at the newly founded Academy of Asian Studies as well as giving many broadcasts and public lectures. He became increasingly famous but still retained his down to earth humor, particularly at himself. At that time, he thought of himself as a teacher-philosopher and also as a bit of a shaman, doing his own "weird."

Watts explored many aspects of existence with his caustic and lively mind. Chiefly he was concerned with bringing people to see that they are not isolated entities "outside" nature, but an essential process of the world itself. He was well aware of the *feeling* of being "a lonely centre of consciousness and action living inside an envelope of skin," but he argued forcibly that this self-existent feeling is a delusion. Ecology, he said, shows that an organism is a continuous field of energy with its environment, for just as flowers and bees cannot exist without each other, so the human organism is a continuous process with all the universe.

He was convinced that the feeling of a separate "I" divorced from nature was the result and also, in a vicious circle, the cause of various fallacies and delusions by which people live. One such fallacy is the idea that the past and the future *actually exist*. He pointed out that our awareness of the past is *now*, in the present. We cannot compare what happened in the past with what is happening now; we can only compare the memory of it with present experience, thus memory becomes *a part of present experience*. Likewise the future can only be supposition felt in the present moment. When this is seen clearly, he said, it can also be seen that the "I" distinct from experience simply does not exist. There is only experi-

ence. To try to separate an experiencer from the experience is as impossible as trying to bite your own teeth:

> You do not feel feelings, think thoughts, or sense sensa-
> tions any more than you hear hearing, see sight, or smell
> smelling. "I feel fine" means that a fine feeling is present. It
> does not mean that there is one thing called "I" and another
> separate thing called a feeling, so that when you bring them
> together this "I" *feels* the fine feeling. There are no feelings
> but present feelings and whatever feeling is present is "I".
> No one ever found an "I" apart from some present experi-
> ence, or some experience apart from an "I"—which is only to
> say that the two are the same thing.[8]

As a practical experiment, he suggested reading, and
then trying to think about oneself reading while doing it.
What happens, as he pointed out, is that the thought "I am
reading" replaces the actual reading as the present experience. Thus, there is always an awareness of experience in the form of thought or sensation, but never an
awareness of a thinker of the thought, or an experiencer of
the sensation for that is just another thought or another
sensation. Why, then, do we believe that such a thing as
the "I" exists?

Watts believes that the feeling of an "I" distinct from
experience is brought about by memory and by the rapid-
ity with which thoughts follow one another. If one falsely
thinks that memory is a reliving of the past, then one has
the impression of knowing the past and the present at the
same time, *both directly*. This gives the feeling of a continuous experiencer who knows both and can connect
them. This in itself might not matter except that humans
build such a life of misery for themselves based on this
illusion:

> The real reason why human life can be so utterly exasperat-
> ing and frustrating is not because there are facts called death,

pain, fear, or hunger. The madness of the thing is that when such facts are present, we circle, buzz, writhe, and whirl, trying to get the 'I' out of the experience.... While the notion that I am separate from my experience remains, there is confusion and turmoil. Because of this, there is neither awareness nor understanding of experience, and thus no real possibility of assimilating it. To understand this moment I must not try to be divided from it; I must be aware of it with my whole being. This, like refraining from holding my breath for ten minutes, is not something I *should* do. In reality, it is the only thing I *can* do. Everything else is the insanity of attempting the impossible.[9]

This struggle to extract the "I" from unpleasant experience, particularly from death, is one reason, Watts thought, why people make an image of God and try to cling to it. But this clinging is in itself intense suffering, which is not to say that there is no God, but that to try and grasp God as a means of alleviating suffering or giving continuous everlasting life, is merely putting oneself in bondage. Death seen as sleep without waking, as the falling away of thoughts and memories and "I"-ness, has something natural and refreshing about it, and should not be confused with "the fantasy of being shut up forever in darkness." Death might also mean waking up as someone else, as one did when one was born, and Watts was convinced that what dies is not consciousness but memory, for "consciousness recurs in every newborn creature, and wherever it recurs it is 'I'."[10]

Another obstacle to man's full understanding of himself is his use of language, a unique and marvelous tool in itself, but not to be confused with the reality it symbolically describes. "... We can easily see," says Watts, "the ways in which it may be splitting organism from environment, and aspects of the environment from one another. Languages with such parts of speech as nouns

and verbs obviously translate what is going on in the
world into particular things (nouns) and events (verbs),
and these in turn 'have' properties (adjectives and ad-
verbs) more or less separable from them. All such languages represent the world as if it were an assemblage of
distinct bits and particles. The defect of such grids is that
they screen out or ignore (or repress) interrelations."[11]
For the reality, which is the basis of everyday life, is
never static or fixed in the way the word that represents it
is. A fleeting, fluid, ever-changing field of experience,
ungraspable because you can only *be* it, not *have* it, frightens many people very much indeed. But mind-con-
structions such as thoughts and ideas, can be grasped and
held and most people not only prefer an idea about the
thing to the thing itself but have actually forgotten or
never understood that the word only symbolizes reality,
and an idea is only a pattern of thought.

As an example, Watts takes the object "tree," points
to it, and says:

> "This is a tree." Obviously *this* and *tree* are not actually the
> same thing. *Tree* is a word, a noise. It is not this experienced
> reality to which I am pointing. To be accurate, I should have
> said, "This (pointing to the tree) is symbolised by the noise
> *tree*."
>
> If, then, the real tree is not the word or the idea *tree*, what is
> it? If I say that it is an impression on my senses, a vegetable
> structure, or a complex of electrons, I am merely putting new
> sets of words and symbols in place of the original noise, *tree*.
> I have not said *what* it is at all. I have also raised other
> questions: "What are my senses?" "What is a structure?"
> "What are electrons?" ... We can never say *what* these
> things are. ... The word and idea *tree* has remained fixed
> currency for many centuries, but real trees have behaved in a
> very odd way. I can try to describe their behaviour by saying
> that they have appeared and disappeared, that they have
> been in a constant state of change, and that they flow in and

out of their surroundings. . . .

But this does not really say what they have done, because *disappear, change, flow,* and *surroundings* are still noises representing something utterly mysterious.[12]

The mysterious reality that we sense both inside and outside of ourselves all the time, and yet which is so difficult to reach because of the miasma of our own confused images and thoughts, is what Watts refers to as IT. IT is the unconditioned, indefinable, real nature of existence before it has been divided up into abstractions and symbols. To be aware of IT is never again to confuse the conventional with the actual, to cease to be swayed by words and ideas, and to realize that the true world is unknowable by the mind. To reach IT demands letting go of the conventional world and this is a step which many people are afraid of. But for others the recognition that one cannot say what the world is, one can only know *that* it is, brings a consciousness of all things as completely concrete yet at the same time numinous and ineffable. This sort of consciousness transcends ordinary self-consciousness and leads to a feeling of oneness with the universe in which all things are seen with extraordinary clarity and love. There is an openness to all that is, and the world is seen as *all* there is (no heavens)—an all that is pure marvel. This can be seen when one loses one's sense of isolation, of being an identity apart from the world.

But words always fall so far short of experience that they are probably better not used, which is why the Eastern religions usually describe by negatives—"not this, not that, nor any thing which can be comprehended." Watts was keenly aware of the misleading nature of words: "But the fact that IT eludes every description must not, as happens so often, be mistaken for the description of IT as the airiest of abstractions, as a literal transparent continuum or undifferentiated cosmic jello."[13] He points out that science has revealed to us a universe so mysterious and so impressive that the Western image of IT as God the Father simply won't fit and the images of a more impersonal or suprapersonal God "are hopelessly subhuman—jello, featureless light, homogenised space, or a whopping jolt of electricity."[14] So how can we think of God?

"I know," says Watts, quoting St. Augustine, "but when you ask me I don't. If you want me to show you God, I will point to the ash can in your back yard. But if you ask, 'Then you mean that this ash can is God?'—you will have missed the point altogether."[15]

Watts took a good many courageous and outrageous swipes at society's hypocrisies and misunderstandings, from the concept of the "Cosmic Male Parent" to the way food is cooked and eaten. His teaching was mainly intellectual and he wrote some twenty books. But he also loved music, both for its own sake and as a way of meditation (which he also did for its own sake). He had a deep and powerfully resonant voice for chanting, and he had trained himself to maintain a sound for an amazingly long time. In a record he made a year before his death, he uses sound as a means of realization by asking questions, such as: "How old is it?" (immediately one realizes that sound has no age) and "How old are you?" (the realization that one is intrinsically ageless comes also).

He said about sound:

... If you just listen, relating yourself to the world entirely through the sense of hearing, you will find yourself in a universe where reality—pure sound—comes immediately out of silence and emptiness, echoing away as memory in the labyrinths of the brain. In this universe everything flows backwards from the present and vanishes, like the wake of a ship; the present comes out of nothing and you cannot hear any self that is listening. This can be done with all the senses, but most easily with the ears. Simply listen, then, to the rain. Listen to what Buddhists call its "suchness"—its *tathata* or da-da-da. Like all classical music, it means nothing except itself, for only inferior music mimics other sounds or is *about* anything other than music. There is no "message" in a Bach fugue. So, too, when an ancient Zen master was asked about the meaning of Buddhism he replied, "If there is any meaning in it, I myself am not liberated." For when you have really heard the sound of rain you can hear, and see and feel, everything else in the same way—as needing no translation, as being just that which it is, though it may be impossible to say what.[16]

Thomas Merton
1915–1969

Thomas Merton was a Trappist monk and a gifted and popular Catholic writer on monastic life who had begun to explore new directions before he died in an accident in a Bangkok hotel, when he was electrocuted by a faulty fan-switch.

His early life was nomadic and insecure. He was born in France of New Zealand and American parents, both of whom were artists. His mother died when he was a young child and from then on he wandered about with his father in France, spending occasional holidays with an aunt in England and with his mother's restless American parents, who would descend on Europe, trailing along with them Thomas's younger brother, John Paul. Eventually Thomas went to a public school in England and then on to Cambridge, where he took a degree in modern languages. But Cambridge was not a success. He was at odds with life and couldn't make heads or tails of it, and he was given to depression. He had no religion, but was deeply impressed by the sincerity of a young Hindu who was able to convey to him some meaning in Christian mysticism. In those early days of his religious quest, Merton's self-

absorption was so great that he could genuinely believe that God, in order to convert him, had specially brought about the Hindu's journey from India.

After the death of his father and the advent of war, Merton went to America and took some more courses at Columbia. Then he began to attend Mass and decided to become a Roman Catholic. He was greatly assailed by his own purposelessness. He could no longer bear to live only for himself. After some retreats at the Cistercian Abbey of Gethsemani in Kentucky, he was received as a novice and was based there as a monk for the rest of his life.

The Trappist life is simple and well-ordered. Merton found in it all the security and sense of purpose which had been so lacking in his rootless wanderings. Book after book flowed from his pen about the especial joys of monasticism and the terrible nature of the world outside the monastery. His autobiography, *The Seven Storey Mountain* (published as *Elected Silence* in Great Britain), was a best seller, and so too was a small book of devotional thoughts and themes called *Seeds of Contemplation*.

Perhaps some of these "seeds" were growing into a different field of flowers than the one Merton thought he was in—a field where active religion is not so important as being still, and where conventional Christianity some-times seems at odds with the truth. Twelve years later he wrote *New Seeds of Contemplation* and became less popular as a Catholic writer for he seemed to query the Christian belief in the uniqueness of the individual self. While describing contemplation (an exercise of inner stillness and receptiveness to God), he said:

> Contemplation is not and cannot be a function of this ex-ternal self. There is an irreducible opposition between the deep transcendent self that awakens only in contemplation,

and the superficial, external self which we commonly identify with the first person singular. We must remember that
this superficial "I" is not our real self. It is our "individuality" and our "empirical" self but it is not truly the hidden and
mysterious person in whom we subsist before the eyes of
God. The "I" that works in the world, thinks about itself,
observes its own reactions and talks about itself is not the true
"I" that has been united to God in Christ. It is at best the
vesture, the mask, the disguise of that mysterious and unknown "self" whom most of us never discover until we are
dead. Our external, superficial self is not eternal, not
spiritual. Far from it. This self is doomed to disappear as
completely as smoke from a chimney. It is utterly frail and
evanescent. Contemplation is precisely the awareness that
this "I" is really "not I" and the awakening of the unknown
"I" that is beyond observation and reflection and is incapable of commenting upon itself. . . .[1]

Christian monasteries are often largely tenanted by two
types of monks. On the one hand, there are pleasant, easy,
talkative men, who simply prefer a monastic way of life,
with its secure routine, to a worldly one, and who are
practical and not particularly mystical; and on the other,
there are men who are more withdrawn, self-absorbed,
and concerned with their experiences, both religious and
secular.

Merton saw a good deal of both types and some of his
books openly criticize the ways and moods of monks. He
repudiated particularly the opinions of those who tried to
define the experience of contemplation in psychological
terms or with scientific definitions. In Christianity there
is a distinction drawn between meditation and contemplation. Meditation is a discussion in the mind, a silent
working-out of a theme. Contemplation is a wordless
nearness to God, an experience of being—unnecessary to
the ways and natures of many monks, just as spiritual
realities are often unnecessary to a busy religious life.

Merton was a mystic, and to him contemplation was the opening up of an inner illumination. But Western religious thought has always been verbal and intellectual rather than intuitive. Many Christians have echoed approvingly Descartes' *cogito ergo sum*, "I think therefore I am." To Merton, this statement and the attitude that went with it were anathemas:

> This is the declaration of an alienated being, in exile from his own spiritual depths, compelled to seek some comfort in a *proof for his own existence* (!) based on the observation that he "thinks." If his thought is necessary as a medium through which he arrives at the concept of his existence, then he is in fact only moving further away from his true being. He is reducing himself to a concept. He is making it impossible for himself to experience, directly and immediately, the mystery of his own being. At the same time, by also reducing God to a concept, he makes it impossible for himself to have any intuition of the divine reality which is inexpressible. He arrives at his own being as if it were an objective reality, that is to say he strives to become aware of himself as he would of some "thing" alien to himself. And he proves that the "thing" exists. He convinces himself: "I am therefore some *thing*." And then he goes on to convince himself that God, the infinite, the transcendent, is also a "thing," an "object," like other finite and limited objects of our thought!
>
> Contemplation, on the contrary, is the experiential grasp of reality as *subjective,* not so much "mine" (which would signify "belonging to the external self") but "myself" in existential mystery. Contemplation does not arrive at reality after a process of deduction, but by an intuitive awakening in which our free and personal reality becomes fully alive to its own existential depths, which open out into the mystery of God.[2]

Teilhard de Chardin regarded the individuality of a person as ultimately real, and many Christians have also always believed this, basing their convictions on the historical existence of God-who-became-man Jesus. But Merton thought this assertion of individuality futile. Far better, he said, to realize humbly our own mysterious nature as persons within whom God exists than to believe that man exists because he thinks.

Belief in the unknowable "I" that is beyond observation and reflection is a constantly recurring theme in this book. Merton saw the unknowable "I" as the true person, whom God had intended, implicit in all created things: "The more a tree is like itself, the more it is like Him. If it tried to be like something else which it was never intended to be, it would be less like God and therefore it would give Him less glory."[3]

It does not mean that created things are imperfect, he said, because they are not exactly alike. On the contrary, real perfection does not lie in conforming to some abstract type; rather, it comes into existence when the individual's identity is with himself—with his own entity, characteristics, and qualities. When he is at one with his own person, he gives glory to God by being precisely what he was always intended to be, just as that one particular tree will give glory to God by spreading out its roots or lifting its branches in a way which no other tree has ever done or ever will do.

This insight of Merton's casts light on the general human habit of trying to conform to some currently fashionable attitude or life style. Instead of being me—here in this present moment and innocent of ideas about any role that would bring me benefit—I habitually think of myself as though there were another person six feet away from me all the time, judging my performance. We live by other people's ideas instead of our own. We are self-conscious instead of conscious.

The discovery of one's own identity distinct from all the conditioning and education which has hidden it, is

the main task of Eastern religions such as Hinduism and
Sufism and is the occupation of such sages as Krishnamurti and Ramana Maharshi. The ultimate discovery
that God, or the Self, is the ground of one's true nature is
seen by Merton as a problem of identity, in much the
same way as Ramana Maharshi saw it. Whereas Ramana
Maharshi believed that one's feeling of "I" was the key to
the question of existence and that once this feeling had
been identified with its Source, the Self, existence would
reveal its true potential, so Merton, in Christian terms,
saw free will as the gift of God to man, to be used as active
participation with God in the revelation of identity with
him:

> Trees and animals have no problem. God makes them what
> they are without consulting them, and they are perfectly
> satisfied.
> With us it is different. God leaves us free to be whatever we
> like. We can be ourselves or not, as we please. We are at
> liberty to be real, or to be unreal. We may be true or false, the
> choice is ours. We may wear now one mask and now another,
> and never, if we so desire, appear with our own true face. But
> we cannot make these choices with impunity. Causes have
> effects and if we lie to ourselves and to others, then we cannot
> expect to find truth and reality whenever we happen to want
> them. If we have chosen the way of falsity we must not be
> surprised that truth eludes us when we finally come to need
> it!
> Our vocation is not simply to *be*, but to work together with
> God in the creation of our own life, our own identity, our own
> destiny. . . . We do not know clearly beforehand what the
> result of this work will be. The secret of my full identity is
> hidden in Him. He alone can make me who I am, or rather
> who I will be when at last I fully begin to be. But unless I
> desire this identity and work to find it with Him and in Him,
> the work will never be done. The way of doing it is a secret I
> can learn from no one else but Him.[4]

His desire for "true identity" led Merton away from the close monasticism which influenced his early writing towards a more compassionate feeling for the suffering world—in contrast to his earlier glad detachment from it. He became aware of people and of the real problems of life. He began to find the distance was lessening between the innate sense of God that came to him in contemplation and ordinary life. He saw that the way to inner spiritual certainty was undramatic, even obscure, and that the monastic everyday routine of "work, poverty, hardship, and monotony" had supreme value.

For a time, he went even further than this and announced that "the surest asceticism is the bitter insecurity and labour and nonentity of the really poor." Many will find this hard to accept. From the security of a monastery it may seem "ascetic" to suffer as the really poor suffer, but no pinched and disheartened parent of hungry children is going to feel his condition as an enviable asceticism. With more insight, Merton added: "Misery as such, destitution as such, is not the way to contemplative union."

As his sense of realism grew, Merton began to take a harder look at the world outside. One of the current phenomena attacked by his pen was the Death-of-God movement which had more of a furor in America than in Europe, and was sparked off by Martin Buber's book, *The Eclipse of God*. When Dr. John Robinson, the Bishop of Woolwich, wrote *Honest to God*, Merton reacted:

To begin with, 'the world' has no need of Christian apologetics. . . . It explains itself to its own satisfaction. That is why I think it is absurd to approach the world with what seems to me to be merely a new tactic and a new plea for sincerity—a "religionless religion" which cheerfully agrees that God is dead. . . . Obvious answers from "the world": "So what?" The world does not need a "religionless religion" any more than it needs the traditional kind.[5]

Merton pointed out that what man needs is not a Christianity that is involved in every worldly issue, but a religion that is "not of this world." Man wants to be freed from the fashionable "myths, idolatries, and confusions" of the world. He can never, of course, be free from the natural created world as such, nor from human society, but a Christian should be free from the obsessions of a society which is governed by love of money and the use of power—"What is important is to show those who *want to be free* where their freedom really lies!"

Many Christians would and did disagree with him over this point. In every religion, but particularly in Christianity, two main groups of people seem to emerge. There are those who believe that God's orders in the form of a vigorous Christian life are to be carried out, but who do not feel the need to contemplate God—who, in fact, are shy and wary of the admonition "Be still and know that I am God." And there is another, perhaps smaller group, who see their own spiritual realization as of first importance although, like Aldous Huxley, they are far from blind to the needs of the world.

Merton was one of the latter type, and it might be fair to say they are more likely to be found in monasteries. But two themes of contemplation seem to have expanded his outlook and perhaps changed the direction of his life. One was the belief, stated earlier, that "each particular being . . . gives glory to God by being precisely what He wants it to be here and now." The full awareness of the moment, which Merton called "nowness," brings the knowledge of the "unknown I" into consciousness. The whole action of awakening is for *now.* Wherever one is, in lonely cell or crowded street, this moment contains all that is needed for "I" to become one with transcendent reality.

The other theme, which he often referred to and expanded, was that of loss of ego; moving away from the individual and toward a state of beingness by means of dropping one's "thinghood."

> As long as there is an "I" that is the definite subject of a contemplative experience, an "I" that is aware of itself and of its contemplation, an "I" that can possess a certain "degree of spirituality", then we have not yet passed over the Red Sea, we have not yet "gone out of Egypt". We remain in the realm of multiplicity, activity, incompleteness, striving and desire. The true inner self, the true indestructible and immortal person, the true "I" who answers to a new and secret name known only to himself and God, does not "have" anything, even "contemplation." This "I" is not the kind of subject that can amass experiences, reflect on them, reflect on himself, for this "I" is not the superficial and empirical self that we know in our everyday life.[6]

Such themes inevitably led a person like Merton, with his wide reading and growingly open attitude to holiness, to the Eastern religions, particularly Zen where the awareness of "nowness" is regarded as essential. Acceptance of non-Christian religions as a real source of the spirit may have entailed some inner struggles but his ability to grasp intuitively the essential teachings of Hinduism and Buddhism were forming Merton into a strong builder of bridges between East and West before his untimely death. He was constantly irked by the unsympathetic attitudes of other Catholic writers who saw the Eastern religions as pessimistic and passive and unsatisfying to the West, and he himself began writing a number of remarkable books, such as *Mystics and Zen Masters* and *Zen and the Birds of Appetite*, to point out the similarities and differences between Christianity and Eastern religions.

His main bridge-building was in the field of Zen. He had illuminating talks with Dr. D. T. Suzuki, the greatest Japanese exponent of Zen in this century, and said afterward that Buddhism (of which Zen is a school) had finally become comprehensible to him, that he had now seen through the rather bewildering cultural patterns of strange rituals, exotic images, and mysterious words to a clear and simple essence—"the simplest and most baffling thing of all: direct confrontation with Absolute Being, Absolute Love, Absolute Mercy, or Absolute Void by an immediate and fully awakened engagement in the living of everyday life. In Christianity the confrontation is theological and affective, through word and love. In Zen it is metaphysical and intellectual, through insight and emptiness."[7]

He came to believe that "the self is not its own centre and does not orbit around itself; it is centred on God, the one centre of all, which is 'everywhere and nowhere,' in whom all are encountered, from whom all proceed. . . ."[8]

This is the great belief of many sages in this book. It is the path to freedom, they say, when the self begins to realize its own powerlessness and limitations and begins to find a new happiness in the surrender of its entity, the giving up of its selfhood.

Merton saw that what replaces the self, the feeling of the small and individual "I," is "an intuition of a *ground of openness* . . . an infinite generosity which communicates itself to everything that is."[9]

This sort of statement made many conventional Catholics view Merton with some suspicion and mistrust, although there was never any Vatican opposition to his views. (I was told by a young English Dominican monk that Merton is not to be read in his monastery and is considered to be "out.") Certainly, although his grasp of the essential likeness between the religions became more masterly, some unusual statements came from his still Catholic pen:

> . . . We begin to divine that Zen is not only beyond the formulations of Buddhism but it is also in a certain way "beyond" (and even pointed to by) the revealed message of Christianity.[10]

Taoism, which formed a large part of the spiritual background to Zen in its early days, also attracted Merton deeply and, after five years of study, he published *The Way of Chuang Tzu*, his own interpretation of the writings of the Chinese sage, in which he was helped by a friend, Dr. John Wu. In an affectionate preface about Chuang Tzu, which has the feeling that it is also about Thomas Merton, he says:

> I simply like Chuang Tzu because he is what he is and I feel no need to justify this liking to myself or to anyone else. He is far too great to need any apologies from me. If St. Augustine could read Plotinus, if St. Thomas could read Aristotle and Averroës (both of them certainly a long way further from Christianity than Chuang Tzu ever was!), and if Teilhard de Chardin could make copious use of Marx and Engels in his synthesis, I think I may be pardoned for consorting with a Chinese recluse who shares the climate and peace of my own kind of solitude, and who is my own kind of person. . . .
>
> Chuang Tzu is not concerned with words and formulas about reality, but with the direct existential grasp of reality in itself . . . the whole teaching, the "way" contained in these anecdotes, poems and meditations, is characteristic of a certain mentality found everywhere in the world, a certain taste for simplicity, for humility, self-effacement, silence, and in general a refusal to take seriously the aggressivity, the ambition, the push, and the self-importance which one must dis-

play in order to get along in society. This other is a "way" that prefers not to get anywhere in the world, or even in the field of some supposedly spiritual attainment. . . . For Chuang Tzu, as for the Gospel, to lose one's life is to save it, and to seek to save it for one's own sake is to lose it. There is an affirmation of the world that is nothing but ruin and loss. There is a renunciation of the world that finds and saves man in his own home, which is God's world. In any event, the "way" of Chuang Tzu is mysterious because it is so simple that it can get along without being a way at all. Least of all is it a "way out." Chuang Tzu would have agreed with St. John of the Cross, that you enter upon this kind of way when you leave all ways and, in some sense, get lost.[11]

Thomas Merton died in Bangkok, where he had been invited to address a conference of Asian monastic orders. His journey through India and Ceylon to Thailand was the fulfillment of a long-awaited dream and as the plane left San Francisco airport for the East, Merton wrote, "We left the ground—I with Christian mantras and a great sense of destiny, of being at last on my true way after years of waiting and wondering and fooling around."[12]

Prophetic words indeed—but Merton had no preknowledge that he was going to his death. Rather, he hoped for confirmation of the sense of kinship he already felt for the Eastern religions—and it came, in what seems to have been a deeply spiritual illumination.

He was on the Buddhist island of Ceylon and was visiting the caves of Polonnaruwa, the site of ancient monasteries and shrines, and of a number of famous carved figures of the Buddha:

The path dips down to Gal Vihara: a wide, quiet hollow, surrounded with trees. A low outcrop of rock, with a cave cut into it, and beside the cave a big seated Buddha on the right, and Ananda, I guess, standing by the head of the reclining Buddha. The vicar general, shying away from "paganism," hangs back and sits under a tree reading the guidebook. I am able to approach the Buddhas barefoot and undisturbed, my feet in wet grass, wet sand. Then the silence of the extraordinary faces. The great smiles. Huge and yet subtle. Filled with every possibility, questioning nothing, knowing everything, rejecting nothing, the peace not of emotional resignation but of *Madhyamika,* of *sunyata* (the Void nature of ultimate reality) that has seen through every question without trying to discredit anyone or anything—*without refutation*—without establishing some other argument. For the doctrinaire, the mind that needs well-established positions, such peace, such silence, can be frightening. I was knocked over with a rush of relief and thankfulness at the *obvious* clarity of the figures, the clarity and fluidity of shape and line, the design of the monumental bodies composed into the rock shape and landscape, figure, rock and tree. And the sweep of bare rock sloping away on the other side of the hollow, where you can go back and see different aspects of the figures.

Looking at these figures I was suddenly, almost forcibly, jerked clean out of the habitual, half-tied vision of things, and an inner clearness, clarity, as if exploding from the rocks themselves, became evident and obvious. The queer *evidence* of the reclining figure, the smile, the sad smile of Ananda standing with arms folded (much more "imperative" than Da Vinci's Mona Lisa because completely simple and straightforward). The thing about all this is that there is no puzzle, no problem, and really no "mystery." All problems are resolved and everything is clear. The rock, all matter, all life, is charged with dharmakaya (law and truth) . . . everything is emptiness and everything is compassion. I don't know when in my life I have ever had such a sense of beauty and spiritual validity running together in one aesthetic illumination.[13]

Teilhard de Chardin
1881–1955

There can be no doubt that we are conscious of carrying within us something greater and more indispensable than ourselves: something that existed before we did and could have continued to exist without us: something in which we live, and that we cannot exhaust: something that serves us but of which we are not masters: something that will gather us up when, through death, we slip away from ourselves and our whole being seems to be evaporating.

Writings in Time of War[1]

The Jesuit priest, Pierre Teilhard de Chardin, spent his life in pursuit of scientific evidence to show the presence of God within the material universe. He was by nature a scientist, interested even in early childhood in all the phenomena surrounding him in the Auvergne region of France where he was born. He relates how, as a very young child, he would collect all objects which seemed to be imperishable. Even at six or seven years old, he longed to possess some finite thing which was unchangeable and absolute. He was dismayed to find that iron rusted, that wood could burn:

I looked for equivalents elsewhere. Sometimes in a blue flame over the logs on the hearth—at once so material and so

44

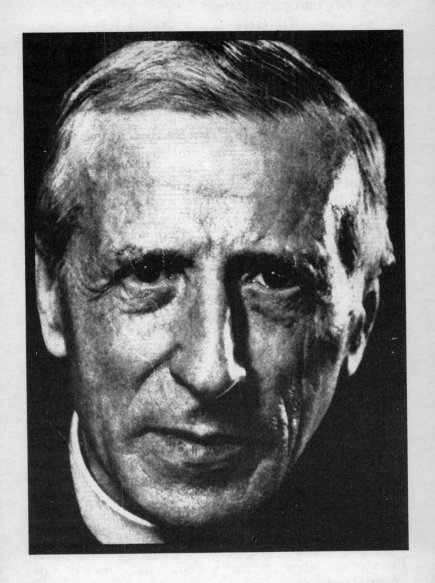

pure and so impossible to get hold of. More often in some stone more transparent or more brightly coloured; crystals of quartz and amethyst, and, above all, shining fragments of chalcedony which I was able to collect in my country of Auvergne. The cherished substance had to be resistant, unassailable and hard.[2]

In the course of time this overwhelming interest in discovering the eternal in the realms of matter brought Teilhard to attempt a synthesis in which he saw God manifest as consciousness throughout the whole of evolution.

His conclusions reached a point which, in some ways, was like the idea of the Self in Hinduism, for he saw the soul (in this sense, the individual self) as nothing in comparison with the power of consciousness which dominates and fills it, and with which it is one.

There is nothing unique about a soul, he said (it was this sort of statement which caused his superiors to refuse publication of his works), for it would contradict the nature of the world's design and development if souls were naturally each one unique. They are legion. But if we turn our attention to that which lies *between* them, by which they subsist, the force of creation which they all have in common, then we meet the really great mystery. We are usually blind to the single unifying force which underlies all manifestation because we tend to look outward and direct our attention to that which isolates and separates us.

This is an important observation, for it certainly seems true that we spend most of our life naming and judging the world in relation to "me," thus creating a false duality. We are distracted by appearances and take the appearance for the whole, so that we come to believe that the material universe we apprehend through our senses is all there is. In this way, always looking outward, we fail to *notice* the unity of all things because we are so intent on seeing their different appearances.

It is this uniting factor that Teilhard was most concerned with. If you were to add up the differences between individuals, he said, you would have no more than a phantom world because differences are so few and ephemeral. But by adding up *all* human qualities and then subtracting the small number which differ from the rest, you are left with a "most impressive residue which belongs to no particular soul but to all souls together."

What is the nature of this residue? Teilhard believed that it was a directing energy which impelled people on to higher and higher states of consciousness and unity. But, like the Buddha, he did not speculate greatly upon its nature. The important thing to him was the fact of its existence which, he felt, *must* be accepted. All living beings, he said, "are grafted upon one and the same Reality as tangible as our own substance. . . ." Whether we concentrate on fulfilling our own personality to its ultimate degree, or whether we surrender our personality to God's will, as soon as we withdraw our attention from the outer world of day-to-day relationships we must find *"immediately behind us, as though it were an extension of ourselves, a soul of the world."*[3]

The "soul of the world" or the "impressive residue" —how can it be recognized? It is manifested, said Teilhard, as consciousness. Throughout evolution, the directing energy of God has impelled organisms to evolve in consciousness, and their consciousness increases in direct ratio to their complexity. He believed that an atom, for instance, has an infinitesimal consciousness of its own existence. As atoms combine, as cells are formed, as organisms develop, so their consciousness grows. The ultimate state of consciousness will be the consciousness of God. Because this is its purpose and the cause of its existence, all consciousness, however rudimentary, is therefore spiritual.

> Spirituality is not a recent accident, arbitrarily or fortuitously imposed on the edifice of the world around us; it is a deeply rooted phenomenon, the traces of which we can follow with certainty backwards as far as the eye can reach, in the wake of the movement that is drawing us forward. As far back as we can recognise a surface of the earth, that surface is inhabited. It is as if no planet can reach a certain stage in its sidereal evolution without breaking into life. But this is not all. The consciousness that we see filling the avenues of the past, does not flow simply like a river which carries an unchanging water past ever changing banks. It transforms itself in the course of its journey; it evolves; life has a movement *of its own*.[4]

If we look at the very lowest forms of life—inert matter—we fall into the error of thinking that it has no consciousness at all, he said. But it may really be that its consciousness is so fragmented and diffused that we can only see it at all through the "laws of nature," the laws of statistical organization which the study of science has revealed.

As we go upward, we can see particles beginning to stand out from the mass as individuals—consciousness appearing in a rather loose form in which recognition of itself is confused by all the mass of mechanisms about it. Such are plants and animals as we see them.

Finally, in what Teilhard thought of as the ultimate development, thought appears. Because the preparation for this phase has extended over such aeons, "nothing quivers when it appears in nature," and because there is no apparent break in the evolutionary chain which binds us to other animals, natural scientists have not, until recently, given a proper importance to the emergence of thinking man. This was Teilhard's contention and undoubtedly he himself was largely instrumental in promoting the belated study of mankind.

For man is not only a new species, he said, he is also the beginning of a completely new era in the history of the earth. There is a much greater gap between man and simple organic life than there is between organic life and inorganic matter. Conscious intelligence has brought about, for the first time, a universe which is aware of itself, which is *"personalized."*

At this point it is easy to lose the drift of Teilhard's theory. What does he mean by a personalized universe? To Teilhard, a devout Christian, God was the ultimate Being, expressed in the perfect man, Jesus Christ. Therefore, he saw the whole of evolution as prearrangedly heading toward the ultrapersonal—toward a point in time when conscious, supremely personal mankind will be united, or oned, with Christ the Omega-point, the heart of the universe.

Catholic Christianity has always believed that in some way unfathomable to man, the person of Jesus Christ contains the whole explanation of existence—not so much in his historical concreteness but as the "cosmic Christ," a spirit of the universe. "The answer to the universe is: Jesus Christ" says Father Corbishley, Superior of Farm Street Church in London; and Teilhard himself says:

> Once we make up our minds to take the words of Revelation literally—and to do so is the idea of all true religion —then the whole mass of the Universe is gradually bathed in light. And just as science shows us, at the lower limits of matter, an ethereal fluid in which everything is immersed and from which everything emerges, so at the upper limits of Spirit a mystical ambience appears in which everything floats and everything converges.[5]

With this belief in mind, it was an easy step for Teilhard to conclude that the direction of conscious intelligence must be toward one personality—the personality of Jesus. Individual differences he thought very little of, as we observed earlier. But ultimate personality, to him, was the expression of divinity—unselfish, creative, and pure. The combined personalities of all men, he thought, would become one, drawn like a magnet towards the end of evolution, towards the *Pleroma* of complete convergence on Christ.

Our worldly conditions, he thought, have been spiritual from the beginning—the divine atmosphere, or *milieu,* in which "God enfolds and penetrates us by creating and preserving us." Thus we have been created for God's activity, which is for one purpose only—that we are to become "one and the same complex thing with him."[6]

Teilhard here raises what is to me, and, I suspect, to many others, a baffling point—why has God bothered to create life if the end result will be the same as the beginning? The *how* of it all we can understand through the revelations of science, but the question of existence itself has not yet been satisfactorily answered by any religion or scientific discovery.

Teilhard's answers perhaps bear some of the shortcomings of a sheltered, academic life, but no one can deny his brilliant insights and fervent yet lucid language. Was he, perhaps, an overdedicated man? As a mystical theologian, his whole interest seemed absorbed by the desire to prove scientifically the links between evolution and the Christian vision of the world. Apart from this overwhelming passion, he seems to have taken little notice of other aspects of life. The arts passed him by. He was not interested in living people, or their conditions. He spent twenty years in China and took amazingly little notice of its culture and philosophies. He visited India and failed to comprehend Hinduism, which he regarded with hostility. All in all, he presents us with a partially self-imprisoned man, whose energy was directed to discovering proof for his theories and syntheses, which is perhaps why some of them seem a bit grandiose and far from reality.

Robert Speaight, a leading authority on Teilhard, says of him: "Now that he was quite fixed in his belief that mankind was carried along by an advancing wave of consciousness, 'does anything,' he asked, 'remain to be disclosed in what has been left behind us?' It was an extraordinarily cavalier view of history. Teilhard was so sure that progress was inevitable that he made little allowance for disaster or decline. It rarely occurred to him that, from his own optimistic point of view, the past might be superior to the present and had much to teach it. For all our conquest of the atom we are still trying to catch up with Socrates. Teilhard envisaged progress in a strictly linear development; he did not seem to realize how it could play ducks and drakes with time."[7]

Teilhard's belief in the inevitability of progress was arrived at through his faith in the magnetic power of Christ at the center of the universe. Having once positioned Christ there, and proved that position to his own satisfaction by what he had observed of evolution, he could then only allow himself to see progress. The future must be better than the present. If it were not, his belief would be wrong. For if mankind is to end up in a great smelting fire of glory, it *can not*, in the meantime, blow itself out in a furnace of radiation.

What is the supreme and complex reality for which the divine operation moulds us? It is revealed to us by St. Paul and St. John. It is the quantitative repletion and the qualitative consummation of all things: it is the mysterious Pleroma, in which the substantial *one* and the created *many* fuse without confusion in a *whole* which, without adding anything essential to God, will nevertheless be a sort of triumph and generalisation of being. . . .

At last we are nearing our goal. What is the active centre, the living link, the organising soul of the Pleroma? St. Paul, again, proclaims it with his resounding voice: it is he in whom everything is reunited, and in whom all things are consummated—through whom the whole created edifice receives its consistency—Christ dead and risen. . . .

And now let us link the first and last terms of this long series of identities. We shall then see with a wave of joy that *the divine omnipresence* translates itself within our universe by the network of the organising forces of the total Christ. God exerts pressure, in us and upon us—through the intermediary of all the powers of heaven, earth and hell—only in the act of forming and consummating Christ who saves and sur-animates the world. And since, in the course of this operation, Christ himself does not act as a dead or passive point of convergence, but as a centre of radiation for the energies which lead the universe back to God through his humanity, the layers of divine action finally come to us impregnated with his organic energies.[8]

There seem to be two ways in which religious people regard the world and time. One is Teilhard's, in which some sort of perfection will be reached at an infinitely distant period. This way regards the present experience of life as incomplete in itself. It is merely a step towards a future goal. It often sees divine patterns revealing themselves—and events which do not fit in are ignored—as Teilhard was inclined to ignore suffering. This religious path demands concentration upon a goal which can never be realized *now*—it is in some vague and far off future. This attitude of mind is shared by all religions —there are many Hindus and Buddhists who believe that merging with the Self, or Nirvana, can only be reached after innumerable lifetimes.

The other way is that of the mystic, such as Thomas Merton, to whom "nowness" is all-important. The true mystic is immensely at home in the world *at this moment*. He is as much at one with the smallest part as with the whole. He does not look for patterns or significant events or future wonders. He does not concentrate upon a goal because he feels no need for one—here and now contains all goals and all wonders. To him the idea of a future Pleroma is meaningless because every present moment is unique, unrepeatable, and timeless.

Because Jesus was a man, Teilhard believed that the cosmic energy of the universe is constantly increasing in man and he saw this "hominized energy" appearing in three ways: incorporated energy, controlled energy, and spiritualized energy.

(a) *Incorporated energy* is that which the slow biological evolution of the earth has gradually accumulated and harmonised in our organism of flesh and nerves: the astonishing "natural machine" of the human body.

(b) *Controlled energy* is the energy around him which man ingeniously succeeds in dominating with physical power originating from his limbs by means of "artificial machines."

(c) *Spiritualised energy* is localised in the immanent zones of our free activity, and forms the stuff of our intellectual processes, affections, and volitions. This energy is probably incapable of measurement, but is very real all the same, since it gains a reflective and passionate mastery of things and their relationships.[9]

It is in this last area of spiritualized energy that Teilhard laid himself most open to attack from other scientists. For he postulated three main spheres in the structure of the universe—the geosphere, which is the sphere of matter; the biosphere, which is the sphere of animate life; and the noosphere, which is the sphere of the mind and is spiritualized energy. It is in the noosphere, he said, that more evolution is going to take place, and he believed that it would:

> The being who is the object of his own reflection, in consequence of that very doubling back upon himself, becomes in a flash able to raise himself into a new sphere. In reality, another world is born. Abstraction, logic, reasoned choice and inventions, mathematics, art, calculation of space and time, anxieties and dreams of love—all these activities of *inner life* are nothing else than the effervescence of the newly-formed centre as it explodes onto itself.[10]

Many scientists could not accept such utterances, particularly when Teilhard envisaged the noosphere as a sort of psychic layer surrounding the globe, a network of communication and thought. But scientific scepticism did not cause Teilhard any hesitation and he went on to predict that from the noosphere would evolve "love, *the higher, universal, and synthesised form of spiritual energy,* in which all the other energies of the soul are transformed and sublimated once they fall within 'the field of Omega.' "[11]

"How could it be otherwise," he said, "if the universe is to maintain its equilibrium?

"A Super-mankind calls for a Super-Christ.

"A Super-Christ calls for a Super-charity."[12]

Super-charity, he believed, is on its way, and is already felt in many places. "At this moment there are men, many men, who by making a conjunction of the two ideas of Incarnation and evolution a real element in their lives, are succeeding in effecting the synthesis of the personal and the universal. For the first time in history men have become capable not only of knowing and serving evolution but of *loving it;* thus they are beginning to be able to say to God, explicitly, as a matter of habit and effortlessly, that they love him not only with their whole heart and their whole soul, but 'with the whole universe.' "[13]

In his precise definitions of God's plans for mankind —a more and more personalized existence in which all men would become one—one begins to sense in Teilhard a need for reassurance. He seems to insist *too much* on the Pleroma, on man's convergence upon himself, his growingly intense and perfect unification as he travels further and further inward to Omega point—as though Teilhard himself was a little uncertain. He spent much of his life, such as the twenty years in China, isolated from contemporary thought and discovery and was further isolated (although not from his friends) by the Vatican's decision to refuse to allow publication of his major works. Whatever the causes, his beliefs about the Pleroma when mankind finally reaches the ultimate convergence in perfection on Omega and Christ is realized and reborn seem ideas hardly related to this world. Yet many people, particularly Roman Catholics, have found in Teilhard a source of courage, and although a very different man from Merton, the two do share a strong spiritual inspiration and revelation; Teilhard's more mystical writings in *The Divine Milieu* and *The Hymn of the Universe* among others, contain a great intensity of feeling which is lacking in the writing of many modern theologians and is perhaps needed in the rational West. He was able to express himself with true depth in poetic prose:

. . . And so, for the first time in my life perhaps (although I am supposed to meditate every day!), I took the lamp and, leaving the zone of everyday occupations and relationships where everything seems clear, I went down into my inmost self, to the deep abyss whence I feel dimly that my power of action emanates. But as I moved further and further away from the conventional certainties by which social life is superficially illuminated, I became aware that I was losing contact with myself. At each step of the descent a new person was disclosed within me of whose name I was no longer sure, and who no longer obeyed me. And when I had to stop my exploration because the path faded from beneath my steps, I found a bottomless abyss at my feet, and out of it came —arising I know not from where—the current which I dare to call my life. . . .

At that moment, as anyone else will find who cares to make this same interior experiment, I felt the distress characteristic to a particle adrift in the universe, the distress which makes human wills founder daily under the crushing number of living things and of stars. And if something saved me, it was hearing the voice of the Gospel, guaranteed by divine successes, speaking to me from the depth of the night: *ego sum, noli timere* (It is I, be not afraid).

Yes, O God, I believe it: and I believe it all the more willingly because it is not only a question of my being consoled, but of my being completed: it is you who are at the origin of the impulse, and at the end of that continuing pull which all my life long I can do no other than follow, or favour the first impulse and its developments. And it is you who vivify, for me, with your omnipresence (even more than my spirit vivifies the matter which it animates) the myriad influences of which I am the constant object. In the life which wells up in me and in the matter which sustains me, I find much more than your gifts. It is you yourself whom I find, who makes me participate in your being, you who moulds me. . . .[14]

O God, whose call precedes the very first of our movements, grant me the desire to desire being—that, by means of that divine thirst which is your gift, the access to the great waters may open wide within me. Do not deprive me of the sacred taste for being, that primordial energy, that very first point of our points of rest: *Spiritu principali confirma me.* And you whose loving wisdom forms me out of all the forces and all the hazards of the earth, grant that I may begin to sketch the outline of a gesture whose full power will only be revealed to me in the presence of the forces of diminishment and death; grant that, after having desired, I may believe, and believe ardently and above all things, in your active presence.[15]

58

References

Aldous Huxley

1 Aldous Huxley, *Those Barren Leaves* (London: Chatto and Windus; New York: Harper and Row), p. 334.
2 Julian Huxley, *Aldous Huxley 1894-1963: A Memorial Tribute* (London: Chatto and Windus; New York: Harper and Row), p. 35.
3 Aldous Huxley, *Eyeless in Gaza* p. 616.
4 Philip Thody, *Aldous Huxley* (London: Studio Vista; New York: Van Nostrand Reinhold), p. 32.
5 Aldous Huxley, *The Perennial Philosophy* (London: Chatto and Windus; New York: Harper and Row), p. 5.
6 Laura Archera Huxley, *This Timeless Moment* (London: Chatto and Windus; New York: Farrar Straus and Giroux), p. 197.
7 Aldous Huxley, *The Doors of Perception and Heaven and Hell* (London: Chatto and Windus; New York: Harper and Row), p. 114.
8 Ibid., pp. 16-19.
9 Ibid., p. 31.
10 Ibid., p. 35.
11 Huxley, L., *This Timeless Moment*, p. 139.
12 Huxley, A., *The Doors of Perception*, p. 121.
13 Ibid., p. 122.
14 Huxley, L., *This Timeless Moment*, p. 23.
15 Huxley, J., *Aldous Huxley 1894-1963*, p. 174.

Alan Watts

1 Alan Watts, *This Is It* (London: John Murray; New York: Pantheon Books), p. 30.
2 Alan Watts, *Beyond Theology* (London: Hodder and Stoughton; New York: Pantheon Books, Random House), p. 109.
3 Ibid., p. 111.
4 Ibid., p. 112.
5 Alan Watts, *Nature, Man, and Woman* (London: Thames and Hudson; New York: Pantheon Books), p. 39.
6 Ibid., p. 45.
7 Alan Watts, *Does It Matter?* (New York: Pantheon Books), p. 37.
8 Alan Watts, *The Wisdom of Insecurity* (New York: Pantheon Books), p. 85.

9   Ibid., p. 86.
10 Watts, *Nature, Man and Woman,* p. 116.
11 Alan Watts, *Psychotherapy East and West* (London:
        Jonathan Cape; New York: Pantheon Books), p. 45.
12 Christopher Isherwood, ed., *Vedanta for Modern
        Man* (London: George Allen and Unwin; The
        Vedanta Society for Southern California), p. 22.
13 Ibid., p. 24.
14 Alan Watts, *The Book on the Taboo Against Knowing Who
        You Are* (London: Jonathan Cape; New York: Pantheon
        Books), p. 136.
15 Ibid., p. 138.
16 Alan Watts, *In My Own Way* (London: Jonathan Cape;
        New York: Pantheon Books), p. 387.

Thomas Merton

1   Thomas Merton, *Seeds of Contemplation* (London:
        Anthony Clarke Books; New York: New
        Directions), p. 5.
2   Ibid., pp. 6–7.
3   Ibid., p. 23.
4   Ibid., p. 25.
5   Thomas Merton, *Conjectures of a Guilty Bystander*
        (New York: Doubleday and Company, Inc.),
        pp. 296–297.
6   Merton, *Seeds of Contemplation,* p. 217.
7   Thomas Merton, *Zen and the Birds of Appetite* (New York:
        New Directions Publishing Corporation), p. 62.
8   Ibid., p. 24.
9   Ibid., p. 25.
10 Ibid., p. 8.
11 Thomas Merton, *The Way of Chuang Tzu* (London:
        George Allen and Unwin Ltd.; New York: New
        Directions Publishing Corporation), pp. 10–11.
12 Thomas Merton, *The Asian Journal of Thomas Merton*
        (London: Sheldon Press; New York: New
        Directions Publishing Corporation), p. 233.
13 Ibid., p. 235.

Further Reading

Contemplative Prayer. New York: Doubleday and Company,
    Inc.
The Wisdom of the Desert. London: Hollis and Carter.

60

Teilhard de Chardin

1 Teilhard de Chardin, *Writings in Time of War* (London: Collins; New York: Harper and Row), p. 181.
2 Robert Speaight, *Teilhard de Chardin: A Biography* (London: Collins), p. 25.
3 Teilhard de Chardin, *Writings in Time of War*, p. 182.
4 Teilhard de Chardin, *Human Energy* (London: Collins; New York: Harcourt Brace Jovanovitch, Inc.), p. 96.
5 Teilhard de Chardin, *Let Me Explain* (London: Collins; New York: Harper and Row), p. 129.
6 Teilhard de Chardin, *The Divine Milieu* (London: Collins; New York: Harper and Row), p. 122.
7 Speaight, *Teilhard de Chardin: A Biography*, p. 213.
8 Teilhard de Chardin, *The Divine Milieu*, p. 122.
9 Teilhard de Chardin, *Human Energy*, p. 115.
10 Teilhard de Chardin, *The Phenomenon of Man* (London: Collins; New York: Harper and Row), p. 165.
11 Teilhard de Chardin, *Science and Christ* (London: Collins; New York: Harper and Row), p. 171.
12 Ibid.
13 Ibid., p. 172.
14 Teilhard de Chardin, *The Divine Milieu*, p. 76.
15 Ibid., p. 79.

2

The Solitary Liberator

      Jiddu Krishnamurti has no religion and no set philosophy for his hope is to liberate men from all systems—from each other's dogmas and opinions as well as from rigid theology and organized religion. He sees man united in mind and body and freed from the bondage and tyranny of the grasping ego. His message is clearly stated but it is a message which many people find difficult to receive. He demands great efforts from his readers and from the many audiences whom he addresses throughout the world.

He talks about the problems which are common to all men—suffering, violence, fear, love, and the passage of time. He sees men caught up in a miasma of false values and he demands that they give up their conceptual ideas about themselves—ideas based on their early conditioning. Men will learn nothing, he says, until they stop comparing the present with the past, for the present is always *new* and must be experienced with a mind that is free from all thoughts and ideas about it.

The feeling of "I" to Krishnamurti, is based on false beliefs. When this feeling is dropped, the awareness of what is here and now is complete and is no longer divided and altered by the choices of the I-ego. To say, for instance, "I am aware" is to put an unnecessary division between the experiencing subject and the experience. The mind is conditioned to believe in "I," says Krishnamurti, but when it can drop its conditioning (the way it has been taught to think) the feeling of "I" changes and becomes at one with existence, no longer separate from it. For many people, this argument is too difficult to understand and so Krishnamurti urges his hearers to become aware of life in a way which is choiceless, and to experience this choiceless awareness *now*.

The key to understanding Krishnamurti's "I" is to remember that he believes it to be an unnecessary and false sensation that leads to division and suffering. He sometimes uses the word *ego* for *I*.

Krishnamurti
1895–1986

I have long been in revolt from all things, from the authority of others, from the instruction of others, from the knowledge of others; I would not accept anything as Truth until I found the Truth myself. I never opposed the ideas of others but I would not accept their authority, their theory of life. Until I was in that state of revolt, until I became dissatisfied with everything, with every creed, with every dogma and belief, I was not able to find the Truth. . . .

René Fouère[1]

The speaker of these words, Jiddu Krishnamurti, had much to revolt against. His story is one of the oddest of the twentieth century. He was born in India, the eighth child of a poverty-stricken Brahmin, Jiddu Naraniah, who had lost his minor post with the British administration. Krishnamurti's mother died when he was young and his father moved the family to Adyar, near Madras, to be close to the headquarters of the Theosophical Society of which he was a member. One of the beliefs of the Society is that from time to time in history a great Being takes on a human form—a body uniquely prepared and waiting for him—and it then founds a new religion, one which will

63

bring out the particular aspect of the Truth needed for
that age. Jesus was the last acknowledged incarnation
(Theosophists do not count Mohammed), and in 1909
they decided that the time had come when an incarnation
was necessary, and they were sure that it was about to
happen.

After the move to Adyar the young Krishnamurti and
his brother Nityananda often roamed the beaches where
the Adyar river joins the Bay of Bengal, and it was here
that they were seen by the librarian of the Theosophical
Society, C. W. Leadbeater, a renowned clairvoyant, and
also the subject of various scandals concerned with
homosexuality. When he noticed the brothers he thought
that their auras were remarkable and he asked for permission to take them to the headquarters and to teach them
himself. Their father agreed to this. Lady Emily Lutyens,
who later became devoted to Krishnamurti, tells us that

> Krishna was a very nervous, shy boy, and it took him a
> long time to feel at ease in the presence of Europeans.
> Frequent absence from school, owing to malaria, had made
> him backward in his studies, and also a great favorite with
> his mother, whom he had adored. He was naturally a
> dreamer—psychic, and spiritually minded, as Indian boys
> can be, without becoming morbid or priggish. His younger
> brother Nitya (as Nityananda was always called for short)
> had, on the other hand, a brilliant brain and was not troubled
> with nervousness. He learned without any difficulty. But
> in spite of their differences in temperament and character
> there was an extraordinarily close bond between the two
> brothers—a great mutual love and respect.[2]

Investigations were then started into their previous
reincarnations and the results were published in *The
Theosophist*. Hopes began to rise that Krishnamurti was
to be the new Messiah and, in 1911, Dr. Annie Besant, the

president of the Theosophical Society, started The Order
of the Star in the East, of which Krishnamurti was made
the head. Although she had by then adopted the boys,
their father now asked for them back on the grounds that
Leadbeater was corrupting them and that their education
was against the rules of their caste. Mrs. Besant took the
boys to England and eventually won her case to keep
them although they had to be hidden at Taormina for a
time in case their father tried to kidnap them.

From then on, all was set for Krishnamurti to be
coached in his role as World Teacher. Mrs. Besant and
Leadbeater were given telepathic instructions by "Masters," supposed representatives of an Occult Hierarchy
governing the world, on what to do with the boys, down to
the smallest items of diet. Perhaps the Masters (two of
whom were said to live on opposite sides of a ravine in
Tibet) were not sufficiently knowledgeable about the best
food for young Indians from Madras, for Lady Emily tells
us that "Krishna suffered very much at that time from
indigestion. Acute pains in his stomach would keep him
awake half the night. C.W.L. [Leadbeater] had laid
down a system of diet for him supposedly under the
direct orders of the Master K.H. [Koot Hoomi]. It was a
cruel diet for anybody suffering from indigestion. Innumerable glasses of milk had to be consumed during
the day, and porridge and eggs for breakfast. I can see
Krishna now, after a sleepless night of pain, struggling to
eat his prescribed breakfast under Mrs. Besant's stern
eye. How I longed to snatch the plate from him and give
his inside a rest."[3]

Food was not the only trouble for Krishnamurti, however. There was the climate—"I . . . well remember at a
garden-party at Oxford the two shivering little Indian
boys trying to keep warm in an English May. They looked
so forlorn and cold and shy that I longed to put my arms

round them and mother them."[4]

But more powerful than any physical trouble was the whole atmosphere of reverence and adoration with which Krishnamurti was surrounded and which must have created abnormal demands on his personality. He *had* to be psychic. It was believed that he roamed about on the astral plane at night, that he could magnetize objects beneficially, that he had passed great occult initiations. Lady Emily tells us, "he accepted his position but never derived any personal satisfaction from it. He never wanted anything for himself—money, power or position. George [Arundale] was always urging him to try to re-member what had happened on other planes. '*Please* bring through,' he would keep saying; but Krishna re-mained unmoved and only 'brought through' when he really did remember something. He was, I think, desper-ately unhappy. He hated publicity; he longed for a nor-mal home life. He often said to me 'Why did they ever pick on me?' "[5]

The crushing burden of this messianic role might have created a dupe or a cynic. Without the support of his beloved brother the depths of his loneliness might have proved too much for his mental balance. Rarely in the history of the world have the good intentions of so many people been centered on one shy, unacademic boy. Krishnamurti's personality remained intact but a healthy rejection of his supporters became necessary.

Spurred on by the expectations of his followers, Krish-namurti had, for a time, come to accept his role and even to speak in the first person as the Lord Maitreya (the head of the Occult Hierarchy). But then doubt and scepticism, heralds of the true Krishnamurti, began to grow and he announced that he disbelieved a great many of the psychic messages "brought through" from the Masters by some of the foremost Theosophists. One of them,

Wedgewood, immediately retaliated by announcing that Krishnamurti was being used by a powerful black magician whom he, Wedgewood, had actually seen standing by Krishnamurti. People began to take sides and the storm grew strong in proportion to Krishnamurti's doubts.

It broke in 1929 when Krishnamurti finally dissolved the Order of the Star—the organization which had been built around his role as Messiah. With that action he deliberately renounced the estates and riches which devotees had tried to thrust on him, the jasmine and rose-filled railway carriages, the camps where thousands listened with bated breath to his every word. Instead he chose an austere integrity, a hard and solitary path, which he outlined in the speech which ended his life as a pseudo-Messiah:

> I maintain that truth is a pathless land, and you cannot approach it by any path whatsoever, by any religion, by any sect. That is my point of view and I adhere to it absolutely and unconditionally. Truth, being limitless, unconditioned, unapproachable by any path whatsoever, cannot be organized.
>
> I do not want followers. *I mean this.* . . . If there are only five people who will listen, who will *live*, who have their faces turned towards eternity, it will be sufficient. Of what use is it to have thousands who do not understand, who are fully embalmed in prejudice, who do not want the new, but would rather translate the new to suit their own sterile, stagnant selves?
>
> Because I am free, unconditioned, whole, not the part, not the relative, but the whole Truth that is eternal, I desire those who seek to understand me to be free, not to follow me, not to make out of me a cage which will become a religion, a sect. Rather they should be free from all fears—from the fear of religion, from the fear of salvation, from the fear of spirituality, from the fear of love, from the fear of death, from the fear of life itself.[6]

For eighteen years, he told them, they had been preparing for a World Teacher who would transform their lives and renew their understanding; but all it had amounted to was the substitution of a new god and a new religion for the old. They were still using the outer forms of religion as crutches and were still barred and limited by them. Their psychological state hadn't changed at all and they depended for their spirituality on somebody else. When he asked them, Krishnamurti said, to put away all religious practices and instead to look within themselves for enlightenment, glory, purification, and incorruptibility, they would not do it.

He then formally dissolved the Order of the Star, telling the Theosophists to go and look for another Messiah and to start afresh with a new organization.

"With that," he said, "I am not concerned, nor with the creating of new cages, or new decorations for those cages. My only concern is to set men free."[7]

From that time on, Jiddu Krishnamurti was on his own, and might well have sunk into oblivion. The fact that he did not, and has instead become the revered and loved teacher of many more thousands than the membership of the Theosophical Society could supply, suggests that Mrs. Besant and C. W. Leadbeater were right when they saw in the young Krishnamurti a remarkable potential. He is now world-famous, the author of many books, a solitary teacher who still refuses to have organizations built around him, and who travels from country to country explaining the nature of man's identity to all who wish to listen.

What is the core of his teaching? The greater part of it is about awareness—choiceless awareness—which means the ability to be aware of exactly this moment now, *as it is*, without trying to pick out of it only what we want to be aware of. When the feeling of "I am aware of this, or of that" is surrendered, given up to make room for an awareness *that does not exercise choice,* the result is an extraordinary clarity and peace of mind in which the habitual feeling of a separate "I" is diminished.

For that "I," or ego, usually lives its everyday life in such a way that it manipulates all circumstances to its own advantage, which means that instead of being generally aware it is constantly particularizing and judging each thing in relation to its own continuance and interests.

What is the basis of the ego? Why does it operate in the way it does? Krishnamurti believes that memory is largely responsible for its existence. Memory, he says, is the storehouse of the past and we, instead of living in the present, spend our lives drawing from this storehouse. Memory responds all the time in the form of likes and dislikes dictated by the storehouse, which is the individual conditioning of each one of us; the way we have been shaped from infancy by our culture, religion, and education. Every moment of the day, memory is pulling out the old established patterns of thought of which we are mostly unconscious—patterns which give rise to the feeling of "me", which build up a seemingly continuous and consistent "me" entity. This "me" appears to use words and thoughts but, says Krishnamurti, it is really that words and thoughts have created the feeling of "me."

Krishnamurti has perhaps uncovered—as did Alan Watts—a valuable light on the structure of the ego, on the sensation of isolated separateness within one's skin which can lead not to humility but to power, not to love but to hatred and destruction. People in the oldest civilizations and in present-day primitive ones seem to have less consciousness of separateness and less feeling of individual ego-centeredness than we do. The sensation of separateness seems closely linked to humanity's increased ability to think in abstract terms, to separate life from the experience of it by the use of a word. Man lives by the symbol of the word rather than by real experience and this endangers his natural humanhood which becomes abstract rather than actual. When he is not actual, not immediately real to himself, man is driven into remoteness and isolation. His ego no longer derives its power from the moment, but from reactions to old storehouse memories which are taken out and dressed in the symbols of a new situation.

Can we quiet down the conditioned mind, asks Krishnamurti, so that the storehouse merely delivers what is needed for recognition of a present situation but does not take over the person and dictate his reactions? Meditation, he says, is to find out whether the brain can become absolutely still. It must not be a forced stillness for this would come from the "I" who is always eager for pleasurable experiences and who still thinks in terms of "I and my stillness" as though each were separate experiences. No, the brain must never be forced to be quiet, but instead must simply be observed and listened to. The way thoughts are formed, the conditioned memories which come to the surface of the mind, the force of fears or desires as they arise—all these can be observed; and the more clearly every movement is seen the quieter the mind becomes. Not the quietness of sleep but more the soundless action of a strong dynamo which is only heard when there is friction.

It is only when the mind is tranquil but alert, Krishnamurti says, that it can really observe things properly. Occasionally we experience this without effort when faced with something awe-inspiring or great, such as a stormy sea, a magnificent sunset, or a superb building. Then the mind becomes completely quiet, if only for a split second. Krishnamurti points out that a child, when given a new toy, is completely absorbed by it. In the same way, he says, the greatness of the sea or the beauty of the sunset can absorb the restless mind and quiet it completely.

But absorption by an object or a situation means that the mind must then depend on something outside itself and beyond its control. Is "losing yourself" the same as "finding yourself?" Can the mind be quieted without outside help?

Yes, says Krishnamurti. Indeed, the brain which can *only* be stilled from without is in a stupefied state, in an unceasingly restless condition which carries on throughout the night in dreams and gives it no peace at all. It *is* possible to calm the immense activity of the brain from *within* without suppression or great effort.

> As we said, during the day it is endlessly active. You wake up, you look out of the window and say to yourself, "Oh, awful rain," or "It is a marvelous day but too hot"—you have started! So at that moment, when you look out of the window, don't say a word; not suppressing words but simply realising that by saying, "What a lovely morning," or "A horrible day," the brain has started. But if you watch, looking out of the window and not saying a word to yourself—which does not mean you suppress the word—just observing without the activity of the brain rushing in, there you have the clue, there you have the key. When the old brain does not respond, there is a quality of the new brain coming into being. You can observe the mountains, the river, the valleys, the shadows, the lovely trees and the marvellous clouds full of light beyond the mountains—you can look without a word, without comparing.
>
> But it becomes much more difficult when you look at another person; there already you have established images. But just to observe! You will see when you so observe, when you see clearly, that action becomes extraordinarily vital; it becomes a complete action which is not carried over to the next minute.[8]

The ability to drop a thought when it is complete and

not to entangle it with succeeding thoughts is an essential
step on the way to self-realization. For to place a problem
in its own niche and not to allow it to affect any other
aspects of one's life is to free oneself from the extraordinarily pervasive way in which problems seem to creep
over one's whole existence, using up psychological
energy and assuming mountainous proportions. When
this happens, the mind becomes stupefied and dull and
can't seem to get out of the habit of constantly going back
to the problem, just as the tongue has to keep touching a
bad tooth. But if one can see the present moment as
completely different to the last one; if one can open one's
mind to all that is *not* the problem, the burden of self-pity
and self-absorption drops away and one feels clear instead of muddled, integrated instead of in pieces.

Watching the movement of the mind, says Krishnamurti, one sees that there is a gap between the presen-
tation of a situation—such as somebody picking a quarrel
with one—and the response to it. In that fragmentary gap
one *can* discard old habits of mind, so that the situation is
seen freshly, without prejudice. If one continues to watch
the mind, one can also see that its main stimulation *is*
problems—and that the very nature of a problem lies in its
incompleteness and the need to carry it over. But if the
mind becomes quiet, if problems are allowed to resolve
themselves and are not dwelt upon, the brain is no longer
stimulated in this way and it becomes rejuvenated and
innocently clear. Spontaneous right action arises from the
uncomplicated brain, which is able to see what is true and
to act upon it fearlessly:

> The innocent mind implies that whole in which are the
> body, the heart, the brain and the mind. This innocent mind
> which is never touched by thought, can see what truth is,
> what reality is, can see if there is something beyond measure.
> That is meditation. To come upon this extraordinary beauty

of truth, with its ecstasy, you must lay the foundations. The foundation is the understanding of thought, which breeds fear and sustains pleasure, and the understanding of order and therefore virtue; so that there is freedom from all conflict, aggression, brutality and violence. Once one has laid this foundation of freedom, there is a sensitivity which is supreme intelligence, and the whole of the life one leads becomes entirely different.[9]

This theme of the thought-free mind pervades Krishnamurti's teaching. As we will see, Ramana Maharshi constantly exhorted those who came to him to look within and find out "Who am I?" in order that they would discover the pure "I" which is different from "I am this" or "I am that"; similarly Krishnamurti tells his pupils to become aware of their conditioning, of the habits based on memory which shackle their minds, and the attachments which bind them to their bodies and give them a sense of continuous existence.

A Zen way of purifying the mind is to exhort a pupil to "See, but don't think!" In particular, Krishnamurti regards the conditioned memories of childhood as responsible for much of our thinking, and for many of our fears. If a fear, such as that for a wild animal, is based on the memory of something read or heard and not on actual experience of the animal, then there can only be the same old reaction of fear when the animal is actually encountered. This sort of fear, which is not based on personal observation (the wild animal may, in fact, be quite friendly), has a paralyzing and destructive effect which would soon be sensed and acted on by the animal. But an action of the mind that makes one merely *aware of the fear* without identifying the mind with it is a complete action and will lead to the right response. So that if one encounters a tiger in the road, one should not feel an automatic fear of it, for this is conditioned fear, but only feel fear if it appears to be hostile, which would be a correctly placed fear.

One can see, if one really does become aware of one's fears in this way, that many of them are old, out-of-date attitudes that one has projected onto present situations. A clear and objective look at them does seem to remove barriers in the mind so that one has the feeling of action flowing rather than being broken up into separate bursts.

Krishnamurti's words of advice bring response from many Westerners whose habits of thought have become compulsive and fear-ridden. But there are also some who find that he proposes no real method besides that of awareness to help the mind become quiet and alert. All that he says is true, they say, but it is theoretical and he gives no practical advice on how to do it.

It is possible that *his* early conditioning put him against all methods. He is outspokenly against any organized religion, and also against many well-tried practices, such as mantra chanting. A person might just as well say Coca-Cola, Coca-Cola, he says.

True to his own principles, a minimum of organization only has been allowed to grow up around him, and little of it bears his name. He has established a school for young people in England but spends little time there, dividing much of his year between America, Switzerland and India. In spite of his impatience with the formal word, at least twenty books appear under his name and more continue to come.

His manner of address has changed little throughout the years. He rejects any form of ceremony, even a chairman to help him cope with the constant questions that come from the crowds who attend his meetings. He comes on to the stage alone, a small slight man with an austerely beautiful face, and sits on an ordinary wooden chair. He talks without preamble and without notes. But there is often an edge of impatience in his voice when he replies to questioners, and sometimes he delivers a sharp verbal cut that can seem unnecessarily severe.

He always returns to the same point: that we must die to our conditioning, die to the known past, in order that we can become fully aware of the present which is the unknown. This is a dying which can take place moment by moment, he says. He most certainly does not mean that somehow we must obliterate memory—even if that were possible it would clearly lead to the end of the human race. There is nothing wrong with memory in itself, he says, but we must put an end to our reactions based *only* on conditioned memory (what Gurdjieff would call our machine reactions). Memory supplies facts, but our minds must be free of the weight of those facts and not charged with emotions about them, which involve us in carrying them with us everywhere. Facts can be used properly, but only if the mind does not desire or reject them in order to create an emotional state for itself.

We certainly seem to cling to emotions quite desperately at times and seem to confuse our psychological states with life itself, so that if we are not "involved" or not feeling some specific emotion we doubt that we are really living. We can even cling to suffering as giving life some sort of meaning, perhaps because we are afraid to contemplate the Emptiness which might be seen if we ceased to cling. Essentially we cling to the known, which we call life, and are afraid of the unknown.

"So the problem," says Krishnamurti, "is to free the mind from the known, from all the things it has gathered, acquired, experienced, so that it is made innocent and can therefore understand that which is death, the unknowable."[10]

But who is it that frees the mind? Who is the observer of the whole process? Many of Krishnamurti's listeners find this the most difficult point to understand.

Is there a thinker, an observer, a watcher apart from thought, apart from thinking, apart from experience? Is there a thinker, a centre, without thought? If you remove thought, is there a centre? If you have no thought at all, no struggle, no urge to acquire, no effort to become something, is there a centre? Or is the centre created by thought, which feels itself to be insecure, impermanent, in a state of flux?

Please, this requires a great deal of insight, meditation, and penetration, because most of us assume that there is a thinker apart from thinking. But if you go into it a little more closely, you will see that thought has created the thinker. The thinker who is directing, who is the centre, the judge, is the outcome of our thoughts. This is a fact, as you will see if you are really looking at it. Most people are conditioned to believe that the thinker is separate from thought, and they give to the thinker the quality of eternality; but that which is beyond time comes into being only when we understand the whole process of thinking.

Now, can the mind be aware of itself in action, in movement, without a centre? I think it can. It is possible when there is only an awareness of thinking, and not the thinker who is thinking. You know, it is quite an experience to realise that there is only thinking. And it is very difficult to experience that, because the thinker is habitually there, evaluating, judging, condemning, comparing, identifying. If the thinker ceases to identify, evaluate, judge, then there is only thinking, without the centre.[11]

Other sages in this book, notably Ramana Maharshi and Alan Watts, have made the discovery that thought does not need a thinker and that if the thinker, the observer, vanishes, there remains a marvelous sensation of release and joy. It is as though all the dualistic barriers of subject and object have melted and the world exists, as it really is, in its pristine wholeness.

"Do not identify the feeling of 'I' with what actually

happens," teaches Zen. But can a person live everyday life in this way? "Can a person afford not to," Zen would say. Krishnamurti believes that it is possible, but only when there is full awareness of life—"an awareness in which there is no motive or choice, but simple observation."[12]

To live without motive immediately sounds a suspect statement to Western ears. Does this mean a permanently happy-go-lucky, no thought for the morrow, kind of existence? Or does it mean no practical attempts to solve world problems?

By motive, Krishnamurti means attachment to results. If we do the best we can for whatever situation turns up, without trying to influence or cling to the result, we will be motiveless in the sense that our motive is not centered on self-interest. Perhaps this sounds drearily austere —we are so used to connecting happiness with acquiring some experience for the self that we rarely step outside this circle. But to serve the situation for its own sake is strangely rewarding. To relate to things without attachment, just for their own sake, means that I am out of their way, allowing them to have their own existence, pure and unstained, no longer derived from the dead fringes of my projected thoughts and feelings:

> Being aware does not mean learning and accumulating lessons from life; on the contrary, to be aware is to be without the scars of accumulated experience. After all, when the mind merely gathers experience according to its own wishes, it remains very shallow, superficial. ... Awareness comes into being naturally, easily, spontaneously, when we understand the centre which is everlastingly seeking experience, sensation. A mind which seeks sensation through experience becomes insensitive, incapable of swift movement and therefore it is never free. But in understanding its own self-centered activities, the mind comes upon this state of awareness which is choiceless, and such a mind is then capable of

complete silence, stillness . . . .

Only when the mind is completely still can it know its own movement—and then its movement is immense, incalculable, immeasurable. Then it is possible to have that feeling of something which is beyond time. . . .

Creative stillness is not the end-result of a calculating, disciplined and widely-informed mind. It comes into being only when we understand the falsity of the whole process of endlessly seeking sensation through experience. Without that inward stillness, all our speculations about reality, all the philosophies, the systems of ethics, the religions, have very little significance. It is only the still mind which can know infinity.[13]

References

1 René Fouère, *Krishnamurti* p. 1.
2 Lady Emily Lutyens, *Candles in the Wind*
       (London: Rupert Hart Davis), p. 25.
3 Ibid., p. 32.
4 Ibid.
5 Ibid., p. 71.
6 Ibid., p. 173.
7 Ibid.
8 Krishnamurti, *The Impossible Question* (London:
       Gollancz; New York: Harper and Row), p. 77.
9 Ibid., p. 78.
10 Krishnamurti, *Talks in Europe 1956* (Krishnamurti
       Writings Inc.), p. 62.
11 Ibid., p. 16.
12 Ibid., p. 18.
13 Ibid., p. 19.

Further Reading

Krishnamurti, *Commentaries on Living*. London: Gollancz;
     New York: Quest.

Krishnamurti, *First and Last Freedom*. London: Gollancz;
     New York: Theosophical Publishing House.

Krishnamurti, *The Urgency of Change*. London: Gollancz;
     New York: Harper and Row.

Krishnamurti, *The Only Revolution*. London: Gollancz;
     New York: Harper and Row.

3

Masters with a Sufi Background

For Gurdjieff, man's feeling of "I" is based *entirely* on his conditioning (heredity, education, environment, etc.) and has no reality at all. Gurdjieff sees man as composed of a mass of contradictory feelings and thoughts, each one of which he mistakenly thinks of as himself. So each man is a whole mass (or mess!) of fluctuating "I's," all of them fleeting and none of them a real "I" at all.

The central core of man, that which he *could* call "I," can only crystallize into existence when man comes to be aware of the impulses which move him—when he can act or 'do' instead of merely reacting.

The crystallized core is there when a man is born, Gurdjieff seems to believe. It is his "essence"—the Sufi word for the true individual. But as he grows up, this unique individuality is dispersed, swallowed up, captured, and lost by the thousands of thoughts and feelings

which assail us all the time and which are produced by
contact with the outside world. The loss of the "I," or the
real individual, means that a central energy is drained
from the person. Instead of being one he is many, and
thus his energies are always being diverted so that he can
never act in harmony with himself. To bring him back to
his essence, Gurdjieff devised many exercises. This
chapter is concerned with Gurdjieff's teaching on these
points, rather than with his more esoteric theories about
the nature of the universe, many of which stem from Sufi
beliefs.

In contrast with the vigorous, powerful, complicated,
and often mischievous Gurdjieff, Pak Subuh seems almost a shadow. This is probably what he would wish, for
he believes that he himself has *no* power—it is the Divine
Life Force which moves him and all his followers. Yet at
Gurdjieff's death, some of his pupils turned to Subuh as a
natural continuation of Gurdjieff's teaching.

The reason for this was that Subuh's understanding of
man's condition resembled Gurdjieff's, and his beliefs
and observations also have a Sufi background. Pak Subuh
sees man as composed of certain forces, about the nature
of which he is mainly unconscious. These life-forces, or
levels, number five. Three of them—matter, plants, and
animals—are lower than man; one, the human, is on
man's own level; and the fifth is the level above man to
which, however, he can aspire.

As did Gurdjieff, Subuh sees man divided and lost,
trapped through his uncontrolled desires and thoughts by
the lower forces which, Subuh believes, actually try to
dominate man. As long as man identifies with one of these
forces, which is only a part of himself, he can never be
whole, and Subuh believes that it is urgently necessary
that man frees himself from the lower levels.

The means by which he is to free himself constitute the

real difference between Gurdjieff's teaching and Pak
Subuh's. For Gurdjieff believed that man must make the
effort himself to realize his essence; whereas Subuh believes that only God, or the Life-Force, can help man—he
cannot do it alone. Pak Subuh has no exercises or methods
except that of emptying oneself of thoughts and feelings
as far as is possible so that the Life-Force can enter and
purify one. This is done during *latihan* (spiritual training)
by a transmission from one who is already opened to the
Force.

Gurdjieff's teaching is difficult to understand, particularly with regard to the use of the word "I," which sometimes means the ordinary self and sometimes means the
essence. Pak Subuh is more straightforward but perhaps
less stimulating.

Gurdjieff
1873–1949

George Ivanovitch Gurdjieff, in almost complete contrast to Krishnamurti, spent most of his early years roaming the East in search of an ancient religion. He belonged to a group of people called the Community of Truth Seekers, who believed that there was once a single world religion that had eventually been divided up among various Eastern countries. Philosophy went to India, theory to Egypt, and practice to Persia, Mesopotamia, and Turkestan. The Truth Seekers were a band of men and women, including many Europeans, who devoted their lives to a quest for this ancient esoteric knowledge of the universe, believing it to be hidden in the symbolism of legends, in music and dancing, in ancient monuments such as the pyramids, and in the oral teachings of remote monasteries. Gurdjieff was one of the leaders of this group. Traveling alone or in couples, the Truth Seekers explored the most remote regions of Asia, frequently in disguise as pilgrims or trad-

ers. They joined secret brotherhoods, studied in monasteries, and gradually pieced together an outline of knowledge which Gurdjieff made famous as the System, or the
Work.

Gurdjieff had always been attracted to the strange and
mysterious. His father was a carpenter of Russian-Greek
extraction, and the family lived in a remote village of the
Southern Caucasus near the Turkish border. The Gurdjieff workshop was the center where the men gathered in
the evenings, for Mr. Gurdjieff was deeply interested in
religion and was also a bard who knew many Asiatic
legends and sagas by heart. These stories and the discus-
sions which they provoked, deeply impressed the young
Gurdjieff. He was fascinated also by the primitive tribes
who roamed the Caucasus with their flocks, and especially by the Yezidis, devil-worshippers, who were so
bound by their own unusual laws and rituals that more
than once he saw Yezidi boys paralyzed, quite unable to
move, because a circle had been drawn around them in
the dust by the village children.

He acquired a good education. The bishop of the district,
a friend of his father, took a great interest in him and
undertook to train him both as a priest and as a doctor, for
in the bishop's opinion it was impossible to practice one
without the other. But the good bishop never saw his
pupil qualify as either, for Gurdjieff left his training un-
finished in order to become a Truth Seeker and find the
hidden meaning of the universe.

His incredible adventures are described in his own
book, *Meetings with Remarkable Men,* although it does
not include his alleged ten-year sojourn in Tibet as a
Russian secret agent and tutor to the Dalai Lama. He was
a brilliant opportunist and could turn his hand to any
trade and make a success of it. He relates how on one
occasion he captured a number of sparrows, painted them

yellow, and sold them as American canaries—having to hurry away before it rained! He learned how to make carpets and sewing machines, and how to hypnotize people and cure them of their afflictions. Typical of his enterprises was his entry into the corset business: having discovered that a fashion of low corsets was sweeping the Caucasus, he offered to alter the old high ones. Among his customers was a stout Jewess. He needed more whalebone as her corset had to be widened as well as shortened, and in trying to buy it, found that it was in short supply. Immediately he bought up all the old corsets he could find—at a greatly reduced price as the shopkeepers were glad to get rid of them—and began to cut them up and reshape them. Soon he was employing girls and producing as many as a hundred fashionable corsets a day, selling them at a high price back to those same, now furious, shopkeepers.

The money from the sale of ultimately six thousand corsets, as well as from other equally ingenious schemes —for Gurdjieff was quick-witted and ruthless in his own interests—was used for expeditions, such as one made with his friend Pogossian in which they tried to find surviving members of an ancient brotherhood, called the Sarmoung Brotherhood, which Gurdjieff claimed had been founded in Babylon in 2500 B.C.

When he had acquired the knowledge for the "System," Gurdjieff went to Moscow intending to teach it to the West. But the First World War began and he could not develop his plans. In 1915 he wrote and produced a "Hindoo" ballet, called *The Struggle of the Magicians*, and a notice of this ballet attracted a journalist, Ouspensky, who was to become Gurdjieff's most renowned exponent. Ouspensky describes his first meeting with Gurdjieff:

I saw a man of an oriental type, no longer young, with a

black moustache and piercing eyes, who astonished me first
of all because he seemed to be disguised and completely out
of keeping with the place and its atmosphere. I was still full
of expressions of the East. And this man with the face of an
Indian rajah or an Arab sheikh whom I at once seemed to see
in a white burnoose or a gilded turban, seated here in this
little café, where small dealers and commission agents met
together, in a black overcoat with a velvet collar and a black
bowler hat, produced the strange, unexpected, and almost
alarming impression of a man poorly disguised, the sight of
whom embarrasses you because you see he is not what he
pretends to be and yet you have to speak and behave as
though you did not see it. He spoke Russian incorrectly with
a strong Caucasian accent; and this accent, with which we are
accustomed to associate anything apart from philosophical
ideas, strengthened still further the strangeness and the un-
expectedness of this impression.[1]

Ouspensky himself had been an unsuccessful "seeker"
of knowledge and had traveled all over India in search of
it. He had returned to Moscow feeling himself frustrated
and at a loss to know what to do next. In Gurdjieff he
found a new beginning and, as his pupil, accompanied
him to the Black Sea. Revolution forced them out of Russia and it was then that Ouspensky and Gurdjieff separated, Ouspensky to continue the Work in London and
Gurdjieff to take his pupils and a large number of his
family and Russian hangers-on to the fourteenth-century
Chateau du Prieuré at Fontainebleau, where they arrived
in 1922. Here the Institute for the Harmonious Development of Man was established and continued until
Gurdjieff's death in 1949. The many American and European intellectuals who studied there became known as
the "Forest Philosophers."

Gurdjieff's basic teaching is simple, almost stark. Man
is a mechanical puppet twitched by every outside event,

he said. He is the prey of his fears and desires which never remain consistent, so that he is constantly changing and is never the same person for long. He is such a bundle of impulses and reactions that his individuality is nonexistent: ". . . all the people you see, all the people you know, all the people *you may get to know*, are machines, actual machines working solely under the power of external influences. . . . Machines they are born and machines they die. . . ."

Ouspensky asked him if it was possible to stop being a machine.

"Ah! That is the question," said Gurdjieff, ". . . It is possible to stop being a machine, but for that it is necessary first of all *to know the machine*. A machine, a real machine, does not know itself and cannot know itself. When a machine knows itself it is then no longer a machine, at least, not such a machine as it was before. It already begins to be *responsible* for its actions."[2]

One of Gurdjieff's constant subjects, referred to at almost every talk, was man's belief that he is a permanent and whole "I." Gurdjieff believed this idea to be one of man's greatest mistakes. How can a "man-machine," a man who cannot act of his own accord and to whom everything "happens," be a single and wholehearted "I," he asked. As every thought or feeling succeeds the one before, man calls this his "I," and his immense error lies in thinking himself to be one and the same "I" all the time when in fact he is constantly changing from the person he was a minute ago. Man believes that every sensation and every thought belongs to *one* "I" and that he *is* this whole "I." So he comes to believe that he operates as a complete person and that his thoughts and feelings are an expression of this total person; whereas in reality each thought or feeling comes and goes quite independently of any such "entire" person, and there is no such thing as an

individual "I." Instead, a man consists of hundreds of
lesser and lesser "I's," some of them incompatible to the
others, some never coming into contact with the others at
all.

> ... Each minute, each moment, man is saying or thinking
> "I." And each time his "I" is different. Just now it was a
> thought, now it is a desire, now a sensation, now another
> thought, and so on, endlessly.... Man's name is legion.
>
> The alternation of I's, their continual obvious struggle for
> supremacy, is controlled by accidental external influences.
> Warmth, sunshine, fine weather, immediately call up a
> whole group of I's. Cold, fog, rain, call up another group of
> I's, other associations, other feelings, other actions. There is
> nothing in man able to control this change of I's, chiefly
> because man does not notice or know of it; he lives always in
> the last I. Some I's, of course, are stronger than others. But it
> is not their own conscious strength; they have been created
> by the strength of accidents or mechanical external stimuli.
> Education, imitation, reading, the hypnotism of religion,
> caste and traditions, or the glamour of new slogans, create
> very strong I's in man's personality, which dominate whole
> series of other, weaker I's.... All I's making up a man's
> personality, have the same origin.... They are the results of
> external influences and are set in motion and controlled by
> fresh external influences.[3]

This may be a novel and helpful way of regarding man's
feeling of "I." It resembles a belief which we will see to
be Ramana Maharshi's that man's "I" is conditioned by
that which he identifies it with. But, ultimately, the two
sages differ. Ramana Maharshi never stated that man's
individuality is so fragmented that he lacks any central
"I" at all: Gurdjieff never said, as Ramana Maharshi did,
that when man ceases to identify himself with his immediate "I," his body-conditioned "I," he will discover
the Self, his true Ground.

At this point one can take note of one's own experience. Do I myself feel a true, unchanging element in myself which underlies all the absorptions and demands of everyday life? On the whole, I do, and perhaps Ramana Maharshi was closer to the real truth when he said that man would not use even the term "I" if this was not his nature—if there was no intrinsic "I" there. Man confuses this eternal, unchanging "I" with all that is superficial and changing, said Ramana Maharshi. There is no profound, underlying "I" at all, said Gurdjieff, it is all a vast mistake.

Whichever view one now takes, there is no doubt that in the thirties and forties many Westerners, brought up to believe in the ego which God was said to have created in order that man should dominate the natural world, found Gurdjieff's shattering attacks on the sacred notion of "I" a revelatory release from outdated and claustrophobic notions.

For there is something innately repugnant and hypocritical in the cozy belief that man is God's chosen creature and is made in His image. The image of the ego? Surely, one feels, God can do a bit better than that. When Gurdjieff told his followers that man has no individuality at all, no single "I" whatever, that all he consists of is a mass of small and separate "I's," many devotees preferred this unhappy estimate of man's condition to the old arrogant hypocrisy.

It is certainly easy enough to arrive at Gurdjieff's conclusion. When I walk, what "I" is telling my legs to move? None that I am immediately aware of. When the door is opened, what curious "I" impels me to turn around? And what "I" gives me love for my husband, irritation with my neighbor, pleasure in the sea and wind? Is each "I" a totally different person, or is it a changing expression of the same person?

It is observably true that when a man is caught up in a quarrel, or a strong and absorbing emotion, his usually integrated personality appears to have been taken over by one aspect or another, and Gurdjieff based much of his teaching on this theme of man's constant identification with what at a given moment has attracted his attention, his thoughts or his desires, and his imagination:

> A man identifies with a small problem which confronts him and he completely forgets the great aims with which he began his work. He identifies with one thought and forgets other thoughts; he is identified with one feeling, with one mood, and forgets his own wider thoughts, emotions, and moods. . . .[4]

It is essential to stop identifying, said Gurdjieff, and the way for man to do this is not to call himself "I" on every occasion. When he can cease identifying with *himself* —and this will happen when he stops using the term "I" for the doer of his actions—he will then remember his "essence," his proper self.

What is man's essence? It would be easy if one could say that Gurdjieff meant God by this term; for the simplest and most penetrating idea about man's existence is that he gains the experience of the beingness of God as he drops his self-absorption, his identification with his small, created self.

But Gurdjieff's ideas of both man and God were much more complicated than that, and followed the Sufi teaching of many veils between man and God and at least four stages of consciousness. Essence, which is a Sufi term, merely refers to all that we are born with, such as the color of the skin and nature of the physique. Gurdjieff believed that character was innate and not acquired, that one was born a certain type of person. But this is arguable, and one cannot help remembering the reply of the Zen master,

Bankei, when a priest asked him how to get rid of the bad temper he had been born with.

"What an interesting thing you were born with!" said Bankei. "Tell me, is your temper quick at this very moment? If so, show me right off, and I'll cure you of it."

The priest replied that he didn't have it at that moment.

"Then you weren't born with it." said Bankei. "If you were, you'd have it at all times. . . ."[5]

Gurdjieff, like the priest, believed that there are certain characteristics we are born with, and that these never change, whereas the personality, which is what we acquire through our surroundings and education, is changing all the time. Personality, he said, resembles a dress or a mask, it comes and goes with the circumstances and can even be changed in a few minutes by hypnosis or a drug. Personality may appear to be strong (as in the case of a loud and dominant person) but the essence beneath may really be that of a child. It was Gurdjieff's teaching that the personality should be dropped so that the essence could be revealed:

> When we speak of inner development and inner change, we speak of the growth of essence. The question now is not to acquire anything new but to recover and reconstruct what has been lost. . . .[6]

So the most important work was to learn to distinguish essence from personality and, while doing this, to discard the personality—the superimposed mask. For Gurdjieff described essence as the real individuality which, he said, is almost entirely dormant in most men. Many people, he said, wander around in a state of semisleep which they call "being awake" although it is only one stage removed from full sleep. These are the only two states that man knows and therefore he thinks of wakefulness as consciousness. But occasionally he is intensely moved, as though he is out of time altogether, and then he experiences a state of consciousness which seems more *real* than his usual state. It carries a sense of freedom and clarity—what Krishnamurti refers to as "astonishingly alive and creative." It is the feeling of being *alive* that is its characteristic, as though true life has not been experienced before. In this state, which Gurdjieff termed Objective Consciousness, the outside world is no less real —in fact it shines forth as though never before seen—but a truly disinterested acceptance of it has taken the place of attachment and dependence, so that it is seen as it is, seen without the colored spectacles of the desiring self.

Gurdjieff outlined four stages of consciousness in man: the state of sleep, the ordinary waking state, the state of self-remembering, and the state of Objective Consciousness. A good deal of his teaching is based on these states. The ordinary waking state is machine-man, and the state of Objective Consciousness is rarely attained. But the third state of self-remembering (which leads on to Objective Consciousness) is, he said, possible for man as a result of hard work and training, and it is man's only way of escape from his machine reactions. True will, the ability to "do," comes with finding the inner self or essence which is the third state. Without the transition to the third state, man is nothing—a mere bundle of impulses.

How do people reach this third state?

In his teaching Gurdjieff was highly aware of three psychological factors. One is that people generally do not take in what they are told; in order to know a thing they must experience it, be it. Another is that an intense experience sharpens the mind and wakes it up. And thirdly, an experience itself, if repeated too often, results in a deadening of the mind so that people will revert to machine reactions—the mind is so caught up in concepts and dreams that they wander through the world without ever really coming into contact with it or seeing that it exists.

Gurdjieff discovered that the way to use these three factors in his teaching was to put people to hard work in circumstances which would cause constant friction. The aim of his establishment at the Prieure was to create the conditions in which men and women would constantly be reminded of what they were really doing and of the unavoidable conflict which would arise between their conscience and their automatic behavior—between sensitive mindful actions and thoughtless reactions. "Fusion, inner unity, is obtained by means of 'friction,' by the struggle between 'yes' and 'no' in a man," he said. "If a man lives without inner struggle, if everything happens to him without opposition, if he goes wherever he is drawn or wherever the wind blows, he will remain such as he is. . . ."[7]

So Gurdjieff insisted on hard physical labor: roads were made, trees felled, buildings constructed, streams diverted, gardens planted, lawns made, cows milked, and chickens fed.

A student relates how he learned to "chop" stones, to break limestone rock into small pieces no bigger than a nut, and to do this as a man and not as an ordinary laborer or machine-man. To begin with he thought the work a terrible waste of time. Gurdjieff reproved him and told him that he was squandering energy on resentment; instead of hating the work, he should make a list of foreign words and memorize them as he worked, at the same time trying to sense his body and become aware of what he was doing.

The student found that the work became satisfying, and undoubtedly Gurdjieff believed that real attention to *any* activity results in wholeheartedness. We are so easily distracted and every distraction brings a feeling of inner division. It is impossible to be wholehearted about anything if one lives in a state of restless comparisons. A child can give his whole self to a new toy. We have so many toys that we lose this ability, and with it the chance to become conscious of wholeness.

After the hard day at the Prieure was over, no rest was allowed. Well into the night, students were expected to learn the elaborate dances which Gurdjieff considered an essential part of the training. The dances were based on the belief that man operates through three centers: the intellectual center that thinks and plans; the emotional center that feels pain and pleasure; and the physical, instinctive center that moves and creates. One of these centers was said to predominate in every person.

The dances were intended to reveal these centers, and indeed to reveal the whole of Gurdjieff's philosophy, in movement. Not only man's real "I," developed by self-remembering and observation of his centers, but also Gurdjieff's more esoteric understanding of the "system" —ideas such as the vibrations of different levels of consciousness; the living nature of the planets; man's role, which is to feed the earth; the negative influence of the moon; and many other complicated ideas which were worked out in mathematical and chemical terms by Ouspensky in his book *In Search of the Miraculous*. Much of the theory is based on the number seven—rays and octaves, worlds and elements, etc. The dances, which were meant to convey all this in movement, had their origins all over the East. Their aim was to teach the dancer to integrate his three centers rather than to express his subjective ideas and feelings. Every movement had to be minutely learned because each limb had to be trained to make actions which were entirely independent of the other limbs. This broke the conventional attitudes of the dancer, for he was no longer dancing to any known rhythm but had to be ready for highly unusual muscular operations; his mental and emotional reflexes became as supple as his limbs.

Because of the formidable concentration needed to learn these dances, the dancers frequently looked as though they were hypnotized. Not only were they to learn the most intricate of movements but they must also be aware of each of their three centers and make sure that they were perfectly and consciously coordinated. This resulted in a curiously blank and zombielike expression.

One of Gurdjieff's most important practices was the Sufi *"ist"* exercise in which, at a word or a gesture from Gurdjieff, all the students stopped whatever they were doing in exactly the position they were in. Not a muscle was to be moved; even thoughts in the head were to remain fixed. This was intended to break up mechanical habits and to keep the mind alert. It was seen in action by hundreds at a famous performance of the dancers in New York when the troupe paused at the back of the stage, facing the audience. Gurdjieff gave a command and they all came racing at full speed towards the footlights and the audience. Everyone expected to see a perfect exhibition of "ist," of frozen movement. But Gurdjieff, instead of giving the word to freeze, calmly turned his back on them, and lit a cigarette. Utterly obedient, the whole troupe continued over the footlights and into the air, leaping across the orchestra and onto the floor, everybody heaped on top of each other with legs and arms at all angles. There they lay, completely immobile and silent, a fallen avalanche of bodies.

Gurdjieff turned around and looked at them and then gave the word of permission to move. The audience was still stunned and unbelieving but when it turned out that no bones were broken, in fact that none of the troupe seemed to have suffered even a bruise, the audience clapped vigorously, if protestingly. The exercise had been rather too dramatic.

On a quieter level, Gurdjieff's training for the fourth state of Objective Consciousness—the state when a man "is"—was felt by many Western intellectuals to be valuable. Louis Pauwels, a student, explains that one of their exercises consisted in being aware of their right arm at a precise time of day, and holding that awareness as long as possible:

> This may seem ridiculous, but it was certainly not so for us. Some people thought that the object of the Teaching was simply to strengthen their powers of concentration and so to help them in all their different activities. . . . But this was clearly an undertaking on a very different scale. I want this to be clearly understood. 'Paying attention' was of little importance. In order to *know* my right arm, from the shoulder to the finger-tips, at a quarter to six exactly, while reading my newspaper in the underground and despite my desires, joys and troubles of the moment, I have to dissociate myself from what I usually call my personality and it is in this act of dissociation that the exercise consists.[8]

He had to disentangle himself from everything he was doing at the moment, he tells us, and refuse to identify himself with any sight or sound or touch, even that of a woman's body pressed against him in the train. If desire arose, he must accept it but keep it at a distance so that he was not overwhelmed by it. All of its accompaniments, such as emotions and fantasies, must immediately be quelled. Then his desire could take second place to the awareness of his arm, and instead of engulfing him it could become an extra tool to be used for self-recollection. The same process must be applied to all the other sights and sounds around him:

> In the effort that I make to keep the awareness of my right arm there is also the effort to keep myself at a distance from

the outside world as well as from myself, and at this distance *I can see objectively* what is going on in and around me; I have reality restored to me in all its purity and all that I see becomes an opportunity of sacrifice indefinitely renewed.

At the same time, this apparently ridiculous effort has begun to give birth to a big "Me" behind the hundreds of restless and identified little "me's." A certain substance is deposited in me, a minute grain of *being*.[9]

It should be pointed out here that this "substance" is entirely different from the Hindu idea of an underlying "I," or Self, which, as we have seen, Gurdjieff rejected.

As well as these day-to-day exercises, the hard physical work, and the dance lessons, Gurdjieff's pupils were expected to observe themselves in situations of emotional friction where conscience and self-will would be at odds. Gurdjieff took a delight in creating situations that would reveal people to themselves. Like Meher Baba, he would request complicated journeys to be organized and then change the plans at the last moment; or, setting out for some distant destination in a cavalcade of cars and devotees, he would misread the map or forget the name of the place they were going to, and they would all be forced to turn up in the middle of the night at some small country inn, where Gurdjieff would ask for beds for perhaps up to thirty people and food to be prepared immediately. His magnetism would give the innkeeper a feeling of privilege to be of service, and Gurdjieff would blame his followers for the difficulties of the situation.

His unpredictability infused every level of his students' lives—he even announced one day that the Prieuré was to close down and that everyone must be out in two days. Students who had given up important careers for his teaching were shattered. Some left, never to return. Others went to Paris and then quietly drifted back and things went on as usual.

He was also generous to the point of fantasy. He once appealed for money for essential needs at the Prieure and then spent it on bicycles for every single person there. The Americans who had donated it were helplessly enraged.

So that his students could become aware of their machinelike minds, Gurdjieff wanted them all to report daily about each other—an infallible way of producing the friction he thought necessary to wake them up. As well, he would deliberately uphold an irritating or un-harmonious personality. One of the boys at the Prieuré, Fritz Peters, remembers how the children would all tease an elderly Russian, Rachmilevitch, "a mournful, dour type, full of prophecies of disaster, dissatisfied with everything."[10] They did all they could to make his life unbearable and he was constantly flying into awful rages. One summer everyone, without exception, was put to remaking the lawns, goaded by Gurdjieff, who "would march up and down among all the workers, criticising them individually, goading them on, and helping to con-tribute a feeling of furious, senseless activity to the whole proceedings."[11]

After some days of this, Rachmilevitch, outraged, put down his tool and told Gurdjieff that with so many people treading on the lawns the grass seed might as well be thrown away—people had no idea what they were doing and were simply raking wherever they could find an unoccupied piece of ground.

Gurdjieff, whose terrifying rages were always con-trolled and could be turned on and off at will, replied furiously that he knew better than anyone how to re-build lawns. The two argued intensely for some minutes and then Rachmilevitch strode off into the woods.

Gurdjieff was concerned. Later on, he sent Fritz Peters to look for the old Russian, telling Fritz that it was essen-tial someone should find Rachmilevitch and ask him to come back, for he would never return of his own accord. Fritz, uncertain of where to go, hitched a horse to a wagon and eventually found Rachmilevitch up an apple tree. After a long protest, Rachmilevitch descended into the wagon and was returned. Gurdjieff was pleased and confided to Fritz that he actually paid Rachmilevitch to live at the Prieuré—"Without Rachmilevitch, Prieuré is not the same; I know no one person like him, no person who just by existence, without conscious effort, produces friction in all people around him."[12]

Looked at from the outside, the Prieuré must have been an unusual but trying place to live in, its community spellbound by their guru and always working self-consciously to please him. Yet Katherine Mansfield preferred it to anywhere and spent the last weeks of her life there; and other writers and eminent people from all walks of life stayed there for months or years.

Gurdjieff himself seems to have been a master showman, a rascal-guru of immense talent; an opportunist with a grasp of underlying truths which he could expound with such force that their impact was perhaps greater than their substance. He made a deep impression on the West and books are still being written about him to this day. To those who knew him he was vividly alive, open to the essence in every person he met. To those who have only read him, his teaching contains some of the great truths to be found in all religions, perhaps the most important being the belief that man as he is, is not perfectible. His personality is always that of a machine. Man himself cannot *do*. But by observing the operations of his personality he begins to abate it, and as it becomes passive so the big "Me" emerges. That is the true "doer," the true life. Gurdjieff believed that the only way out of man's dilemma is to change his consciousness of who he is, and in this he agrees with other teachers such as Krishnamurti,

Ramana Maharshi, and Dhiravamsa, who all suggest awareness of the self as the way to find out what transcends it.

"Remember yourself always and everywhere,"[13] Gurdjieff said.

"All energy spent on conscious work is an investment; that spent mechanically is lost forever."[14]

"The highest that a man can attain is to be able to *do*."[15]

Pak Subuh
1901–1987

Pak Subuh is a native of Java, a country which is watered by the religious streams of Hinduism, Buddhism, Christianity, and Islam. The result is a theosophically fertile soil, exceptionally given to esoteric cults and the development of psychic faculties. When, for instance, Subuh was born, his first name was changed from Sukarno to Muhammad because a wandering beggar foretold that the delicate child would otherwise die. And his health improved from that moment on. Predictions of death, however, continued to shadow him, and when he was a young man he heard a firm prophecy that he would die at the age of twenty-four.

Believing, then, that he had no time to waste he went in search of all the spiritual guidance he could find before it was too late, and as he was (and is) a Muslim, he went to various teachers within the Islamic tradition. One well-known Sufi teacher accepted him as a pupil but refused to initiate him or give him any training, saying that Subuh would receive all he needed from a nonhuman source. So Subuh gave up the search for spiritual knowledge and re-entered everyday life, training as a bookkeeper and getting married.

In 1925, the year when he was supposed to have died, a strange thing happened to him which altered the course of his life.

He was walking with some friends on a dark, moonless night, when, he says, a ball of light seeming to resemble the sun appeared above his head. It then seemed to enter him and he was filled with the feeling of vibrating forces. Believing that this would be his death, he went home and lay down, but as soon as he relaxed an unknown force impelled him to stand up and go through the Muslim ritual of prayer. He recounts that for the next three years he rarely slept but was visited every night by visions and by the same impelling force which moved his limbs without his volition. During this time, an understanding grew in him that the extraordinary force was cleansing and purifying his body and soul, and that the movements he made and the sounds which emerged from him were the expressions of inner purification. He became certain that his experience was a *latihan*, the Javanese word for training, and that the force which manipulated him was divine. He believed that his own submission to this force and his surrender to it had allowed it to "open" him. He realized that surrender was the great key which unlocks the human heart to the will of God.

"In truth the surrender you make when you have been opened or at the time of the opening is not the surrender to God that people ordinarily make, with their emotions only, with their thoughts, or with their desires. That which is required is not the surrender of your heart or mind; it is rather the power of God that is working and manifest within your being. . . .

"In its essence you can come to the surrender . . . only when your heart is emptied and void of everything, such as your hopes, desires, and wishes, even your wish to surrender to God, for that part of you which wishes to do so in this way is nothing but your own heart."[1]

You must allow God to act within you through the working of the great Life Force, says Pak Subuh. The action is similar to allowing a friend to take you by the hand and guide you—whatever he wants to do, you submit to it. This is the meaning of surrender to God, in Pak Subuh's view.

At the end of his three years of illumination, Subuh received a revelation that it was to be his mission to transmit the divine force to others. Accordingly, he gave up his job—by that time he had five young children—and told his wife that they must trust that God would look after them. He felt intuitively that he must not even look for pupils or talk about his revelation unless asked to; but, at the same time, the transmission should be given to all who wanted it.

Soon afterwards the pupils of a Sufi teacher arrived to receive it, having been directed by their master to come to Subuh—who was thenceforward called *Bapak*, the Javanese for father, of which Pak is an affectionate abbreviation. This was the beginning of Subud.

Subud is the abbreviation of three words—*Susila, Budhi, Dharma. Susila* means man's true character when he acts in accordance with the will of God; *Budhi* is man's divine life-force as man encounters it within himself; *Dharma* means man's full surrender to the will of God.

Thus Subud is a term which describes the whole content of the action of the *latihan:* the total submission to God which results in the growth of man's true nature.

Subud has now become known throughout the West, as

well as in Indonesia. After a slow growth in Java itself, it was brought to the West by Husein Rofé, a pupil of Bapak's. In 1956, the late J. G. Bennett, a pupil of Gurdjieff's, met Rofé and thought he saw in Subud a further development of Gurdjieff's teaching. He provided a house close to London for a center and, before long, Bapak and his wife came for a visit. This led to a number of world tours for the Javanese couple, and to the formation of Subud groups in over thirty countries, although Bennett himself did not remain a member of the Subud Association.

Why should Bennett have seen Bapak as Gurdjieff's natural successor? Perhaps because both Bapak and Gurdjieff were in touch with Sufi masters in their youth, there do seem to be some resemblances in their teachings. Whereas Gurdjieff saw man as a multiplicity of "I's," each "I" living briefly and solely as a reaction to external conditions, and all of the "I's" adding up to a sort of machine personality which man superimposes on his own true and unique human individuality; so Bapak sees man as composed of a number of lower forces which he allows to dominate him, thus submerging his own humanity.

There are five life-forces, or levels, he believes, which dominate the ordinary human being, and of whose presence he is usually unaware because he believes himself to be his own master. The three lower forces comprise the very nature of the physical world itself and at the same time each one—matter, plant, and animal—is a sphere on its own. Above them is the human, or fourth, level; and the fifth level is comprised of those expressions of the life-force that are superior to humans.

Bapak makes it clear that the lower forces constitute the physical world itself and thus man is an *expression* of the total world beneath him. When the three lower forces dominate him and he behaves as their slave, the world itself falls out of balance and everything suffers; for man's destiny, as the most evolved of all the creatures, is to reconcile the forces within his own nature. To accomplish this, he must rely on the creative power of God, which releases man's human understanding and gives him compassionate but firm mastery over the lower forces.

Bapak has much to say about this mastery. He believes that inanimate matter has a great attraction for man and that man's everyday thoughts reflect his obsession for material objects and his enslavement by them. They exert an immense power over him so that he forgets that they are just things, and imbues them with all sorts of qualities. Because of this, possessions dominate people, and those people lose their understanding of what they are doing with things.

Bapak even believes that men who are blind to the real purpose of material possessions—which is to serve as common benefits to mankind—actually become impregnated with the quality of matter, its heaviness and inertness. Such men fall below the level of humanity and even below the level of matter itself, for they have lost all awareness of the spirit.

Within its own sphere, matter is capable of worshiping God, he says. Though without an intellect, it is spiritually aware, and it longs for mankind to allow it to enter his thought and thus raise it to his level. Man must understand this desire of matter to connect itself to him if he is to recognize the impulses of which he is composed.

Plants, which, directly or indirectly, provide all man's food, are even more intimately part of man than is matter, and they exert a greater influence upon him. When man's inner feelings are purified and he is free from desire for the plant-force—in other words, when he is no longer

enslaved by his stomach—the plant life-force of which he
is partly composed is able to make contact with the plant
world outside and this, says Bapak, "resembles a long-
awaited meeting between husband and wife." Because
man can accomplish this plant reunion, his wisdom is
worshiped by the lesser power, who has longed for
his help.

Both the forces of matter and of plants bring about
disruption within man when he allows them to dominate
him—not purposely, but because they are not naturally
on his level and will therefore drag him down. Worse than
either of those, however, is the animal force, which
penetrates more deeply. Until a man becomes conscious
of his animal nature he assumes that all he does is by his
own will. But, says Bapak, in reality almost all his actions
are sparked off by one of the three lower forces, usually
the animal force.

The way in which these three levels exist in man is by
being eaten. Humans, however, do not eat each other so
the human level of the life-force arises in a different way.
Interaction on the human level comes about through sexual intercourse. Sexual union implies the act of creation
and Bapak sees man becoming the creative field in which
the world can develop—he likens the human body to that
of a soil which varies in its fertility so that different
people correspond to different soils, the highest being
the "golden earth."

Bapak believes that the act of sexual union gives man a
chance to be influenced by the force which is properly
human because, in the moment of orgasm, the innermost
self of the man or woman becomes isolated from the lower
forces. At this instant, if a man can be free of desire, and of
thinking, he will become aware of an inner awakening to
his true nature.

How is it that we are unaware of the lower forces?

When they arise, says Bapak, they seem to man to be a single stream of stimuli, although in fact they have come from different places. Because they have flowed through a common path when they entered his ordinary consciousness, man is not aware of their sources. But when his consciousness is raised to a purely human level, as can happen in the sexual act, he can become aware of the behavior of the lower forces and can detach himself from them. Their domination over, he is then their master and can direct them into their proper paths. He will no longer be deceived after that, by meeting a level which seems to be human but is really a lower force wearing a human mask. Once he is in charge, the needs of each force will be properly met—the human force in the human and the animal force in the animal.

> There is a way by which man can come to a knowledge of all this—indeed there is possibly no other way—by abandoning his thoughts which are ever groping after phantoms of the imagination.[2]

It is a man's imagination and thought which dominates his waking day, and only when he can empty himself of these will he be able to be conscious of his inner condition. When he does become thus empty, he will find himself aware of a sensation of vibration throughout his whole body, and he will feel as though he has been touched by an altogether new and unique power. Gradually, as he begins to receive this power more fully, he will learn the nature and make-up of his personhood.

This theme of emptying one's mind of thoughts and imagination is one of Bapak's most important teachings. To him, the separation of thinking and feeling from the reception of the Divine Power is essential. For thinking and feeling belong to the realm of the lower forces— *everything* that we do, which includes the actions of thinking and feeling, is conditioned by these forces. But they must be transcended if the Divine Power is to work unimpeded. How can this be done?

The way to receive the Power, says Bapak, is to become empty and still within the mind and heart, so quiet that all thoughts and emotions die down. The thinking mind, in particular, is the instrument of whatever powers are uppermost—man can never apprehend his spiritual inner feelings with his superficial thinking-mind. It must quiet down and be replaced by the powerful Life Force of God. This Life Force, the nature of which is entirely beyond his capacity to grasp, is the only true help man has. His thinking brain is an excellent tool and should be developed to its full strength by ordinary methods; but its field of operation is the outer world and it cannot be used to understand the reality of God. One remembers, "Render unto Caesar what is Caesar's, and unto God what is God's."

When man can abandon his thinking-mind, says Bapak, only submitting his will to God, he will become properly human, at one with himself and with the forces of which he is composed.

How can this submission come about? Bapak's answer lies in the *latihan*, the spiritual training which is the core of Subud, and is also its great distinguishing feature. For the power of the Life Force is transmitted during the *latihan*, in the first instance only, by the people called "helpers," who are appointed by Bapak to "open" their fellow men. This "opening" is not, however, anything personally to do with Bapak or the helpers. They are merely the channel through which the force is transmitted. Anyone may attend a *latihan* and be opened in this way. It is a classless and race-free aid to religion in which few are refused, although it is occasionally felt advisable that a person should not receive the *latihan* until his present circumstances have altered. There is a three-month waiting period for *every* applicant before the *latihan* takes place, so that his sincerity can be tested and so that he can become properly informed about the nature of Subud and of the brotherhood he is joining. As there is no formal teaching in Subud, there is no required form of belief. At his "opening," however, the applicant makes the simple affirmation that "he believes in Almighty God, and in his power."

What actually happens in the *latihan?* Twice a week for life, men and women go to separate rooms in their nearest Subud center, take off anything liable to be broken, and, standing relaxed with eyes shut, empty themselves as far as possible of all thoughts, perceptions, and desires. They then feel themselves urged to move about by a force which they believe to be the power of God. The *latihan* is said to be at one and the same time the worship of God, and a means of purification which clears out stage by stage the results of wrong actions, bad heredity, and so on. Members do not try to understand what is happening to them, but allow everything to proceed as it arises —whether it be slight movements, dancing, talking in foreign tongues, singing, weeping, and even shouting and screaming and making strange animal noises; or they may stand in complete stillness. At no time are they in any kind of trance, nor do they pay attention to what is going on around them. Every possible movement or sound may occur, because every person has his own combination of lower forces to master. But nobody is ever so possessed that he is out of his mind, and he is aware all the time as an observer. At the end of half an hour the helper declares the *latihan* is finished.

The *latihan* will, says Bapak, give a man the opportunity to arrive at a state of reality in which the lower forces will inevitably be separated from him. He takes care to point out that the exercise itself, the *latihan*, is entirely tailored to the individual in that it arises in accordance with each person's strength and capacity. Because of its complete appropriateness to that person it cannot, therefore, be in any way harmful. In fact, it is more likely to bring about good health, he says. What is experienced seems to the individual beneficial and natural, and it appears to be the heritage of every man.

One of the bonuses to those who do the *latihan* is a new ability to discover how to direct their lives. The way is called "testing," and the method is to become as internally quiet as possible, to formulate a question in words, and then to put it completely out of the mind and to go, with the aid of the helpers, into the *latihan* state. The answer then is said to make itself clearly known. This has proved a great boon to many people whose thinking minds have not proved successful at helping them to live well.

What is this strange force that seems to attract different types of people including, for instance, the many Quakers who are Subud members?

Although it is constantly referred to as the power of God, Bapak takes care not to claim that the force actually does come from God for, he says, only God can know this. What is received, he says, comes from a stream of life beyond the reach of the lower forces and also beyond anything that could be termed magic. But he cannot explain or categorize this stream. In fact it is useless to talk about it, he says, for explanations, however highsounding, are only projections of the thinking mind and the imagination. The proper answer to those who want to know what it is, is that they must come and experience it for themselves. They will then know the facts, rather than words about them.

The facts include, says Bapak, a beneficial change in all

who practice the *latihan*. Illnesses decrease, age is held back, the mind becomes clear and supple, and the emotions easy and open. In time, people should be able to receive the fifth power, the level of life which lies above the human. On this level are the saints and prophets, the rare men and women whose awareness and love embraces all forms, although they themselves have evolved into a spiritual state which is formless, "comparable to the vastness of the ocean."

Subud is not a separate religion. Its members come from all the established religions and find that, because of the *latihan*, their understanding of their own religion is greater (perhaps, as well, because they have learned to surrender their self-will). Bapak, himself, as the instigator of Subud and the original "transmitter" of the force, is regarded as a prophet by many of his "children," although he refuses to think of himself as anything but the most ordinary of men. For it is not he but the Life Force which is the dynamic opener, he is merely a family man and lives in that way.

He puts it this way: "Bapak is willed by God to be simply as Bapak is—to drink coffee, to eat butter, bread and cheese, also to smoke—because this is what people ordinarily do; and it will not close my way to God because He wills me to be so."[3]

Bapak's complete confidence in the Life Force, rather than in man's own efforts at self-transcendence, may seem deceptively submissive to those of us who have not been touched by it. For although man must, perhaps, ultimately see himself as nothing and the power of God as everything, although he should eventually surrender himself wholly—yet are not his struggling attempts to do so the very rungs of his ladder? To replace his own insights and affirmations which often arise from setbacks and doubts, by a force seemingly transmitted effortlessly from an outside source seems, in some way, to miss the point of being human.

But perhaps Bapak has disposed of this criticism, for he is a firm believer in daily life in the world as the best arena for the force of God, and his teaching these days emphasizes the growth of enterprises. In the seventeen years since he brought Subud and the *latihan* to the West, he has gradually laid more and more emphasis on outer activities, and particularly on the enterprises which are now beginning to finance the social aims of Subud. He has given guidance in his talks to members about working for better social conditions, and he urges them to start Subud schools, hospitals, homes for the elderly, and so on. This is the only publicity for Subud that he is prepared to consider—"We should not make propaganda, but there should be evidence in ourselves for others. It is of the greatest importance," he says, "to make use of our minds and hearts as long as we live on this earth, since our minds and hearts and our five senses are indeed given to us by God to serve the needs of life as long as we live on earth."[4]

And after this life? We not only need happiness in this life, but also happiness after death, says Bapak, for death is the continuation of life. It is absurd to think that we come to an end when we die. Certainly, he says, our minds and hearts stop working, but there is an inner feeling which continues to exist. If that inner feeling is not ready for the next life, if it is not yet purified and has not discovered the power of God, then it will be left rigid, inflexible, and lifeless by the ending of the mind and heart.

It is otherwise if the Power of God has been active within you in your exercise, for your inner feeling has begun to wake up and come to life; and coming to life means not owing to the influence of heart, mind and desires, but, on the contrary, owing to liberation from all these influences. Having come to life, the inner feeling is able to recognise and to be aware of life free from the influence of mind, heart and desires, which cannot possibly guide or accompany our inner life or our soul to the realm of life after death.

As your inner feeling (or inner self) comes alive, freed from mind, desires, and heart, it becomes able to receive what you need and what is God's will for you, so that you are able to receive within your inner self [a knowledge of] what life is like after death and "before I was born."[5]

116

References

Gurdjieff

1   P. D. Ouspensky, *In Search of the Miraculous* (London: Routledge Kegan Paul; New York: Harcourt Brace Jovanovitch), p. 7.

2   Ibid., p. 19.

3   Ibid., p. 59.

4   Ibid., p. 150.

5   Lucien Stryk and Takashi Ikemoto, *Zen Poems, Prayers, Sermons, Anecdotes, Interviews* (New York: Doubleday and Company, Inc.), p. 81.

6   C. S. Nott, *Teachings of Gurdjieff* (London: Routledge Kegan Paul; New York: Samuel Weiser, Inc.), p. 65.

7   Ouspensky, *In Search of the Miraculous*, p. 32.

8   Louis Pauwels, *Gurdjieff* (London: Times Press Ltd.; New York: Samuel Weiser Inc.), p. 86.

9   Ibid., p. 88.

10   Fritz Peters, *Boyhood with Gurdjieff* (London: Gollancz; New York: Penguin), p. 56.

11   Ibid., p. 67.

12   Ibid., p. 72.

13   Kenneth Walker, *A Study of Gurdjieff's Teaching* (London: Jonathan Cape), p. 212.

14   Ibid., p. 213.

15   Ibid., p. 211.

Pak Subuh

1   Muhammad Subuh, *The Meaning of Subud* (Subud Publications International), p. 57.

2   Muhammad Subuh, *Susila Buddhi Dharma* (Subud Publications International), p. 353.

3   Subuh, *The Meaning of Subud*, p. 35.

4   Muhammad Subuh, *Subud in the World* (Subud Publications International), p. 25.

5   Gordon Van Hien, *What Is Subud?* (London: Rider and Co.), p. 145.

Further Reading

Vittachi, Tarzie, *A Reporter in Subud,* New York: Dharma Book Company Inc.

4

The Hindu Messiahs

There are two main strands in Hindu teaching—perhaps in all religious thought. One strand advocates complete love of God and surrender to him. All activities are not done for the self but are done for God. The other strand, although acknowledging the need for love and surrender, is not concerned with God as a recipient of devotion but more with the nature of his being, the ground of his existence.

The majority of Hindus find the first way the easiest, and their religion has developed a wonderful number of gods and goddesses, who are worshiped not for themselves but for what they symbolize. Thus Kali, the Mother of the Earth, can be identified with and worshiped because through her the devotee knows he is reverencing life itself. In her destructive aspect, he reverences the cleansing force of death. As well, there are cosmic gods such as Rama, Krishna, Vishnu, etc.—legendary figures

118

who embody all the personal aspects of God himself.

Following this tradition of embodiment, a Hindu guru, or wise teacher, is supposed to embody great wisdom and power and a pupil goes to him in a state of surrender. If he is a Bhakti guru, a devotional teacher belonging to the first strand, he will expect total obedience and devotion from his pupil.

Bhakti gurus abound in India, but some have greater depth or more charismatic qualities than others. These come to be reverenced by thousands and are then invested by public opinion with even more holy power, for they are thought of as avatars or messiahs, self-realized when born, direct incarnations of God, as uniquely God-become-man as Christians consider Jesus to be.

The two such messiahs in this book are divided from each other by age and by teaching. Meher Baba, brought up a Parsee, offers little in the way of concrete methods; his advice is sometimes good but is generalized and not very original. His teaching was entirely concerned with devotion to himself—as an incarnation of God, of course.

Maharaj Ji is a very young man still and although he too asks for devotion, it does not contain the element of obedience demanded by Meher Baba. In contrast to Meher Baba, he has a definite set of awards to be won by those who make the effort to surrender themselves to him. One is the seeing of a light, the Divine Light, from which his movement takes its name.

Neither messiah taxes the brain unduly. But then, perhaps quite rightly, neither believes that the intellect is any help when it comes to apprehending Reality.

Meher Baba
1894–1969

The key provided by Meher Baba does not quite fit the door. Somehow he is too frenetic, his demands and promises too overwhelming and improbable. He insists that he is God, all-knowing and all-powerful, that he is the messiah of this age, as much God-man as Jesus:

> I am the Ancient One. When I say I am God it is not because I have thought about it and concluded that I am God—I know it to be so. Many consider it blasphemy for one to say he is God; but in truth it would be blasphemy for me to say I am not God.[1]

He speaks of himself as having appeared in the past as Krishna and as Christ, and he promises that through his mediation the world, especially America, will change and become more spiritual. He forecast for himself a violent death at the hands of his countrymen, the Parsees, but he died peacefully in 1969.

Yet in spite of the many prophecies of wars and other world-shaking events which never came true, and in spite of his grandiose claims of divinity and infinite power, one senses a warm and potentially good person who failed to fulfill his own nature—distracted perhaps by attempts to live up to a role to which he was not temperamentally suited.

India is a country where, if one says "I am God," one does not provoke either laughter or scepticism. The goal of all Hindus is to realize that this transitory body is not the final "me." The body, mind, and senses die but my true nature is the Self, sublime and eternal, the one Reality which, because of illusion and ignorance, I see as a multitude of separate beings and things, including that which I think of as myself. Aldous Huxley once said that Western religion tries to "know" God, whereas Eastern religion tries to "be" God. The awareness of God, the Whole, as the undifferentiated ground of himself is the moment when the Hindu comes home to his true nature at last.

Thus to say "I am God" means "I have made the trip—I am there." Meher Baba pointed out that only the man who is really there can say whether he is or not. An avatar, the nearest a human can come to God while still in a body (a list may include Krishna, the Buddha, Zoroaster, Jesus, and Mohammed) is the only one who can pronounce on his own status because nobody else has the qualifications to do so. Meher Baba said he was an avatar and many people believed him.

His religion was mostly Sufi although he was born and brought up in Poona and absorbed a Hindu background. His parents had come to India from Persia and his own name was originally Merwan (nicknamed Meher) Sheriar Irani. It is said that he had a light skin, soft warm eyes, a hooked nose, and a rather Georgian, drooping moustache.

A strange experience in his late teens sparked off his spiritual career. Until then he had been, apparently, a carefree, clever young man, uninterested in anything but his studies at the university and his social life. One evening, cycling back from college, he drew close to the small hut of an old Muslim woman, Hazrat Babajan, who was said to be a fakir. To his surprise she appeared and beckoned to him. He got off his bicycle and went up to her. They didn't speak but she clasped his hands and then kissed his forehead.

This kiss affected Baba profoundly and he was drawn to her "as steel to a magnet." He visited her every evening until one night, he relates, she "made me realise in a flash the infinite bliss of Self-realisation (God-realisation)." He went home to bed and lost consciousness of his body.

For the next few months he lived as a moving corpse, unconscious of life around him. He was able to walk but little more. He hardly ate, and tried to give away all his food to dogs and beggars. His parents thought his mind had gone and he was put under doctors, but to little avail. At last he began to regain consciousness and to live "as an automaton possessing intuition." Gradually, he is said to have recovered completely, although Paul Brunton, one of his critics, seriously doubts this.

The whole course of his life was now changed. The "veil" between himself and God had been rent by Babajan's kiss. He had been in a state of ecstasy during the unconscious months, and had felt he was one with God in such a way that the whole universe, with all its levels of consciousness, became apparent to him. But coming down from this bliss to the earthly level was great agony, so painful that he would spend hours each day knocking his forehead against walls and windows, the physical pain relieving the spiritual torture. He said:

> In reality there is no suffering as such—only infinite bliss. Although suffering is illusory, still, within the realm of illusion, it *is* suffering. In the midst of illusion, Babajan established my reality. My reality, although untouched by illusion, remained connected with illusion. That was why I suffered incalculable spiritual agonies.[2]

At last he resolved to ask Babajan what he should do next. She signified that he should find a spiritual teacher. When asked where he should go, she waved her hand vaguely.

His whole longing now was to spiritualize himself. He went to several masters, including the famous Sai Baba, a fierce guru who would demand money from any rich-looking visitor and then hand it to the waiting poor. Sai Baba looked at him and immediately called him the God-Sustainer. Meher went with Sai Baba to a temple where a guru called Upashni (Upasani) was living as Sai Baba's disciple, in a state of fasting and nakedness.

This was a historic occasion. As soon as Upashni set eyes upon Meher he picked up a stone and threw it at him with great force. It hit him on the forehead and drew blood. This ended Meher's torn state of being in between bliss and "gross consciousness" and brought him down into "the ordinary consciousness of the realm of illusion." Unfortunately, however, the more conscious he became of this ordinary world, the more his suffering increased, and he says that for years afterwards he continued to knock his head against stones, eventually loosening all his teeth and prematurely losing them.

The blow had the effect of confirming him in his belief that he was the "Ancient One," God incarnate, and he regarded Upashni as his master, staying near him for six months. Then Upashni announced: "Meher, you are the Avatar and I salute you." He then became know as Meher Baba, *Baba* meaning Spiritual Master.

He accepted a number of disciples from Upashni, and in 1922 he started the first of his ashrams, a simple house in Bombay, where he received devotees of all persuasions, Parsee, Hindu, and Muslim. There were strict diet rules and no furniture was allowed. But a year later he closed this ashram and told forty inner disciples, whom he called the *mandali* (in Sufism, it seems, it is a master's duty to train forty followers), that they must prepare to go with him to Persia. With immense difficulty the journey was arranged and visas obtained. They set off but never got there. Most of the mandali fell ill on the boat and Baba turned back. For some eighteen months, the group then traveled continually about the country. Often Baba would announce that they were going to settle in a place but no sooner were the arrangements in hand than he would start them all moving again. His temper was erratic in those days, and he would occasionally lash out and give one of the mandali a beating or a blow on the ear. On one occasion, he threw an over-fat disciple down a flight of stone stairs.

After this, the whole group reestablished themselves in a disused army camp a few miles outside Bombay. It was christened Meherabad—*abad* meaning flourishing—and Baba soon organized his followers into building a hospital out of old army huts—"The Meher Charitable Hospital and Dispensary," and a boarding school for up to a hundred boys—"The Meher Ashram." This school was entirely free and Baba welcomed Untouchables as well as Hindu and Muslim boys.

At that time it was unheard of for a guru like Baba to have anything to do with the Untouchables. Such distinctions, however, meant nothing to Baba, who was not particularly Hindu and who believed in the universality of God. He not only accepted the boys but personally cleaned their latrines and cut their hair and bathed them when they arrived.

In 1925, he announced that he would remain silent for a year. He never spoke again.

> My Silence and the imminent breaking of my Silence is to save mankind from the monumental forces of ignorance, and to fulfil the divine Plan of universal unity. The breaking of my Silence will reveal to man the universal Oneness of God, which will bring about the universal brotherhood of man. My Silence had to be. The breaking of my Silence has to be—soon.[3]

Although he never did break his silence, his followers were kept in a continual state of expectation that he would and were promised great dramas when it happened:

> When an atom is "split" an infinite amount of energy is released. Similarly, when my Silence is broken and I utter the WORD infinite wisdom will be released.
>
> When an atom bomb strikes the earth it causes vast devastation. Similarly, when the Word I utter strikes the universe there will be a great material destruction; but there will also take place a tremendous spiritual upheaval.[4]

Much has been written about Baba's silence, and he himself wrote a great deal on it. Silence it may have been, but it was certainly not lack of communication. After some time he gave up writing as well but grew extremely agile with an alphabet board, flicking his fingers from one letter to another while a disciple took it all down. Eventually he abandoned even the alphabet board and relied upon gestures to express himself. A disciple would translate the gesture and ask Baba if this was correct.

In 1926, he suddenly and without warning closed Meherabad altogether, putting an end to all the thriving enterprises. He said:

> Usually a temporary scaffolding is set up around a big

building which is under construction, and when the building is completed, the scaffolding is removed. Often my external activities and commitments are only the external expression of the internal work I am doing. In either case, my external activities and commitments may be continued indefinitely or I may end them promptly at the end of the inner work, depending upon the prevailing circumstances.[5]

But the ashram was reopened later.

He embarked upon an interminable series of journeys. By this time he had disciples from the West as well as from Persia and India. Once more he and a group set out for Persia, now hiring a bus to go overland across difficult desert terrain. Many were ill, the bus broke down, there was a forced stay at Duzdab because of visa trouble, but at last the party actually crossed into Persia. After this accomplishment, he traveled all over India with the purpose of opening ashrams, and then began a series of world tours in 1932.

Hollywood welcomed him and he became very popular in America, more so than in Europe. All in all, he paid some seven visits to the West and made at least two world tours.

Many of these trips were made excruciatingly difficult for the mandali by their master's constant, capricious changing of plans. These often major reorganizations tested his followers and sometimes found them wanting, particularly the Western women, who disagreed among themselves. Baba reminds one of Gurdjieff in this respect, and undoubtedly it is a Sufi teaching that disciples should have their conceptual and reactive ("machine") minds jolted, shaken, and battered by their master's apparently illogical whims.

The adulation of America, however, did not keep Baba permanently there. At the end of his world tours he started a new phase which seems to have been more humble in intention. At Rahuri, near Ahmednagar, he founded the "mad ashram" for the treatment of the Indian insane, particularly those who were "God-intoxicated" and who lived in a state of squalor and filth, their minds so removed from reality that they were unconscious of their surroundings. Various of the mandali were sent to search the district for both holy and ordinary madmen, and when they were brought back to the ashram Baba would personally shave, bathe, feed, and clothe each one. He also scoured the latrines each day, and bathed the old before sitting in seclusion with them.

This work of a servant to those in need was a spiritual task which Baba would not talk about. All he said was that he loved the God-men and they loved him. The ultimate purpose of this work was never known to anyone except Baba.

In 1937, the mad ashram was moved to Meherabad, but shortly afterward, except for intermittent periods of enthusiasm, Baba's interest in it began to decline. A year later, most of the inmates were sent back to their homes and Baba began an extensive tour of India to find genuine *masts,* the word used for those God-intoxicated men whose ordinary minds have been driven into disintegration by, supposedly, the revelation of Truth which they have received. Whenever one was found he was added to the party and consequently, when Baba eventually started back for Meherabad, he was accompanied by the mandali, twenty or so madmen, half a dozen *masts,* a gazelle, a peacock, a sheep, a rabbit, geese, dogs, monkeys, and pet birds, all of whom had to travel by train. There was also a vast assortment of trunks, tables, chairs, and cooking equipment, which occupied the carriage with them.

A few months after this, Baba closed the mad ashram altogether, from then on working only with the more advanced and highly spiritual *masts*, moving around India with the mandali and sending them off for the local *masts* wherever they stopped. Sometimes the mandali were put into great difficulties by *masts* who refused to cooperate, and there are stories of taxis standing by while *masts* were clothed and persuaded to enter them only to get out the other side, or to sit with their legs out of the window. Baba would say that he must contact a certain number of *masts* in one place, the onus being on the mandali to find them. Frequently this entailed great hardships—rides in bullock carts or on camels, treks over miles of dust or mud, in every sort of weather until, in the end, seventy-five thousand miles had been covered, twenty thousand contacts made, and seven *mast* ashrams founded.

No one can judge how much good this did to the *masts*. Baba put tremendous energy and, so it is said, love into sitting with them and caring for them. He oiled the scale-covered body of one "crocodile" *mast* until his skin was healthy again. He fed them and sent them back with fresh clothes. He listened to them and believed in their spiritual state. It would be impossible to do all that without love.

As well as being a Sufi teacher, Baba followed the traditional Hindu *Bhakti* path of devotion in which he, as a guru, expected a disciple to give up his life to serving him, thus enabling the disciple to approach God through him, who was God-man. A guru of this type does not think of himself in a personal way, and it is not to him as a person that the disciple submits.

In theory Meher Baba was such a guru, but he somehow fails to convince. His authority over his disciples sounds frequently querulous, as though struggling to believe in itself. His teaching, when read, is not particularly original but is mainly a series of discourses on straightforward Sufi and Hindu doctrines. His cosmology, also derived from these sources, takes the form of evolutionary charts which show six different levels of consciousness in man, the attainment of which resembles a set of spiritual "O" Levels.

What, then, gave him a world audience of devotees? Foremost, undoubtedly there was a magnetic, charismatic quality about him which was genuinely felt as love radiating from him. People often wept when they first saw him. He laid himself open to everybody—not, perhaps, with the divine love which he attributed to himself, but with a genuine if sometimes strangely expressed empathy with many ordinary people.

Secondly, his teaching, at its best, was designed to break down intellectual barriers and to reach the heart. It was not a philosophy so much as a way of cutting through philosophical reasoning to intuitive feeling, to where a deep response can be elicited—"The moment you try to understand God rather than love Him you begin to misunderstand Him, and your ignorance feeds your ego. Mind cannot reach that which is beyond it. God is infinite and beyond the reach of mind."[6]

Perhaps it is true that the theorizing intellect is a hindrance to spiritual response. Buddhism is quite clear that this is so. To a disciple who wanted to speculate on the afterlife, the Buddha replied emphatically that this sort of query is not profitable and has nothing to do with the fundamentals of religion. Zen says, "Don't think—just look," and the Hindu sage, Ramana Maharshi, said, "You know that you know nothing. Find out that knowledge. That is liberation." The mind, itself a marvelous tool for ordinary living, must be dropped when the nature of life is sought for. The observer in us who analyzes and makes value judgments, must give way to the total "I" who wants to respond to what is. Methods for letting go of the

discriminating mind and for coming to such a response
are described by other sages, such as Krishnamurti and
Trungpa. Meher Baba's way was to expect devotion from
his followers to such an extent that their analytical,
evaluating intellect would be replaced by a selfless
love—selfless because Baba was put in the place of the
self. When a decision had to be made the devotee was to
summon his image of Baba into his mind and to ask it what
to do. When there was a moment of leisure, Baba should
be thought of. In this way, the ordinary ego was supposed
to diminish. Baba made it clear that his disciples must not
blindly copy him, but must always *obey* him:

> Do not try with your limited mind to understand the sig-
> nificance of my actions, nor try to imitate them. You must not
> do what I do, but do what I tell you to do. To try to bring my
> every action within the orbit of your understanding is but to
> understand the limitations of your own understanding![7]
>
> What is meant by becoming footless and headless? It
> means implicitly obeying the Perfect Master: following His
> orders literally and not using your head to analyse their
> significance; doing only what He wants you to do—your feet
> moving at His command and your life being lived in the way
> of His love.[8]

"God can always be captured by love," said Baba. Certainly it would be hard for many people if God had to be
captured by intelligence or reason. Perhaps Baba spoke
good sense, for the real abandoning of self occurs when
you or I cease trying to better the "self" in any way, even
the most spiritual way. When I drop, or gladly cast aside,
my sense of separate selfhood, I do so because I want
direct experience of being, of reality. I want to *be* actual
and real, without barrier or guard, and my urge to do this
is a·revolution, felt completely and not only intellectually. To call it love is true but it also transcends ordinary
love as the sun pales a candle. "God is captured by love"

is so, in the sense that all I have is given up and gladly forsaken; and *it appears* as though there is a reciprocal action of acceptance and immeasurable love by something—God, the heart, life, the real world. All is felt to be right, to be wholly good.

There are many people for whom this state of openness is reached, as nearly as it can be reached, through a "messiah," a personal Christ, one with whom a relationship can be established, on whom the weight of sorrows can be laid, to whom devotion is offered. Love must be experienced if it is to grow, and the cosmic image is sometimes easier to love than one's neighbor. Hindus are well aware of this human need for an object of devotion and provide deities for every type of person, each image being the embodiment of a virtue rather than an actual god. Krishna, the mythical avatar of the Bhagavad Gita, sets many hearts afire. But the sort of avatar who gets into actual history, such as Jesus of Nazareth, tends, perhaps, to create complications, for his humanhood is not always at all easy to reconcile with his "divine" nature.

Meher Baba rather fell into this historical trap. He frequently seemed to try too hard to live up to an avatar image and perhaps as many people were turned off by him as were turned on. But now that he is dead, young devotees who never met him are thrilled with their image of him in the same way that some Christians respond to the Jesus of their imagination.

One wonders how much of Baba's teaching will survive. His cosmology may, because a number of people of theosophical inclination are always fascinated by intricate charts, such as Sufis and Hindus produce. And Baba's cosmology is quite specific. There are always, he says, five Perfect Masters on earth. God becomes man as an avatar, such as himself, and the five men become God as Perfect Masters who fetch the avatars when there is need of them. "It is because of the five Perfect Masters that I appear here before you," he said. "They fetch me down, and I experience myself as everything and tell you that I am everything."[9]

Three of the Perfect Masters we met earlier in this chapter—Babajan, Sai Baba, and Upashni. A fourth was Sadguru (Perfect Master) Narayan Maharaj, whom Baba visited once, without much impact on either side; and a fifth was Tajuddin Baba, an ex-soldier in the Indian Army who gave up his military career when he became God-realized. Constantly irritated by people who came seeking advice and blessings, he appeared naked one evening on a European tennis court and thus had himself sent to a lunatic asylum where he lived happily for seventeen years. Baba's one visit to him seemed to be unimpressive.

Below the Perfect Masters in the chart, who live as both God and man, are a "very, very few people" who experience the Perfect Master state without actually putting it into daily practice; and below these again, are a very few who "pass away into God" and experience infinite power, knowledge and bliss. Below these are a number of planes of existence, Mental and Subtle for the few, and Gross for most of us. In the outer universe are planets which contain Seven Kingdoms of Evolution below our own.

Apart from these categories of existence (all straightforward Sufi teaching) can one say that Baba said anything else which might have a life of its own?

A small selection of possibles might be made. One in particular, clarifies the position of the heart (openness, fearlessness) in relation to the intellect (analytical, evaluating):

> The difference between love and intellect is something like that between night and day: they exist in relation to one another and yet as two different things. Love is real intelli-

gence capable of realising truth; intellect is best suited to know all about duality, which is born of ignorance and *is* entirely ignorance. When the sun rises, night is transformed into day. Just so, when love manifests, not-knowing (ignorance) is turned into conscious-knowing (knowledge).

In spite of the difference between a keenly intelligent person and a very unintelligent person, each is equally capable of experiencing love. The quality which determines one's capacity for love is not one's wit or wisdom, but one's readiness to lay down life itself for the beloved, and yet remain alive. One must, so to speak, slough off body, energy, mind and all else, and become dust under the feet of the beloved. This dust of a lover who cannot remain alive without God—just as an ordinary man cannot live without breath—is then transformed into the beloved. Thus man becomes God.[10]

But perhaps Baba will be remembered by his followers more for his teachings prepared for them than those for the world at large:

Truth is simple, but Illusion makes it infinitely intricate. The person is rare who possesses an insatiable longing for Truth; the rest allow Illusion to bind them ever more and more. God alone is Real and all else that you see and feel is nothing but a series of nothings.

I am Infinite Knowledge, Power and Bliss. I can make anyone realise God if I choose to do so. You may ask, why not make me realise God now? But why should it be you? Why not the person next to you or the man in the street, or that bird on the tree, or that stone—who are all but one in different forms? The more you love me the sooner you will discard the falsehood you have chosen to hide under that hoodwinks you into believing you are what you are not. I am all in all and love all equally. Your love for me will wear through your falseness and make you realise the Self that you truly are.

Mere intellectual understanding does not bring God nearer to you. It is love, not questioning, that will bring God to you. Questioning nourishes pride and separateness. So do not ask questions, but strive to become a "slave" of the Perfect Master.

When your life presents an honest and sincere picture of your mind and heart just an embrace from a Perfect Master is enough to quicken the spirit. When I the Ancient One embrace you I awaken something within you which gradually grows. It is the seed of Love that I have sown. There is a long period and great distance between the breaking open of the seed and its flowering and fruiting. Actually the Goal is neither far nor near and there is no distance to cross nor time to count. In Eternity, all is *here* and *now*. You have simply to become that which you are. You are God, the Infinite Existence.[11]

Maharaj Ji
1958–

Guru Maharaj Ji was born in 1958 and has been a *Satguru*, a revealer of the Divine Light, since the age of eight.

Like Meher Baba, his disciples believe him to be an avatar, an incarnation of God, and the most realized and holy among men. Unlike Meher Baba, he appears to have some quite concrete techniques to offer as aids to the transcendent, and it is the effects of these techniques that have brought him immense popularity among the young, as well as a vast American audience and a decidedly comfortable style of life.

Older and more reticent Europeans and Americans are repelled by a form of religion which seems to resemble show business more than spirituality, which promotes a star—the young Satguru—and loudly proclaims him as he travels about in his Rolls Royce to be an avatar, on the level of Jesus, the Buddha, and others.

But before one reacts too far against the credulity of the young and the pop-starlike adoration they feel for their guru, perhaps one should look more carefully at the background from which he has emerged, and at the teaching he offers.

Maharaj Ji's "divinity" comes in direct line from his father, Shri Hans Ji Maharaj, of Badrinath in North India. Shri Hans, who died in 1966, was the true Bhakti type of guru, not so much interested in philosophy as in teaching devotion to God and the realization of Him. He has his own place in this book as a sage for, like other sincere gurus, he attracted many devotees.

Briefly, the story about him goes that he was changed from a rather arrogant, guru-less young man to a devoted follower of the path after hearing a teacher who was called Dada Guru speak. He begged for knowledge and for *Updesh*, initiation, and was told that he must hear *Satsang*, the spiritual discourses of his master. Eventually the time came for him to receive his initiation. On his way to Dada Guru he had to cross a stream which had swollen in the recent rains to a torrent. He was carried away by the current and gave himself up for dead, his one regret being that he had not received the Guru's knowledge. Suddenly he was pulled out of the river and on to the bank. In good Hindu fashion, when he looked for his rescuer, no one could be seen.

He believed this episode to be a sign from God that he was doing the right thing. He went on to Dada Guru and was given the four *krijas*, truths, which constitute the Knowledge. At first he did not know what to do with it, but after reading the Bhagavad Gita the whole mystery of existence became, apparently, crystal clear to him. He surrendered totally to his Guru, and was known to be "austere and simple, his whole being bent upon truth." After the death of his master, he began to disseminate the

Knowledge in Sindh, Lahore, and Delhi, spending much time with laborers in the Delhi Cloth Mill, to whom he taught methods of meditation in action so that they could realize God at all times.

He refused to accept differences in caste, fully believing that all men are entitled to receive the word of God. On one occasion a sweeper in the household of a Brahmin disciple asked to be initiated. Shri Hans accepted him and gave him Updesh, but when the Brahmin heard of this he was infuriated. It was unthinkable, he said, that both he and a sweeper could be disciples of the same Guru. Shri Hans replied that the blame must be laid on God, who places divinity in the heart of every man, Brahmin and sweeper alike, and there was nothing Shri Hans or the Brahmin could do to alter that.

This sort of episode brought him respect and popularity in many parts of India although he did have enemies, and the fact that he married was viewed as an imperfection.

His aim became clearer as time went on. He wanted to teach direct spiritual experience without the usual formalities of ritual and worship. He seems to have been like an early Quaker among the Hindus. He spoke strongly against the Indian love of metaphysical argument and philosophical debate describing these as time-wasting pastimes for the intellectual, as games that destroy the intuitive realization of Reality. He asked, rather, for loving surrender to himself, the Guru, for no spiritual understanding, he said, could be acquired without a teacher.

Surrender to one's guru is basic to Hindu tradition. Is it a genuinely religious path? At a certain stage in man's growth he seems to need to lean on a divine figure, sometimes an image, to whom he can attach feelings of love which otherwise could not be expressed. The very pouring out of reverence, joy, and intense love may carry him perhaps to a more open and trusting acceptance of daily encounters.

On the other hand, total reliance on a human guru (sometimes all too human) must often lead to emotional overdependence, in the same way that an excessive devotion to the formalities of religion quenches the seeking spirit. The Buddha, originally a Hindu, spoke sharply against Brahmin practices and refused to allow his followers to regard him as anything but the teacher of a path that all could follow with or without him there to guide them. His was an austere way of self-reliance, of finding out for oneself as one goes along, the validity of the truths he gave tongue to.

Westerners, hooked by their own insistence on a historical Christ, have been caught for centuries in the dilemma of owning a supreme guru and yet not being able to carry out his teachings. Because he was an unrepeatable, once-and-for-all guru, no modern one can be acknowledged. And yet what Christ is reported to have taught, although it has a generally profound application, is moral rather than spiritual and does not seem to bring about self-transcendence and God-realization. Worship of a bearded and stern moralist or of a meek and forgiving Savior fails to satisfy many in the world today. But the image of Christ can not yet be dropped to make way for the living illumination.

The young Maharaj Ji, who has taken on Shri Hans' guruship, has a reply to this Christian dilemma. The knowledge that he imparts is universal, he says, and is the pure essence of all religions. It is not specifically Hindu, and so his messiahship is not limited to any one religion.

In London, in 1971, he said:

This Knowledge is so holy, so perfect, that one spark that comes out of this Knowledge is so perfect, so, so perfect that wherever it goes, it hits, it makes it perfect, and wherever it goes again, it hits and again makes it perfect. Wherever one spark of this Knowledge shines out it makes it perfect. And that Knowledge, I have got it here.[1]

In Colorado in 1972 he spoke again about the Knowledge and his giving of it to mankind:

I am not scared to tell this point to everyone because it's true, it's a true point. The time is coming soon when the world is going to see a great, strange thing happening, a really far-out thing happening. The time is very near when the world will be able to realise who God is—not only believe in God but *know* that God exists.[2]

To *know* that God exists would surely be, for many people, a reassurance so profound that all life would be transfigured by it. It is partly the lack of external, objective evidence of God that causes such terrible existential doubt. If this doubt could be assuaged by some form of supreme knowledge, how many could resist it? Who would not want to go and obtain it as soon as possible?

And this is just what happens to those who think that Maharaj Ji will give it to them. Whether they get real knowledge of God or not, every day there are hundreds of young people who believe that they will, and who queue up to get it, longing for the moment when they will feel a vibration, see a bright light, smell nectar, hear a divine sound: these four experiences make up the Knowledge of God which Guru Maharaj proclaims.

The most important is the first of the four, the vibration. This is also known as the Word of God, and it is said to be the vibration of cosmic energy which activates the universe. It is here within us already, says Maharaj Ji, but we are not conscious of it, we do not know how to realize it. The realization can only be gained by initiation from the Guru himself, or from one of his Mahatmas, chosen transmitters of the Knowledge.

When there is consciousness of the vibration, the body moves with it and then a light can be seen that is said to be startlingly brilliant (the eyes are shut). This is the Divine Light of God and has given its name to Maharaj Ji's movement, the Divine Light Mission. It is this light which seems particularly holy to those who see it, but not everybody does—it is not automatically seen after the vibration is felt, and it is said that those who are "intellectual," such as school teachers, have great difficulty in seeing it at all. It is also referred to as the third eye.

The nectar which enters the mouth from within is said to taste sweet and to be the origin of all the fluids in the body.

The divine sound is said to be music, faint and wonderful.

Those who have received the initiation are known as "premies," which literally means lovers of God and disciples of Maharaj Ji. Morning and evening, they practice putting themselves into the vibration and seeing the Light.

It is hard to judge as yet the effect that Maharaj Ji is having on the West. He is a very young man and almost all his devotees are also young. Many are carried away by the highly emotional atmosphere of gurudom and he appeals particularly to those who long for bliss without strings, a teaching based on sensations rather than words:

And I must tell you that you don't meditate for me, you meditate for yourselves. *You* should get high. I am high. I am high enough. But you should get high. You need to do this meditation because you want to get high. Not me. I am high. I am in the infinite state. You must get high, you must get to this point where you can also go to the infinite state. I have given you this Knowledge, therefore your duty is to meditate on it.[3]

Maharaj Ji addresses his followers in modern American words and accent and in a high, rather breathless voice. His discourses consist largely of pointed stories which reveal aspects of straightforward Hindu teaching, although he is not thought at all highly of by other Indian gurus, who consider him to be unlearned in the scriptures. But sometimes Maharaj Ji's stories come straight from the scriptures; at other times they have no acknowledged origin (such as the following):

There was once a man and he went into this big exhibition where people were selling things and he had only two coins in his hands; one was ten cents and the other was five cents and he was holding them like this. And what happened was that there was a man there advertising these polishers which were very good for your teeth, really excellent, they made them really sparkle. And the guy was saying, "Anyone who has got bad teeth, please come up to me," and an old man comes up who was also visiting the exhibition. He goes up there and the salesman takes some stuff out of a bottle, puts it on the old man's teeth, gives him some water and says, "All right, gargle!" The old man gargles and then he opens his mouth and his teeth are absolutely shining! Immediately people start buying it like anything, buying, buying, buying until there are about four or five bottles left. So the man says to himself, "Mmm. I think I should buy some because my teeth are pretty dirty." So he takes out his ten cents and his five cents from his pocket because that's the cost of the bottle—fifteen cents—and now he's there thinking whether to take it or not to take it. See, he's twisting his fingers also, he is actually rubbing the coins together. "Shall I take it or not, take it or not, take it or not, take it or not? I'll be losing my cents but I'll be getting white teeth. Shall I take it or not, take it or not, take it or not?"

Finally when there was one bottle left, he said, "All right, give it to me," and he gives that fiteen cents and the man takes them. But they are just plain pennies—nothing else. They have been completely rubbed off. They are no longer ten cents and five cents, they are nothing, because that guy just rubbed them off. They don't mean anything any more.

So this is the same thing. You live all your lifetime doing this, just thinking, "Should I realise God or not, should I realise God or not, should I realise God or not?" Then when the last moment of your life comes, you say, "All right, I'll realise Him." But then this body has already got only fifteen seconds to live, and it is too late.[4]

The style of this story is more that of a Fundamentalist preacher than that of a subtle Indian guru. Perhaps the great American audiences of the Midwest have imposed their style on him.

He does not advocate the use of drugs and these, together with cigarettes and alcohol, are forbidden in the Palaces of Peace where Satsang (discourse) is held. The atmosphere at these Palaces is dreamy and ecstatic —immense, blown-up photographs of Maharaj Ji and of other gurus line the walls, pop music plays softly, and the "spiritual" discourses go on and on, nonstop, from nine in the morning till nine in the evening. The Knowledge is given free to anyone who asks for it, which contrasts pleasantly with the Maharishi's high fees.

All that the disciple is asked to give (besides a voluntary donation) is his time—and many of the young seem to have more of this than their elders. One is expected to devote two weeks at least to hearing Satsang. One must hear it and hear it until one is consumed by a longing for the Knowledge and is ready to give up all one's attachments, such as drugs, smoking, eating meat, etc. Then, if one has sufficiently surrendered one's personality to Maharaj Ji, a Mahatma will perceive this with his inner eye, and the Knowledge will be given. If he continues to pass one over, this means one is not ready for the transmission.

Such stringent conditions (if you are working or have a

family, it is impossible to spend every day for two weeks at Satsang) builds up a hysterical feeling that you *must* be chosen by a Mahatma. The premies, those who already have the Knowledge, conduct the Satsang and discourse endlessly on the corruptness of society, the futility of modern life, and the grossness of the body. One premie may intersperse his discourse with cracking, uncovered yawns, as though he has been dragged out of bed to speak. Another can be overcome by an emotional devotion to the young Maharaj and tell her audience that he is "love, just love—he actually created Jesus and the Buddha— if any of you have a guru, and he took one look at Guru Maharaj, he would fall down in front of him."

Again one senses the Fundamentalist attitude when one hears a discourse consisting of long lists of mankind's sins; and a revivalist feeling in the whipping up of devotion. It does not seem surprising that after a continuous fortnight of this, those who take the Knowledge feel vibrations and see white lights. The giving of the Knowledge takes six hours—two of which are spent in meditation. The basis on which the whole exercise rests is a mantra, the holy name of God, concentrated on at the tip of the nose. This is said to put one on a vibration wavelength.

The four experiences of "divine" pleasure—the vibration, the light, the smell, and the sound—are the goodies offered in exchange for devotion. Those who follow the plump young Maharaj are uncritical, even when they do not see white lights. They do not want philosophy or scholarship, which is fortunate. The Maharaj seems to base what doctrine he has on a few well-known sayings taken from Christianity as well as Hinduism, and he does not always interpret them properly. One such saying is: "In the beginning was the Word and the Word was with God." Guru Maharaj, who rests much of his advice on this saying, has taken it to mean literally that the first thing that occurred in the universe was a word, whereas the Greek *logos* is rather more complicated than that.

Such oversimplifications do not matter to the Guru's followers, and perhaps they are right. What does a mere reinterpretation matter in comparison with divine bliss? And it is true that it is the experience of illumination that matters and not its description. In any case, soon we may all be able to decide for ourselves on the truth of his statements, for he has forecast that shortly the whole world will have the Knowledge.

Although so young, the Guru has recently married an American girl named Marlene, some eight years older than himself. As his message seems profoundly different from his father's, it will be interesting to see if Maharaj Ji and the American sons yet to be born to him will found a dynasty of Hindu revivalism. This seems doubtful; the Guru's image has slipped considerably since he was photographed passionately kissing an admirer—a divine action that did not please his supporters. Nevertheless, in 1988 he is still the revered head of this movement, but the movement itself has changed its name. It is now Elan Vital.

References

Meher Baba

1   Meher Baba, *The Everything and the Nothing* (The Beguine Library), p. 48.
2   Meher Baba, *Listen, Humanity* (New York: Harper and Row), p. 248.
3   Baba, *The Everything and the Nothing*, p. 75.
4   Ibid., p. 76.
5   Dr. Donkin, *The Wayfarers* (Adi K. Irani), p. 254.
6   Baba, *The Everything and the Nothing*, p. 45.
7   Ibid.
8   Ibid., p. 10.
9   Baba, *Listen, Humanity*, p. 61.
10   Ibid., p. 17.
11   Baba, *The Everything and the Nothing*, p. 50.

Further Reading

Baba, Meher, *God Speaks*. New York: Dodd, Mead & Co.
Baba, Meher, *Discourses. Sufism Reoriented*
Purdom, C. B., *The God-Man*. Sheriar Press
Hopkinson, Tom and Dorothy, *Much Silence*. London: Victor Gollancz

Maharaj Ji

1   *Satguru Has Come*, presented by Shri Hans Productions
2   *Satguru Has Come*
3   *Satguru Has Come*
4   *Farewell! Satsang of Shri Guru Maharaj Ji*, Divine Light Mission Magazine, 1973.

Further Reading

Satgurudev, *Shri Hans Ji Maharaj*. Delhi: Divine Light Mission

5

The Hindu Sages

The second strand of Hindu guruship comes from the teachings of Advaita Vedanta, where the divine being is seen as impersonal, as pure Reality without attribute, limitation, or definition. At the same time, he is THAT from which all has emerged, and which sustains it eternally. THAT is the fundamental nature of all things, but only man has been given the power to find this out. The ways of discovering his true Self, which is the name given to man's apprehension of the transcendent (it is called the Self because a man feels as though he has found his real self when he realizes the true ground of his nature) are not so much those of devotion to an object (human or inanimate) as in the preceding chapters, as of realizing the difference between the appearance of things and their reality.

The two *Jnana* (intuitive knowledge) gurus in this book have very different ways of helping their followers to make this discovery.

The great theme of Ramana Maharshi's teaching is Self-enquiry. When people asked him what would happen to them after death, he would say: "Why do you want to know what you will be when you die before you know what you are now? First find out what you are now." Who am I? was the essence of his teaching, and some people found this hard to understand.

He believed, as do other mystics in this book, that the feeling of "I" is given by its experiencer a wrong identification. Each of us thinks of our bodies as "I," of our minds as "I." But if bodies and minds are examined, no trace of self-entity can be found in them. Where, then, does the feeling of "I" come from? It arises with the body, said Ramana Maharshi, but it is not caused by the body. The "I" feeling has its origin in pure consciousness. When the "I" feeling is identified with the body it becomes known as sensations, when with the mind it becomes thoughts. To realize the feeling of "I" without identifying with anything other than consciousness is the aim of Ramana Maharshi's teaching.

The Maharishi, without Ramana Maharshi's brilliant use of the human faculties of intellect and understanding, nevertheless belongs to the Jnana school of gurus for he, too, queries the sense of self and points out that to identify the "I" with any of the self's worldly attributes is to take the appearance for the reality. His method for finding the nature of "I" is not so penetrating and ego-shattering as Ramana Maharshi's, for he relies on an easy technique.

Nevertheless, this technique—which is the substitution of a *mantra* (a word which supposedly has a divine origin and, as well, no intellectual connotations) for each and every thought as it arises—has helped many busy and self-identified people to approach a wordless peace of mind, which at least may be a step on the way to a greater wisdom.

Ramana Maharshi
1879–1950

In the desolately rocky and sun-baked Tamil country of South India there is a twin-peaked hill called Arunachala, the Hill of Light. For many centuries this hill has been sacred to the Hindus. They believe that our world has been in existence for three complete eons, called *yugas*, and we are now in the fourth. Throughout all this time the hill has been there, but has changed its nature according to its age. In the first yuga, the purest, called the Age of Truth, the hill was a pillar of light. As the universe gradually declined and entered the Age of Trinity, when creation, disintegration, and renewal were manifested, it became a heap of rubies. In the Age of Duality, when right and wrong came into existence, it was a pile of gold; and now, in Kali-Yuga, the present Age of Darkness, it is a mountain of stones. Throughout its history, it is believed to have been the seat of Shiva, the god of sleep and death, who embodies the darkness which comes before the light and the ending which precedes a new beginning.

Stories of this strange sacred hill stirred the mind of a seventeen-year-old Brahmin schoolboy, Venkataraman, who later came to be called Ramana Maharshi (*Maharshi* meaning *Great Sage*). But it was not until an unusual preexperience of death came to him that he decided to forego the education that his parents had planned for him, and instead to journey as a *sadhu*, an ascetic, to the Hill of Arunachala. The experience of death, which was his turning point, came to him as he was sitting alone one day in his uncle's house. He had rarely been ill and there was nothing at all wrong with his health on that day. But a sudden unmistakable fear of death swept over him. There was no apparent reason for this strong feeling and he did not try to explain it to himself. Nor did he panic, but instead began to wonder what he should do. It did not occur to him to consult anyone else; he felt it to be his own problem, and he said to himself, "Now death has come. What does it mean? What is it that is dying? This body dies."

Immediately afterward, we are told, he lay down stretching his limbs out and holding them stiff as though rigor mortis had set in. He held his breath and kept his lips tightly closed, so that to all outward appearances his body resembled a corpse. Now what would happen? This was what he thought:

Well, this body is now dead. It will be carried to the burning ground and there burnt and reduced to ashes. But with the death of this body, am I dead? Is the body I? This body is silent and inert. But I feel the full force of my personality and even the voice of the "I" within me, apart from it. So I am the Spirit transcending the body. The body dies but the Spirit that transcends it cannot be touched by death. That means I am the deathless Spirit.[1]

When Ramana Maharshi narrated this experience later on for the benefit of his devotees it looked as though this was a process of reasoning. But he took care to explain that this was not so. The realization came to him in a flash. He perceived the truth directly. "I" was something very real, the only real thing. Fear of death had vanished once and for all. From then on, "I" continued like the fundamental *sruti* note that underlies and blends with all the other notes."[1] Absorption in the awareness of "I" continued from then on.

Ramana's experience of what he took to be death may seem to some people to be incomplete. After all, what do we know of death, and what could he know? To shut one's eyes and hold one's breath and then discover that the feeling of "I" continues is hardly evidence that it will still be there when one is unable to shut any eyes or hold a single breath.

At this point and taken on its own, the experience does not seem sufficiently profound to have brought about a life of wisdom and deep understanding, any more than the fairly common psychic experience of being outside one's body (usually suspended above it) seems to lead to any great spiritual profundity.

But since Ramana Maharshi attached supreme importance to this early experience of "death," it is possible that it acted on him by giving him an illumined insight into "I," the inner person—whom we so readily identify with our body.

Hindu thought has always believed that ignorance lies in false identification, that we misunderstand our real nature when we identify it with the feelings and sensations of the body and call every body sensation "mine." If we can see beyond this possessive thinking, and see beyond the feeling of "I am this body, which is named so and so," our insight will be accompanied by intimations of bliss and liberation.

For the initial act of ignorance about our own self-

nature leads to ignorance about everything else. Because
we think of the body as the self, we think that the world is
composed of a multiplicity of other bodies all containing
separate selves. We dwell only on outward appearances
and are misled by them. A universe of names and forms
dominates our thinking.

Hinduism teaches that the creative force which upholds the world is neither name nor form but is consciousness itself. And the way for each one of us to
experience this consciousness is to give up identifying
ourself with all the *objects* of consciousness—with the
body-centered world.

Yoga practices are intended to bring about the end of
the feeling that "I am my body." Perhaps Ramana Maharshi, in a great leap of insight, arrived at that realization by
the intensity of his feeling that his body had died and was
no longer "him." He found that consciousness continued,
and that it was expressed in the feeling of "I am." From
then on he took the theme of self-enquiry—Who am
I?—as his lifework, and his discoveries and teachings
about it led to his fame as a guru.

After his "death" experience, Ramana left home and
went to Tiruvannamalai, a town which lies at the foot of
Arunachala, the Hill which he had imagined so often. He
never left there again. At first there was no question of
his being considered as a teacher. All he did was to sit
absorbed in the consciousness of Being, indifferent as to
whether his body lived or died. This was a state known
and respected by Hindus, who have always treated their
holy men with care and reverence; and a daily cup of food
was brought to him. Gradually he left the condition of
ineffable bliss and returned to the everyday life of those
around him.

Although still a very young man, his understanding was
so clear that he was soon recognized as a teacher, and

disciples formed an ashram about him. For the next fifty
years he expounded his one central message—Who am
I?—in language which was simple and penetratingly
direct.

The sense of "I" is natural to every being, he said
—thinking along the same lines as Alan Watts, who pronounced that life is continually reborn in every "I." Our
feelings, said Ramana Maharshi, are always expressed in
"I" terms—"I went," "I am," "I do." Usually these feelings are connected with the body and its actions—"I did
some gardening," "I read a book"—and so we come to
think of the body itself as "I." We identify ourselves with
all its functions and activities and call them "mine." But
the sense of "I" is vaster, more profound than the vehicle
of the body in which it arises. The body on its own is a
mere collection of bones and tissue, alive for a time and
then dead. If the body *caused* the consciousness of "I,"
we would be bound to feel this consciousness all the
time, but when we are deeply asleep there is no feeling of
"I."

The sense of "I" arises with the body, but is not caused
by the body. This was Ramana Maharshi's teaching. Because we are not aware of this, he said, and identify
consciousness with the body, it takes on the characteristics of bodily feelings and becomes what we think of as
our individual self or ego.

For all feelings pertain to the body; and they inevitably
give rise to the verbalized mind-chatter which we call
thoughts. When identification with the body is total, the
thoughts which arise are primarily for body-survival,
such as thoughts about food, housing and money. This is
ignorance of the real nature of "I." As realization begins
to take place (which may not occur in this life, according
to Hinduism) the sense of "I" becomes purified and
ceases to be identified so strongly with the body. More

unselfish and more abstract thoughts then occur. The feeling of "I" is not so much weakened as liberated into pure consciousness.

It is not the "I" sense itself which is the cause of suffering. A Zen master, Bankei, once asked his pupils why they "sold" their marvelous and deathless sense of "I" for the passing transformation into a greedy mind or a selfish mind. Instead of dwelling in the whole and acting from it, we become involved with the part and bind ourselves to its limitations.

What, then, is "I," and what has caused us to feel it? This question, said Ramana Maharshi, is the basis of all the scriptures. How can one ignore such a question? How can one go through life without bothering to enquire what the nature of the "I" is? "I," he says, shines within the heart, and the feeling of "I" is a continuous, unspoken, and spontaneous awareness which underlies all the flow of thoughts. If it is discovered and held to, the ignorance which mistakes it for its bodily attributes will disappear. This is liberation.

Even complete ignorance can never completely hide it, says Ramana Maharshi. The most unenlightened speak of "I." Ignorance only hides the reality of pure consciousness, and confuses the "I" feeling with the body.

The teachings on self-inquiry attracted many seekers to Tiruvannamalai. Although the Maharshi—frequently called *Bhagavan*, meaning endowed with sublime attributes—wrote very little, his answers to questions were taken down and compiled into several books by the late Arthur Osborne, as well as other, Indian, writers. Everyday he received visitors, among whom were many Westerners; and everyday he gave *darshan*, or audience, to many Indians and people of other nationalities. He was fragile and saintly and aroused great devotion among his followers. A Buddhist monk, Sangharakshita, who came to visit the ashram, describes the daily *darshan*:

By the time we arrived the Maharshi was generally established in his usual place on the couch at the far end of the hall, where he would either recline against a bolster or, though more rarely, sit up crosslegged. Sometimes we arrived early enough to hear the chanting of the Vedas by a group of Tamil brahmins, with which the morning darshan began. . . . After the chanting was over, and the brahmins had filed out of the hall, not much seemed to happen. The Maharshi sat on his couch. From time to time someone would approach him with a question or a request, would receive a brief reply, sometimes no more than a look or gesture, and would then return to his place. That was all. The rest of the time the sixty or seventy people sitting in the hall either simply looked at the Maharshi, which was what the word *darshan* literally meant, or else closed their eyes and meditated. Talking was by no means prohibited, and muted greetings would sometimes be exchanged between new arrivals and friends in the congregation, but for the most part the devotees sat quiet and motionless, hour after hour and a great silence reigned in the hall. One could not sit there for long without becoming aware that this silence was not mere absence of sound but a positive spiritual influence, even a spiritual force. It was as though a light breeze blew down the hall, or as though a stream flowed through it, a stream of purity, and this breeze, this stream, seemed to emanate from the silent, nodding figure on the couch, who did nothing in particular, only reading the letters that were brought to him or glancing, every now and then, at some member of the congregation with keen but kindly eye. Sitting there in the hall . . . I felt the stream flow over me, felt it flow over body and mind, over thoughts and emotions, until body, mind, thoughts and emotions had all been washed away, and there remained nothing but a great shining peace.[2]

One of the questions continually being put to Ramana Maharshi was, "Who am I? How can I find this out?" On one occasion he answered sharply, "If you don't know who you are, who else can tell you?" for he felt that people muddled themselves up with conceptual thinking and that if they could only become simple they would see the truth in a moment. But usually he replied patiently and at length to those who asked this troublesome question. He described two ways leading to Self-realization (the Hindu term *Self* means the One Reality, the Unity in which the world lives and moves, and which is also the undifferentiated Ground of the individual man. Awareness of this Ground gives a feeling of true identity, of having come home to one's real self at last. Hence it is often spoken of as the Self, the knowledge of one's own being).

The two ways that the Maharshi taught were (1) enquiring into who it is that undergoes this destiny and lives this life; then making the discovery that only the ego is bound by destiny and that the ego does not exist in the way we believe it to. And (2) surrendering the ego to God by way of realizing one's own limitations and helplessness, and by substituting God's will for one's own; by accepting all that is to be done without ever claiming any action as one's own, thus removing all sense of "me" and "mine." (The Maharshi frequently used the term *God* for the Self.)

Most Hindu gurus are by nature inclined to one or other of these paths, as has been pointed out. Ramana Maharshi was exceptionally clear about both, but was primarily concerned with the first, self-enquiry, although he was very firm that mind discrimination alone would only take one part of the way, and that the second way, development of the heart, was essential.

On the discrimination path, he would answer the question "How can I find out who I am?" by saying: "The body and its functions are not 'I'. Going deeper, the mind and its functions are not 'I'."[3]

These statements seem startling, even alarming, to the person who has always identified himself with both mind and body, particularly the mind. If the mind is not "I," what is "I"? This is exactly the right question to ask, says Ramana Maharshi. Clear observation will show that thoughts and feelings arise independently of the will in rather the same way that the sympathetic nervous system works. We digest our food without "I" being involved at all. Our blood circulates without will power. In the same way, mind and memory seem to have a natural autonomy which has little or nothing to do with the feeling of "I."

Two hundred years ago, on the other side of the world, the philosopher Hume discovered this and said:

> For my part when I enter most intimately into what I call 'myself,' I always stumble on some particular perception or other, of heat or cold, light or shade, love or hatred, pain or pleasure. I never can catch *myself* at any time without a perception, and never can observe anything but the perception. . . . We are nothing but a bundle or collection of different perceptions, which succeed each other with an inconceivable rapidity and are in a perpetual flux and movement.[4]

And far farther East, Zen Buddhism teaches its followers not to project the feeling of "I" onto thoughts, feelings, or the outside world. As thoughts begin to be clearly seen as arising and dying in the same way that the body is born and dies, the sensation of "I" becomes more profound and less personal. It transcends me and yet it *is* me. This sensation can no longer be called a thought or a feeling—it is an awareness of a changeless state of being, about which there can be no doubt. It does not *seem* to be, it *is*. No words can ever capture the immense marvel of this certainty.

The discriminatory path to it is by the gradual realization of the transitory nature of all created things so that

eventually they are seen as empty of all the attributes of
self, and upheld only by God or the Self—That which is
beyond all human understanding.

Sometimes this realization occurs suddenly and
uniquely without any preliminaries of training. It came to
the young Ramana Maharshi in this way when he saw that
the death of his body was inevitable but that That which
created and upheld it does not die. It was then that he
understood the great Hindu saying "Thou art That" and
realized that his feeling of "I," in its purest form, *was*
That, was pure Being without attribute.

He taught his questioners to trace this feeling back
through all the sheaths of intellect and personality which
enfold it, through the three states of consciousness
—sleep, dreaming, and waking—which occur to it, and to
see it as the substratum, the unqualified and unaffected
ground of all its manifestations, which include the mind
itself.

"The essence of the mind," he said, "is only awareness
or consciousness. However, when the ego overclouds it,
it functions as reasoning, thinking or perceiving. The
universal mind, not being limited by the ego, has nothing
outside itself and is therefore only aware. This is what the
Bible means by 'I am that I am.'"[5]

When questioners said that they could not trace the 'I,'
that when they looked within themselves they could not
see "I," Ramana Maharshi told them that this was because of habitual false identification—that the individual, limited to the waking state, is so used to looking
outward and expecting to see something different from
himself that he cannot believe that he who is seeing, the
objects he sees, and the act of seeing them are all the same
manifestation of one Consciousness.

"How do you recognise yourself now?" he would ask.
"Do you have to hold a mirror up in front of yourself to

recognise yourself? The awareness is itself the 'I.' Realise it and that is the truth."[6]

He taught that even the *perception* of "I" at the root of thoughts is still associated with forms, even with the physical body, and is not the pure consciousness of Self, with which no thing can be associated. "The Self is the pure Reality in whose light the body, the ego and all else shines. When all thoughts are stilled, pure Consciousness remains over."[7]

Some of his followers found the discriminatory path of Self-enquiry hard to follow, and Ramana Maharshi would then advise the way of surrender to God. Surrender, in his way, does not involve the intellect so much as the will, for it is a continual giving up of identity; a longing for God's will to be done rather than one's own; a complete giving away of the feeling of oneself as the "doer" of one's actions.

"Egoism in the form of 'I am the doer' resembles a great black and poisonous serpent. The antidote to its poison is recognition of the fact 'I am not the doer.' This knowledge leads to happiness,"[8] says the Ashtavakra Gita.

The sensation that there is no self to perform one's acts comes as a miraculous release, a feeling of having dropped a heavy and unnecessary burden—the sea rises and falls and the wind blows but not because of me; in the same way, the steps are taken, the food is eaten, the book is read, but there is no self involved:

"Reality is only one and that is the Self," says Ramana Maharshi, "All the rest are mere phenomena in it, of it and by it. The seer, the objects and the sight, all are the Self only. Can anyone see or hear, leaving the self aside? . . . If you surrender yourself . . . all is well. . . . Only so long as you think that you are the worker, are you obliged to reap the fruits of your actions. If, on the other hand, you surrender yourself and recognise your individual self as only a tool of the Higher Power, that Power will take over your affairs along with the fruits of actions. You are no longer affected by them and the work goes on unhampered. Whether you recognise the Power or not the scheme of things does not alter. Only there is a change of outlook. Why should you bear your load on the head when you are travelling in a train? It carries you and your load whether the load is on your head or on the floor of the train. You are not lessening the burden of the train by keeping it on your head but only straining yourself unnecessarily. Similar is the sense of doership in the world by individuals.[9]

"To live with the true consciousness of life centred in Another is to lose one's self-important seriousness and thus to live life as 'play' in union with a Cosmic Player," says Thomas Merton. "It is He alone that one takes seriously. But to take Him seriously is to find joy and spontaneity in everything, for everything is gift and grace. In other words, to live selfishly is to bear life as an intolerable burden. To live selflessly is to live in joy, realising by experience that life itself is love and gift. To be a lover and a giver is to be a channel through which the Supreme Giver manifests His love in the world."[10]

"Surrender to Him and abide by His will whether He appears or vanishes: await His pleasure," said Ramana Maharshi to an anxious questioner, who felt that surrender was not bringing the comfort he had hoped for. The Maharshi pointed out to him that to desire anything, even spiritual assurance, is not true surrender. "If you ask Him to do as *you* please, it is not surrender but command to Him."[11]

Perhaps the essence of arrogance and self-assertion lies in thinking that we know what is best for ourselves. We then take nothing on trust and direct our energies to acquiring at all costs the best possible conditions for ourselves. The very opposite of this attitude is a real trust that life is intrinsically good and right, and that what is provided for one right now is the proper and appropriate condition at this moment. To attempt to manipulate it one iota for one's own benefit is to impose a stultifying and deadening concept onto a living reality.

"To be aware of reality, of the living present, is to discover that at each moment the experience is all," says Alan Watts. "The art of living . . . consists in being completely sensitive to each moment, in regarding it as utterly new and unique, in having the mind open and wholly receptive."[12]

Complete acceptance of the moment does not mean, however, that one never *does* anything. Real surrender means a surrender to what needs to be done. This was once the basis of Christian life, and remains today an ideal in the mind of many Hindus who have not always seen, however, that surrender to a present situation requires a great effort of active awareness to help one to *do* as well as to be.

Because of the apparent indifference of Hindus to the value of life itself, which they display to shocked Western eyes in the rotting, death-laden streets of Calcutta and Bombay, the more energetic Westerners have concluded that a spuriously divine attitude of acceptance is to blame. That may be partly true. But another factor enters into Hindu philosophy which is apt to confound Western thinking altogether—*maya*—the world thought of as illusion, not really there at all.

Hindus are just as apt to misinterpret their own scriptures as are the followers of other religions. In the case of maya, what was once a valuable spiritual understanding has frequently been debased into a distorted belief that everything, finally, is the creation of the finite individual mind, and is therefore not worth bothering about.

Ramana Maharshi explained to his followers that the

physical world is absolutely real, for the Self manifests in
every creature and to disbelieve in the existence of the
world is to deny the manifest Self. What gives falseness
and unreality to the physical world, however, is to ascribe
to any part of it a separate, self-subsistent life—which, in
fact, is the error most of us fall into when we identify with
the body and think of ourselves as mortal, think of the
other as friend or enemy, think of all life as having its own
separate powers over us. When we do this we create a
conceptual illusory world, a dream world which replaces reality. Ramana Maharshi likened the process to a
film or movie, where one sees characters and events that
are not real in themselves, but are real in the imagination
as a shadow show. And just as only the light of the lamp is
visible when there is no film, so the Self alone shines
when mental illusions are absent.

It is the same when one dreams, he said. The people of
the dream are created by one's mind but one loses nothing by their creation nor gains anything by their
reabsorption—so the Self manifests in all creatures without ever changing from its eternal Self, and without ever
ceasing to be Itself.

Some of the Maharshi's followers felt this to be a cold
vision of a mere force of energy, creating but not caring for
its manifestations. But Ramana taught that if one could
discover the Self existing always as the true nature and
ground of one's own being, one would find eternal life.

The Self is the Heart. The Heart is self-luminous. Light
arises from the Heart and reaches the brain, which is the seat
of the mind. The world is seen with the mind, that is, by the
reflected light of the Self. It is perceived with the aid of the
mind. When the mind is illumined it is aware of the world.
When it is not itself so illumined, it is not aware of the world.
If the mind is turned in towards the source of light, objective

knowledge ceases and the Self alone shines forth as the Heart.[13]

And he said, "You now think that you are an individual; outside you there is the universe and beyond the universe is God. So, there is the idea of separateness. This idea must go. For God is not separate from you or the cosmos."[14]

The Maharshi was, perhaps, the greatest exponent in this century of the Hindu doctrine of Nonduality or Advaita. His teaching on the nature of the mind is clear and explicit and bears a close resemblance (as we will later observe) to Martin Buber's doctrine of "I and Thou"; Ramana Maharshi says:

> The "I"-thought arises first and then all other thoughts. They comprise the mind. . . . It is only after the "I"-thought has arisen that the thoughts of "you" and "he" and "it" can enter the mind, and they cannot exist without the primary "I"-thought. The "I"-thought itself is therefore not one of them, but is their cause. It is the subject while they are the objects. Since the mind is nothing but a collection of such thoughts, it will only subside when its cause is looked for by the enquiry "Who am I?"[15]

The method that the Maharshi taught for self-enquiry was that every thought should be noted as it arose. He believed that there was no such thing as a mind apart from thoughts and that as a thought arose one should not bother about its content or try to finish it, but should enquire "To whom has this thought occurred?" The answer will be "me"; and then, when you ask "Who am I?" the mind turns inward, ceases to be concerned with the thought, and the thought subsides. Constant practice of this technique gives the strength of truth to the feeling of "me." It ceases to be distracted by thoughts arising and is able to "abide in its Source."

Hard work indeed, and the Maharshi told his followers that their detachment from the ego must be very strong to do it, as strong as the craving of a man for air when he is drowning. Perhaps the mantra system of the Maharishi (p. 172), which resembles Ramana Maharshi's method in that the mantra replaces other thoughts and shows the practitioner the emptiness of mind without thought—perhaps this technique is easier for most Westerners, even if it is less dynamic, far-reaching, and profound.

The Maharshi died in 1950 of a long painful illness caused by an inoperable tumor. His own philosophy upheld him to the end, and he is remembered by many for words spoken within hours of his death: "They say that I am dying but I am not going away. Where could I go? I am here."[16]

Although he wrote very little, he was prevailed upon by the poet, Muruganar, to condense the essence of his teaching into forty verses. Of these forty, three are presented here which, perhaps, transmit the Maharshi's insight most clearly:

Although the world and its awareness rise and set as one, it is by the awareness that the world shines. The *Whole*, wherefrom the world and its awareness rise and wherein they set, but which shines without rising and setting—that alone is the real.[17]

The duality of subject and object and the trinity of seer, sight and seen can exist only if supported by the One. If one turns inwards in search of that One Reality they fall away. Those who see this are those who see Wisdom. They are never in doubt.[18]

Under whatever name and form the omnipresent nameless and formless reality is worshipped, that is only a door to realisation. Understanding one's own truth in the truth of that true reality, and being one with it, having been resolved into it, is true seeing. Thus should you know.[19]

The Maharishi

(The Maharishi has never disclosed his age, as he does not think it right to talk about himself. He is probably between sixty and seventy.)

The fifty-dollar mantra. Is it worth it? Does the repetition of a single, intellectually meaningless word have the liberating, tranquilizing, and efficiency-making effect that the Maharishi claims for it? Many people find, apparently, that it does, and the Maharishi's organization is now worldwide and steadily growing.

The Maharishi is a small Hindu from North India whose impact on an audience comes largely from a total lack of self-consciousness combined with a hypnotic gaze. He is very picturesque, always dressed in a white dhoti, about which flows his long, graying hair and thick beard. His English is excellent and he speaks in the high voice which seems to belong to Indian gurus everywhere. He is not a *bhakti* (devotional) guru and does not demand adoration and loyalty from his followers; he is more the *jnana* (discrimination) type of guru, a type to which Ramana Maharshi belongs, and his aim is to pare away the

chatter of the mind to reveal the always-present depths of creative awareness.

He does not display Ramana Maharshi's profound grasp of truth; the Maharishi's teaching seems to be of a more conventional and superficial nature, but he does have a technique—and it is an admirable and valid one, particularly for Westerners. It may not have the mind-shattering effect of following to the very end Ramana Maharshi's great query of "Who am I?" but it gives a quick and certain experience of tranquility to thousands of people who have never heard of Ramana Maharshi. The Maharishi's technique is the use of a mantra, carefully taught.

From time immemorial, mantras have been used to harness the mind and bring it back from its endless and erratic thought journeys. Focusing the mind on a mantra (the most famous is OM, which Hindus believe to be the word of God, the primordial sound) allows the mind to rest and, in that rest, supposedly to deepen. As thoughts arise they are replaced by the mantra and in this way the process by which they come to birth and fill the consciousness can be observed.

The process can be seen equally well without a mantra. Buddhist meditation (Vipassana, or Zen) in which internal thoughts, images, and daydreams, as well as external sounds and interruptions, are merely noted without involvement in them, is as quieting to the nervous system and as revealing of the nature of thought as is mantra repetition. But it is harder.

For the mantra is essentially a crutch or device to help the mind release its grip on the thoughts which distract it. The Maharishi is honest about his mantra system and does not attribute any mystical or supernatural power to the mantra itself. It is, he declares, an easy method of bringing the mind down from its usual superficial thought ruts to a deep level of transcendental, creative intelligence.

To those who have not made the experiment, various questions now arise. Is the mind separate from thoughts? When thoughts subside, what is left? Is the true nature of the mind really that of creative intelligence?

In answer to the last question, the Maharishi says yes. He believes that the purpose of man is also the purpose of the entire universe, and that that purpose is the expression of divinity. A divine, creative intelligence has caused the world to exist and man is "a bridge of abundance" between God and the whole of creation:

> To live a life of freedom is the purpose of life in the human species. If one is not able to live such a life, the very purpose of life is blurred. Man is born to live a perfect life holding within its range all values of the transcendental absolute divine of unlimited energy, intelligence, power, peace, and bliss, along with the unlimited values of the world of multiplicity in relative existence. He is born to project the abundance of the absolute state of life into the world of relative existence.[1]

The true nature of man's mind, says the Maharishi, is pure consciousness, a transcendent state of existence. It is pure being, which man knows as a state of *is*-ness. This state of pure Being is the very Ground of creative intelligence. Man is fulfilled when he knows himself as pure consciousness and lives from that knowledge in intelligent creativity.

What we habitually think of as our mind is a superficial consciousness which is not separate from thoughts, but is comprised of them. There are many levels of thought but they all belong to the relative world and can, if we survey them clearly, all be attached to objects or conditions in the outside world. Even the subtlest thoughts are about *something*. However, when thoughts subside and the superficial, conditioned mind becomes still, when it transcends the relative world of experience altogether and becomes empty, what is left is its essential nature, which is pure Being. In this experience of pure consciousness, the superficial mind becomes one with its Ground. After that, the mind will go back to relative thoughts in the world but it will feel the urge to return to pure Being and the constant journey from one state to another will deepen its familiarity with its own essential nature. It will then become capable of retaining that consciousness of Being while it is engaged in thought or speech or action. In this way, man serves the universe by becoming the bridge between unconditioned and conditioned life, and he also serves himself by fulfilling his own individual nature and purpose.

For the realization of Being does not mean giving up everyday life, but enhancing it. The Maharishi is emphatic that people throughout time have been mistaken in believing that God-realization is incompatible with ordinary existence; that in order to know absolute bliss consciousness you must deny the life of the senses—which the Maharishi calls the force of Karma, the continuous action of relative life seen in the cycle of birth, death, creation, evolution, and dissolution.

No, says the Maharishi (whose attitude to the nature, or Suchness, of life seems more Buddhist than Hindu), you must not split life into two opposing forces, Being and Karma. This leads directly to suffering. Instead, you must bring the glory of Being into the field of Karma and thus transform and harmonize all activities. This is the purpose of life, which hundreds of generations have missed. Because they have not understood how to realize Being and how to bring it into everyday life, the amount of misery and suffering, tension and negativity in the world has increased.

But now, he says, with his own technique, there is a chance to end suffering.

He makes it seem very simple and many people will laugh at his claims. But he does not ask for belief. He stands or falls by the effectiveness of his method, which anyone (who has enough money) can try. How does it all work?

A person who wants to be given a mantra must, in England, pay £20. It is a large amount of money, but it is perhaps better than a week's wages, the price in 1967 at the time that the Beatles made the Maharishi famous.

Having given the money, the aspiring customer will then take part in a short initiation ceremony, which consists of offerings of flowers and fruit to the Maharishi's guru predecessors, the names of whom are chanted by the initiator. The initiator and the client then kneel together in front of a photograph of Guru Dev, the affectionate name for Swami Brahmananda Saraswati, the Maharishi's teacher, and when they get up the client will be given his mantra, which he must immediately repeat for a few minutes in quieter and quieter tones. Each mantra is selected according to age, sex, and other variables, and the right one (chosen from a historically ancient stock) is supposed to be of particular help to the meditator.

Having now bought his mantra, the customer then learns how to use it, and must return daily for four days for constant teaching, checking, and advice. The way to use it is to sit in a relaxed position, thinking of nothing in particular, until the mantra comes into the mind. If it has not come of itself after half a minute, then the meditator must silently say it. After this he lets it go and ceases to cling to it or to worry about what is happening to it. If it is replaced by a thought, it doesn't matter, this is still meditation. If, at the end of twenty minutes, the mantra has been obscured by thoughts all the time, this still doesn't matter.

On the other hand, if the meditator comes to the end of a thought and then remembers to substitute the mantra, this too is right. The mantra, the Maharishi says, should arise as spontaneously as thoughts arise. When the meditator becomes conscious that he is thinking, or has been thinking, then the mantra will replace the thought as naturally as would any other thought. For the mantra too is a thought; but it is a thought without content and so it does not give rise to more thoughts.

In this way there is nothing that can go wrong and there is no burden of learning a difficult technique. The only absolute rule is the twenty-minute period twice a day during which the mantra is thought of at least once.

The reason why this technique appears to be so successful is, according to the Maharishi, that it is the nature of the conscious mind to want to return to that level of transcendent Being where it is happy, creative, and free. He bases the whole theory of his system on the Rig Veda, one of the oldest Hindu scriptures. The central theme of the Rig Veda—the science of creative intelligence—is, he says, brought out in the Bhagavad Gita (part of the epic Mahabharata), when Krishna instructs Arjuna and says: "Open your awareness to the absolute field of life (the infinite value of creative intelligence), and, established in that awareness, perform action" (Maharishi's translation, verses 11, 45, 47).

The alternation of activity and deep rest (even though it is only forty minutes a day) brings, says the Maharishi, the true fulfillment of a person's natural creative intelligence. Sleep alone cannot provide the depth of real rest which comes with meditation. This is not an idle claim, for a great deal of research has been going on into the effects of Transcendental Meditation, the Maharishi's technique, and it now seems well established that there are physiological changes in the body and the brain, which

do not occur in sleep, for sleep merely dissolves physical
fatigue. Experiments at Harvard Medical School and at
the Maudsley Hospital in London, show that the
metabolic rate falls below the level of sleep, the heart rate
falls, the rate of oxygen flow increases (because the activity of the sympathetic nervous system is so reduced that it
secretes less norepinephrine, a biochemical which
causes the blood vessels to constrict), and the brain-wave
patterns show a surprisingly simultaneous pattern of
sleep-level rest (as though the meditator were actually
asleep) and complete alertness.

These patterns are brought forward to substantiate the
Maharishi's claim that during meditation the mind is
opened to the awareness of Being as a state of timeless-
ness and space, empty of attributes. The mind, he goes
so far as to say, is enabled to unite with the origin of life
before it reenters its relative and manifest state. He sees
Absolute Being as resembling the center of a seed which,
seemingly, is hollow. But in that hollowness, the "abstract area of the seed," is contained the whole potential
of the tree—"the unexpressed source of all its expressions."

Because it is the source of life, the nature of the unexpressed and "hollow" potential is to create, and it stays
eternally at the center of each one of its changing cre-
ations. Thus a potential creativity is always latent within
us, as it is within all living things, and the Maharishi
regards this potentiality as pure creative intelligence, the
basis of life.

Separation from this basis leads to the rootless, restless,
disturbed, and negative world that we know. A daily
return to it brings the mind home to its source, refreshes
and re-invigorates it, and gives it a feeling of stability and
endurance, of having found a permanent resting place

and source of happiness independent of the vagaries of life.

The Maharishi seems to have become enraptured by the methods of science and, like Teilhard de Chardin, uses scientific discoveries to confirm his own understanding. He quotes the third law of thermodynamics—as activity decreases, order increases—to affirm the transforming effects of Transcendental Meditation—known as TM. As the stresses dissolve, he says, physical and mental order increases, and the conscious mind expands into creativity. He explains the process by likening a thought to a bubble. A thought is formed at the deepest level of the subconscious mind—the part of our mind that is most out of reach as it is composed of innumerable old memories, feelings, and reactions which we have stored from earliest childhood. In the same way as a bubble starts from the mud at the bottom of a pond, so the thought emerges from the subconscious waters of the mind. As a bubble, or a thought, comes up, it becomes bigger. When it reaches the surface it becomes big enough to be perceived.

This process, says the Maharishi, is not usually apparent to us because the thought bubbles come up in a rapid stream, each following the other indistinguishably. But the TM technique trains the mind to experience an oncoming thought at an earlier and earlier stage of its growth. In this way, the attention is taken down deeper and deeper until it reaches the source of thought, the source of creative energy.

What is the main cause of suffering, asks the Maharishi? It is the inability to adapt; it is the adoption of rigidly fixed ideas, beliefs, and routines that frustrate the very nature of life and its creative intelligence. Material progress depends on routine, and once routine has become established there is very little opportunity for the flow of unbounded creative intelligence. Routine soon becomes rigidity—the unbounded is diminished and the full flow of life is lost. The supple, enduring mind becomes stiff and easily broken.

This is the age-old problem of how to enter a new dimension of consciousness while still living an ordinary life; the problem of bringing together bliss and all the everyday things and events of which our life is made up; the problem of affirming one state while not denying another. Many people never reach the stage of seeing this problem at all. Others give up the attempt to solve it by retreating to monasteries, or living in drug-land, or devoting all their energy to making money. Some, like Aldous Huxley, carry the problem with them to the grave.

Is the Maharishi's answer too simple? All that is necessary is to establish another routine, he says. You can't live without routine, it is natural to human life, so don't attempt to. Break open your rigidity instead, by allowing your mind to become unbounded twice a day. Just a bit of extra routine.

Perhaps this is indeed the way for modern man to solve the problem. There are well over a million TM practitioners in America alone, and the Maharishi's technique is considered so successful that it is being adopted by civil aviation authorities, by educational authorities, by private industry, and officially by several U.S. states. It is available in many prisons throughout the world. Certainly, from all the evidence now available, TM can make a major contribution to the treatment of stress illnesses such as hypertension and to drug addiction, where it has been found that drug users prefer the effects of meditation to drug-induced sensations.

Perhaps, for the ordinary man and woman, there is an element of big-business showmanship about all the glossy propaganda produced by TM to deliver its message. One can't help remembering some of the American growth campaigns for various dubious religious groups. But the Maharishi gives an impression of complete sincerity and considerable understanding, even if he is a little over-impressed by the miracles of science. Perhaps the naughty, negative world will really be changed by TM.

178

References

Ramana Maharshi

1   Dr. T. M. P. Mahadevan, *Ramana Maharshi and His Philosophy of Existence* (T. N. Venkatarman), p. 6.
2   The Venerable Sangharakshita, *The Thousand Petalled Lotus* (William Heinemann Ltd.), p. 197-198.
3   Arthur Osborne, ed., *The Teachings of Ramana Maharshi* (London: Rider and Co.), p. 116.
4   David Hume, *Treatise of Human Nature* (London: J. M. Dent & Sons), Vol. 1, p. 239.
5   Osborne, *The Teachings of Ramana Maharshi*, p. 23-24.
6   Ibid., p. 24.
7   Ibid., p. 24.
8   Hari Prasad Shastri, *The Ashtavakra Gita* (London: Shanti Sadan), p. 3.
9   *Talks with Sri Ramana Maharshi* (India: T. N. Venkataraman), p. 487.
10 Swami A. C. Bhaktivedanta, *The Bhagavad Gita as It Is* (London: Collier-Macmillan Ltd.), p. 19.
11 *Talks with Sri Ramana Maharshi*, p. 425.
12 Alan Watts, *Why Not Now?* (a record)
13 *Talks with Sri Ramana Maharshi*, p. 94.
14 Osborne, *The Teachings of Ramana Maharshi*, p. 46.
15 *Talks with Sri Ramana Maharshi*, p. 234.
16 Arthur Osborne, *Ramana Maharshi and the Path of Self-Knowledge* (London: Rider and Co., New York: Samuel Weiser Inc.), p. 185.
17 Mahadevan, *Ramana Maharshi and His Philosophy of Existence*, p. 60.
18 Arthur Osborne, ed., *The Collected Works of Ramana Maharshi* (London: Rider and Co.), p. 73.
19 Mahadevan, *Ramana Maharshi and His Philosophy of Existence*, p. 64.

The Maharishi

1   *Transcendental Meditation* (original title: *The Science of Being and Art of Living)*, (London: George Allen and Unwin; New York: New American Library, Inc.), p. 65.

Further Reading

Maharishi Mahesh Yogi on the Bhagavad Gita. London: Penguin Books; New York: Gannon.

Forem, Jack, *Transcendental Meditation.* New York: E. P. Dutton and Co. Inc.

Campbell, Anthony, *Seven States of Consciousness.* London: Gollancz, New York: Harper and Row

Olson, Helena, *A Hermit in the House.* Los Angeles.

Kroll, Una, *TM: A Signpost for the World.* London: Darton Longman and Todd

6

The Middle Way
of Buddhism

The two Buddhist masters in this book are from different countries and different traditions, but both are concerned with techniques and ways for finding out the true nature of the self. Buddhism is the most practical of all the religions. It does not ask its followers to believe in anything at all, it simply says: follow the teachings and see what happens.

The Buddha lived and taught in the sixth century B.C. He pronounced that the main cause of suffering is the belief in a separate ego which persists through time and change. In truth, there is no such thing as a "self," he said. There is only the endless flux of sensations and thoughts and feelings that we take for reality and believe to be self-powered. The flow of endless appearances that make up the "world" are all proceeding from each other in a minutely determined chain of cause and effect, including our own bodies and minds. But there is also that which is not part of the chain; and enlightenment is the experience of finding existence to be unconditioned and timeless.

His teaching was the basis of two distinct schools in Buddhism. One, the Theravada school from which Dhiravamsa comes, believed in a strict segregation of monks from laymen, and thought that withdrawal from the world through meditation was the way to enlightenment.

The other school from which Trungpa, the Tibetan, comes, was the Mahayana—the Greater Vehicle—in which a compassionate return to the world was advised, in order that all sentient beings might be liberated.

The two ideals of Wisdom and Compassion dominate Buddhism, and the two Buddhists here, although they have both moved a long way from the strictly traditional teaching, reflect its ideals in their practices. Dhiravamsa's ways are the quietly serene ones of a meditation master. Trungpa's are the more colorful and dynamic statements of a Tibetan sage. Both emphasize the importance of insight into the nature of "I" and both frequently use the word ego for the feelings and demands of "I."

Their teaching is direct and profound without being complicated.

Chogyam Trungpa
1938–1987

To look at Trungpa is to smile. There is a quality of
unshakeable happiness in his broad face and solid walk.
There is also the feeling of a great reserve of strength. His
personality reveals an easy balance, like a well-oiled
machine, but this equilibrium has not come without formidable effort.

The impact of Western life on three newly arrived
Tibetan abbots in 1963 was felt as a jarring shock. Each of
them, Trungpa, Chime, and Akong, had spent his life
until then almost entirely in study and meditation. They
had come from the vast silence of mountain monasteries,
from the radiantly clear air of Eastern Tibet, from the
brilliance of flower-covered hills and ineffably blue sky,
first to the hot steamy plains of India, and then to
London—crowded, polluted, and shatteringly noisy.

The three Tibetans were young, in their early twenties,
and they were each a tulku, a reincarnation of a long line

of great religious teachers. Trungpa was the eleventh reincarnated lama, and the supreme head of the Surmang group of monasteries. All his life he had been trained for his task of high-ranking abbot of the Karma-ka-gyu school. Quite literally all his life, for he had been found at the age of one year by monks who were searching for him, after the death of the tenth Trungpa Tulku in 1937.

He was then the second child of a farmer, who had met Trungpa's mother when she was looking after yaks belonging to her relatives. Trungpa was thus a peasant boy, and his whereabouts had been seen in a vision by Gyalwa Karmapa, the head of the Karma-ka-gyu school. He had told his monks that they must look for the small reincarnation of the tenth Trungpa in a village five days northward from Surmang, in a house whose door faced south, and with a father whose name was Yeshedargye, who owned a big red dog. Truungpa was discovered exactly as foretold and greeted the monks in the prescribed way, as though he already knew what to do, by taking a scarf from one of them and hanging it round the monk's neck.

Trungpa and his mother were established in a house near the monastery and he was taken to it every day. A few months later he was enthroned in front of an audience of some thirteen thousand monks from all parts of Eastern Tibet. When he was five, his mother left him at the monastery and returned to their village. He says: "I missed her as only a small boy can."

The years which followed were filled with study. At the age of eleven he took the Bodhisattva vow, which says:

"In the presence of all the Buddhas and Bodhisattvas and of my teacher, Rolpa-dorje, I vow to proceed towards Enlightenment. I accept all creatures as my father and mother with infinite compassion. Henceforth for their benefit I will practice the transcendental virtues (*paramitas*) of liberality, discipline, patience, diligence, meditative concentration, wisdom (*prajna*), skillful means (*upaya*), spiritual power, aspiration, gnosis (*jnana*). Let my master accept me as a future Buddha, but as remaining a Bodhisattva without entering Nirvana so long as a single blade of grass remains unenlightened."[1]

He and his tutor sometimes lived at a center for retreats on the slope of a mountain. Their home was so high up that every morning the mists would cover the sides of the valley below, so that they called it the Garden of the Mists. It was here that Trungpa's program of Buddhist metaphysics included:

1) 100,000 full prostrations
2) 100,000 recitations of the Triple Refuge
3) 100,000 recitations of the Vajra Sattva mantra
4) 100,000 symbolic offerings
5) 100,000 recitations of the mantra of Guru Yoga, or "Union with the Teacher"

At the same time five subjects were contemplated.

1) The rare privilege given to one to receive spiritual teaching in this life.
2) The impermanence attaching to life and to everything else.
3) The cause and effect of *karma*.
4) The understanding of suffering.
5) The necessity for devotion.

He says that he was deeply affected by all this: "Living in this place, studying these teachings and constantly meditating, I began to develop greater depths of understanding as a preparation for the way of life that lay ahead of me."[2]

During these years the Chinese army had begun to enter Tibet and to establish garrisons at many places. Their increasing economic and political hold on the country threatened the life of the monasteries, which were often regarded by the Chinese as spy strongholds. Lamas were tortured and killed, monasteries burned, and, finally, when the full invasion of Tibet came in 1959, Trungpa escaped over the mountains to India. He was then twenty years old.

It was once prophesied in Tibet that its religion would travel to the West and become that of the pink-faced people. Certainly Tibetan Buddhism has begun to attract many Westerners who are eager for a positive religious teaching based on meditation practices and on the intensified use of the senses.

The whole unique and very practical teaching of Tibetan Buddhism revolves around the understanding that each one of us lives in an illusory world of self-projection, isolated from reality by our grasping at ideas and beliefs, which includes the belief that "I" exists as a separate, autonomous entity. This description of personal existence is, the Buddha said, the cause of all suffering, and the way out of suffering is to realize that "I" does not derive its power from itself, is not self-subsisting, but is, in truth, Buddha-mind, the natureless nature of all things, empty of self-nature altogether. The complete realization of this emptiness is known as Nirvana. It is transcendent wisdom.

But wisdom alone is not enough. There must also be transcendent compassion for all life. "One single self we shall tame, one single self we shall pacify, one single self we shall lead to Nirvana" is not the way of the Bodhisattva, the embodiment of Compassion. A Bodhisattva, said the Buddha, should train himself in this way: "My own self I will place into Suchness, and, so that all the world might be helped, I will also place all beings into Suchness, and I will lead to Nirvana the whole immeasurable world of beings."

Suchness is the reality, ungraspable by the human intellect, which the world is *in itself*. It is a dimension of existence, formless and unknowable, but which we feel to be *there*. One cannot *understand* Suchness, but it is experienced when we drop what stands between ourselves and it—the observer in us who is always reporting and making judgments.

The ways for reaching Nirvana and for placing the self in Suchness belong to the whole field of Buddhism, but the practices of compassion for placing all beings in Suchness belong only to Mahayana Buddhism, the teaching that spread north from India and found its greatest exponent in Tibet.

It was the doctrine of ultimate compassion which Trungpa learned during the intensely hard-working years of his childhood, and it is the formidable understanding of the use of energy, stillness, sound, silence, rhythm, and visualization, which he is now translating into Western terms. He is so much at home now in America that language is no problem, and what he says emerges with the clarity of the authentic master.

He is particularly keen to cut through "spiritual materialism," the devices of the ego to better itself by spiritual conquests:

The problem is that ego can convert anything to its own use, even spirituality. Ego is constantly attempting to acquire and apply the teachings of spirituality for its own benefit. The teachings are treated as an external thing, external to "me," a philosophy which we try to imitate. We do not actually want to identify with or become the teachings. . . .[3]

Whenever we begin to feel any discrepancy or conflict between our actions and the teachings, we immediately interpret the situation in such a way that the conflict is smoothed over. The interpreter is ego in the role of spiritual advisor. The situation is like that of a country where church and state are separate. If the policy of the state is foreign to the teachings of the church, then the automatic reaction of the king is to go to the head of the church, his spiritual advisor, and ask his blessing. The head of the church then works out some justification and gives the policy his blessing under the pretence that the king is the protector of the faith. In an individual's mind, it works out very neatly that way, ego being both king and head of the church. . . .

It is important to see that the main point of any spiritual practice is to step out of the bureaucracy of ego. This means stepping out of ego's constant desire for a higher, more spiritual, more transcendental version of knowledge, religion, virtue, judgement, comfort or whatever it is that the particular ego is seeking. One must step out of spiritual materialism. If we do not step out of spiritual materialism, if we in fact practice it, then we may eventually find ourselves possessed of a huge collection of spiritual paths. We may feel these spiritual collections to be very precious. . . But we have simply created a shop, an antique shop.[4]

A questioner said to Trungpa, "It is difficult not to be acquisitive about spirituality. Is this desire for acquisitions something that is shed along the way?"
Trungpa answered,

You should let the first impulse die down. Your first impulse towards spirituality might put you into some particular spiritual scene; but if you work with that impulse, then the impulse gradually dies down and at some stage becomes tedious, monotonous. This is a useful message. You see, it is essential to relate to yourself, to your own experience, *really*. If one does not relate to oneself, then the spiritual path becomes dangerous, becomes purely external entertainment, rather than an organic personal experience.[5]

Relating to oneself is a form of surrender. The word surrender has, for some people, an emotional content slightly tinged with hysteria and perhaps connected with the ecstatic writings of Christian or Sufi saints. But surrender in Trungpa's definition, is openness, a giving up of ego defenses, a positive acceptance of here and now, the perfectly ordinary:

> Surrendering does not involve preparing for a soft landing; it means just landing on hard, ordinary ground, on rocky, wild countryside. Once we open ourselves, then we land on *what is*.
>
> Traditionally, surrendering is symbolised by such practices as prostration, which is the act of falling on the ground in a gesture of surrender. At the same time we open psychologically and surrender completely by identifying ourselves with the lowest of the low, acknowledging our raw and rugged quality. There is nothing that we fear to lose once we identify ourselves with the lowest of the low. By doing so, we prepare ourselves to be an empty vessel, ready to receive the teachings.[6]

Trungpa sees the avoidance of surrender as leading one into self-deception.

> If one searches for any kind of bliss or joy, the realisation of one's imagination and dream, then, equally, one is going to suffer failure and depression. This is the whole point: a fear of separation, the hope of attaining union, these are not just manifestations of, or the actions of, ego, or self-deception, as if ego were somehow a real thing which performed certain actions. Ego *is* the actions, the mental events. Ego *is* the fear of losing openness, the fear of losing the egoless state. This is the meaning of self-deception, in this case—ego crying that it has lost the egoless state, its dream of attainment. Fear, hope, loss, gain—these are the on-going action of the dream of ego, the self-perpetuating, self-maintaining structure which is self-deception.
>
> So the real experience, beyond the dream world, is the beauty and color and excitement of the real experience of *now* in everyday life. When we face things as they are, we give up the hope of something better. There will be no magic, because we cannot tell ourselves to get out of our depression.

Depression and ignorance, the emotions, whatever we experience, are all real and contain tremendous truth. If we
really want to learn and see the experience of truth, we have
to be where we are. The whole thing is just a matter of being a
grain of sand.[7]

In this way, Trungpa teaches that the openness of real
surrender implies an attitude of trust and confidence in
"what is." But the usual human way of operating is one of
considerable distrust. Every day when you or I wake up it
is to a world comprised of names and places and set times,
and to a jumble of plans with which I hope to dominate
this world. For either I must dominate my sphere of
action or it will dominate me. As I believe that I would not
survive were the world to overcome me, I attend with all
the ways I can think of to mastering it. In all this planning
(often vague and semiconscious) there is a general feeling that I can't trust anything to go according to my
wishes (which I call "right") unless I push it along and
make it do so.

But just suppose I gave up this struggle? Suppose I
trusted that *whatever happened* was "right," even for this
almighty me? Suppose I continued to live in an ordinary
way but making no demands, just letting things occur as
they wanted to? Would the world get the better of me?
Would I suffer? Perhaps I would in some ways, but I
might find that I was becoming extraordinarily peaceful
and happy as well. Because real trust in another, or simply in what is "other," is a creative action and brings
immediate response from the world.

To trust is to surrender oneself to the situation, not to
hold anything back. We often think that we love, but our
love is rarely capable of simple trust. Trust diminishes
the ego in a way that thought can never do, for by opening
myself to whatever is here at this moment I am creating a

space—the space where all the machinery of my defenses was—in which the other can be received:

The action of the bodhisattva is like the moon shining on one hundred bowls of water, so that there are one hundred moons, one in each bowl. This is not the moon's design nor was it designed by anyone else. But for some strange reason there happens to be one hundred moons reflected in one hundred bowls of water. Openness means this kind of absolute trust and self-confidence. The open situation of compassion works this way rather than by deliberately attempting to create one hundred moons, one in each bowl.[8]

Trungpa calls trust the open path—"a matter of working purely with what is, of giving up altogether the fear that something may not work, that something may end in failure. One has to give up the paranoia that one might not fit into situations, that one might be rejected. One purely deals with life as it is."[9]

When he was asked how one could trust if one was afraid of somebody, he said:

Compassion is not looking down upon somebody who needs help, who needs care, but it is general, basic, organic, positive thinking. The fear of someone else seems to generate uncertainty as to who you are. That is why you are afraid of that particular situation or person. Fear comes from uncertainty. If you know exactly how you are going to handle this frightful situation, then you have no fear. Fear comes from panic, the bewilderment of uncertainty. Uncertainty is related to distrust in yourself, feeling that you are inadequate to deal with that mysterious problem which is threatening you. There is no fear if you really have a compassionate relationship with yourself, because then you know what you are doing. If you know what you are doing, then your projections also become methodical or predictable, in some sense. Then one develops *prajna,* knowledge of how to relate to any given situation.[10]

A lot has been said in this book about the ego, most sages believing that it is the principal delusion of man, resulting in all his wars and divisions. To understand the real nature of the ego is the basic aim of Buddhism, and Trungpa explains how the ego develops from the primary openness of our real nature—a limitless clarity which we sometimes catch a glimpse of when our separate ego feeling is overwhelmed by beauty or strangeness, so that we no longer perceive in the usual analytical way, but drop perception for the simple act of seeing. But then, almost immediately, we try to attach a name to that experience so that we can freeze it into a form and store it in our memories as something belonging to us, a possessed knowledge, which, if it is labeled, can be brought out and looked at again. Clear space disappears then, and the world becomes solid with names.

Trungpa uses an old Buddhist metaphor of a monkey's activities to describe the process of ego development and the way we lose our inborn and marvelous sense of freedom and space. The monkey, he says, finds himself locked into an empty house (the body), a house which has five windows (the senses). Instead of swinging through the leafy trees of the jungle—free, and at one with his surroundings—he now finds that the trees have solidified around him and become his prison. "Instead of perching in a tree, this inquisitive monkey has been walled in by a solid world, as if a flowing thing, a dramatic and beautiful waterfall, had suddenly been frozen. This frozen house, made of frozen colors and energies, is completely still. This seems to be the point where time begins as past, future, and present. The flux of things becomes solid tangible time, a solid idea of time."[11]

Having peered out of all five windows, the restless, bored monkey tests the walls to see if they are solid. When he finds they are, he either grasps at the space he is in, trying to possess it as his own fascinating experience, his own unique understanding—feeling desire for it; or he feels claustrophobic and frustrated and tries to batter his way out, feeling hatred for all that hems him in. Or he might even try to ignore or forget that he is in a prison and simply give up all feelings about it, becoming indifferent, slothful, and insensitive in a stupid way.

The monkey (ego) develops primarily in one of those three directions—desire, hatred, or stupidity—and, having got himself going, he then begins to label the house (or the world) he is in: "This is a window. This corner is pleasant. That wall frightens me and is bad. He develops a conceptual framework with which to label and categorize and evaluate his house, his world, according to whether he desires, hates, or feels indifferent to it."[12]

From these concepts he then begins to create a dreaming imagination which sees events not as they really are but as the monkey wants them to be. We all seem to do this. Trungpa says:

We have definite opinions about the way things are and should be. This is projection: we project our version of things onto what is there. Thus we become completely immersed in a world of our own creation, a world of conflicting values and opinions. Hallucination [or misapplied imagination], in this sense, is a misinterpretation of things and events, reading into the phenomenal world meaning which it does not have.[13]

There is a possibility for the monkey to question the obsession of relating to something, of getting something, to question the solidity of the worlds that he experiences. To do this, the monkey needs to develop panoramic awareness and transcendental knowledge. Panoramic awareness allows the monkey to see the space in which the struggle occurs so that he can begin to see its ironical and humourous quality. . . . The clarity and precision of transcendental knowledge allows the monkey to see the walls [of his prison] in a different way. He begins to realise that the world was never outside of himself, that it was his own dualistic attitude, the separation of "I" and "other," that created the problem. He begins to understand that he himself is making the walls solid, that he is imprisoning himself through his ambition. And so he begins to realise that to be free of his prison he must give up his ambition to escape and accept the walls as they are.[14]

To his story about the monkey, Trungpa adds the comment: "The tremendous energy that drives the monkey is the primeval intelligence which pushes us outward. This intelligence is not like a seed which you must nurture. It is like the sun that shines through gaps in the clouds. When we allow a gap, the spontaneous, intuitive understanding of how to proceed on the path suddenly, automatically comes to us."[15]

When Trungpa arrived in England in 1963 he was a young but full-fledged meditation master. He studied at Oxford and combined this with setting up one of the first Western Tibetan meditation centers, Samye-ling, in Dumfriesshire, Scotland. Here he was joined by the tulkus who had come to England with him, Chime Rinpoche and Akong Rinpoche.

It was during these first years at Samye-ling that Trungpa fell ill. First he had a bad car accident and it was thought he might not recover, but he did. Then he seemed to become remote from his friends. It was as though the more venal influences of the West had hit him and temporarily floored him. Hippies flocked to Samyeling and the older English Buddhists frowned in fierce disapproval.

But Trungpa resembles in every way the solid doll whose center of balance always brings it to an upright position. With the permission of the Dalai Lama, he married a young English girl and took her to America in 1970, where he founded the Tail of the Tiger Meditation

Center in Vermont and Karma Dzong Meditation Center in Colorado. He also founded the Naropa Institute in Colorado, a unique college where Eastern and Western intellectual traditions can interact.

His intrinsic understanding of the Bodhisattva path has now developed—perhaps helped more than anyone could guess by his knocked-out period—and today he lives and writes straight from the heart, with a direct simplicity and understanding which brings him many disciples.

His greatest intuition has always been towards "accepting the walls of the prison as they are." As they are, and also for their own sake. To transcend them, to see them in the clear light of space as insubstantial, is only half the story. They must be looked at in ordinary daylight, in their conditioned nature, *as themselves*. They must be seen without the burden of our imposed ideas of what they are. In this connection, the painter, Turner, once said, "My job is to draw what I see, not what I know is there." In the same pristine way, we must allow our senses to observe without mind-interpretation.

Form is that which *is* before we project our concepts onto it. It is the original state of "what is here," the colourful, vivid, impressive, dramatic, aesthetic qualities that exist in every situation. Form could be a maple leaf falling from a tree and landing on a mountain river; it could be full moonlight, a gutter in the street or a garbage pile. These things are "what is," and they are all in one sense the same: they are all forms, they are all objects, they are just what is. Evaluations regarding them are only created later in our minds. If we really look at these things as they are, they are just forms.

So form is empty. But empty of what? Form is empty of our preconceptions, empty of our judgements. If we do not evaluate and categorise the maple leaf falling and landing on the stream as opposed to the garbage heap in New York, then they are *there,* what *is.* They are empty of preconception. They are precisely what they are, of course! Garbage is garbage, a maple leaf is a maple leaf, "what is" is "what is." Form is empty if we see it in the absence of our own personal interpretations of it.

But emptiness is also form. That is a very outrageous remark. We thought we had managed to sort everything out, we thought we had managed to see that everything is the "same" if we take out our preconceptions. That made a beautiful picture: everything bad and everything good that we see are both good. Fine. Very smooth. But the next point is that emptiness is also form, so we have to re-examine.

The emptiness of the maple leaf is also form; it is not really empty. The emptiness of the garbage heap is also form. To try to see these things as empty is also to clothe them in concept. Form comes back. It was too easy, taking away all concept, to conclude that everything simply is "what is." That could be an escape, another way of comforting ourselves. We have to actually *feel* things as they are, the qualities of the garbage heap*ness* and the qualities of the maple leaf*ness,* the *isness* of things. . . . It is a question of seeing the world in a direct way without desiring "higher" consciousness or significance or profundity. It is just directly perceiving things literally as they are in their own right.[16]

Even words—such frequent deceivers of the mind, as Watts and Krishnamurti point out—even they regain their benefit when all preconceptions have been cleared out. ". . . When a person is completely exposed, fully unclothed, fully unmasked, completely naked, completely opened—at that very moment he sees the power of the word. When the basic, absolute, ultimate hypocrisy has been unmasked, then one really begins to see the jewel shining in its brightness: the energetic, living quality of openness, the living quality of surrender, the living quality of renunciation.

Renunciation in this instance is not just throwing away but, having thrown everything away, we begin to feel the living quality of peace. And this particular peace is not feeble peace, feeble openness, but it has a strong character, an invincible quality, an unshakeable quality, because it admits no gaps of hypocrisy. It is complete peace in all directions, so that not even a speck of a dark corner exists for doubt and hypocrisy. Complete openness is complete victory because we do not fear, we do not try to defend ourselves at all.[17]

When the current of thoughts is self-liberated
And the essence of Dharma is known,
Everything is understood
And apparent phenomena
Are all the books one needs.[18]

Dhiravamsa
1935–

The two Buddhists in this book, Trungpa and Dhiravamsa, both seem to emanate characteristics of serene cheerfulness and calm good sense. This latter quality belongs, in particular, to Dhiravamsa. Although not physically large or imposing, as soon as Dhiravamsa stands up to speak, his personality quietens and brings together a waiting audience. When he addresses groups of people in his clear careful style, even the most irrational or persistent questioner is transported to an area of practical common sense.

Dhiravamsa comes from Thailand, and was born the eldest of eleven children. His family owned the small piece of land from which they made their living, and they shared the local village life. When Dhiravamsa was thirteen he attended a village temple festival—a common occurrence, but on this occasion an exceptional one. For he was singled out by the elderly temple monk, who then

spoke to him about some of the profound truths that are the basis of Buddhism.

Thai country peasants are not, as a rule, very spiritual people. They love their religion of Theravada Buddhism—the strict Buddhism of ascetic monks, meditating on imperfections and the hollow, transient world of the passions—and they take much contrasting pleasure in noisy, cheerful, colorful festivals and ceremonies during which large, ornate statues of the Buddha are decked with flowers and offerings. Many Thais feel such reverence for the Buddha that they have given him the status of a god, and frequently attach ancient superstitions and strange beliefs to him. They also have great respect for the Sangha, the order of yellow-robed monks, who carry their begging-bowls around the village once a day to be filled with food. And there is a complete belief in the Dhamma, the Buddha's teaching—but not much understanding of it.

Dhiravamsa, until the monk singled him out, had not looked at life in an introspective way at all. But although their conversation was brief, it made a great impression on him. He found himself constantly thinking of it, and longing to know more about a matter he had never considered before—the real nature of existence.

He went to the small temple and presented himself to the monk. He was invited to stay for four weeks. He was told to sit in one corner while his friend, the old monk, meditated in another. He was to learn to sit still—not an easy task for a thirteen-year-old—and nothing else was asked of him except for one thing. He had a fear of the dark, and the monk requested him to get up every night and to walk away from the temple to a certain tree until his fear left him, which it soon did. At the end of his four weeks he was ordained as a novice monk.

The course of his life was beginning to shape itself. He

continued to spend some months every year at the temple until he was old enough to go to Mahachulalongkorn Buddhist University in Bangkok, where he started to study the historical Buddhist texts. As well, he began to learn more and more about meditation. Every day he cleaned the room of his Abbot and sometimes came across unusual books describing methods of meditation. One such outlined a way called the tranquility meditation and Dhiravamsa immediately started to practice it on his own. First, the head and shoulders of the Buddha had to be visualized in every detail—no small undertaking. Then the Buddha had to be visualized seated on the head of Dhiravamsa. From there, the stages of visualization took the Buddha to the throat, to the heart, and down the body to the solar plexus. Dhiravamsa accomplished all this. But his interest began to turn away from absorption and visualization states to another, more active, form of meditation called *Vipassana*, "insight into things as they really are." It was Vipassana which attracted Dhiravamsa most and he still sees this as the best means for realizing the truth. Vipassana is the meditation of awareness and attention.

Watch any state of mind, whether it be worry, anxiety, wandering, thinking, talking—any condition of mind—watch carefully, closely, *without thinking about it,* without trying to control it and without interpreting any thought; because this is very important when you come to the deeper level of meditation. Naming is the main obstacle to coming to the deeper level because the moment you give identity to what you are watching, ideas come into being. Then you have to work with ideas again and you come back to the superficial level. You fail to remain deep down in the reality of what you are watching. In the deep state, all concepts and all names or words must be given up completely so that the mind can remain silently watchful and because of that, creative energy comes into being. All impurities can be cut off through the power of understanding and the presence of creative energy. You can sense creative energy in the state of passive watchfulness or in the state of stillness and complete tranquillity.[1]

In 1966, Dhiravamsa was appointed Chao Khun (chief incumbent monk) at the Buddhapadipa Temple in London. Here was another turning point in his life. Not only a new language but a totally foreign way of thought had to be learned if he was to communicate successfully with Westerners. But in less than a year he had mastered the language and was writing books in English. In the course of three years he had founded a meditation center at Hindhead in Surrey and became its meditation master. In 1969 he was asked to conduct a meditation workshop at Oberlin College in America, and has spent several months of every year in both the United States and Canada since then.

In 1971, he gave up the robe and ceased to be a monk. This is less dramatic than it sounds for no life-vows are taken in Buddhism and there is no stigma attached to such a decision. Dhiravamsa still remains a meditation master, but now feels himself free to know people in their ordinary lives. He considers the monk's robe to be a barrier to real communication—

Robes are a symbol, a form, and when we put them on we are in a certain role where we try to conform to an ideal or to rules without looking into all aspects of life. It therefore fragments life, creating a division between the holy and the ordinary, and tends to prevent the individual from experiencing the wholeness of life. People think that the holy man should be dressed in a certain way, and they link holiness with form. This is contrary to reality, because in reality the holy is very ordinary, very simple. When we overlook simplicity we shall not find the holy, but instead just find the idea of holiness and worship this, in a religious way.[2]

Dhiravamsa's teaching on Vipassana meditation has grown more dynamic since his arrival in the West. A good many of the old traditional Buddhist observances have been pruned, and what is now emerging is a new form of teaching, one that is wholly in accord with modern life and therefore with "what is." Its theme is insight, to be attained by simple awareness of what is here and now, a perfect alertness of attention to the present moment:

The whole spirit of it (Vipassana meditation) lies in full attention or complete attention. This is very important. If we actually attend to what we do, what we see, what we come across, what we experience, then there is no waste of energy, no waste of time for seeing the truth, the living movement of life. In the Satipatthana Sutta (Sutra) you can see that the Buddha advises us to attend to all the things we do in our life; whether we are walking, eating, lying down, standing, talking, looking forward, looking backward or keeping silent. All this must be done so that you do not miss the point, the target, of meditation practice and you do not live in the past or in the future, but fully in the present. The Buddhist teaching emphasises the full living in the present.

Now in life we should examine ourselves, whether we are attending to everything fully, and find out what is the obstacle to attending to everything fully, if we cannot do this. It may be because we have thoughts, fantasies, we have so many things going on in the mind that we are not really there; the body is there but the mind is somewhere else, wandering around seeking something, or entertaining some thoughts. So the mind is not attending to what is actually going on at that moment, and then there is no attention.

One other thing we should understand is that when we pay attention to something we tend to be serious in the sense of being tense, being stiff somewhere in the mind or in the body. When there is no relaxation of the body or the mind, attention is a kind of mental creation, not the natural process of paying attention. The natural process of paying attention is to let things flow, not to obstruct, not to exclude yourself or anything else and then the whole process of attention is an inclusive process, which is the dynamic process of living, the dynamic process of life. Some people may call this a kind of movement in silence, or movement in the unknown. The unknown is that which cannot be given a name, a concept . . . so meditation in your daily life is to be very attentive to everything. . . . Then you can feel lively with your life, with your experiences, without being attached.[3]

When Dhiravamsa talks of being lively with one's life, he is referring to the extraordinary sense of freedom one sometimes gets when a scene—perhaps a moment when one looks out of the window, or turns a corner in the road—is experienced without any value judgment or any expectation. When it is just seen, without the interference of one's mind in any way, it then IS.

We tend to be possessive about our individual worlds. We *know* what is going to be around the corner—it already in some way belongs to us. But if, for a minute, we can let go of this known and self-occupied scene, it will create itself in a magically new fashion.

When one attends to things in this way, for the first time, it can be very difficult. It seems so simple, just to attend, but one finds that hosts of impressions, ideas, feelings, and thoughts—all that the Hindus call mind chatter—rush in and one's actual time of real attention is infinitesimal. One can then become aware that most of one's life is spent in a state of semiconscious confusion, hardly ever noticing the moment *as it is*. The Buddhist way out of this dilemma is not, however, to reject the contents of the mind when they crowd out actuality, but to become aware of *all* that is going on, mind as well, in a judgment-free way:

. . . You are not attached, you do not grasp and hold on. You are also not detached in the sense of escaping from the reality of life. You will become realistic, looking at life, seeing it for what it is. You have learnt to accept whatever arises and to practise acceptance in action, not in the idea. Beliefs, doubt and uncertainty are replaced by understanding and seeing. . . . The way of meditation tells us to observe with awareness any situation we come across so that we can learn and remain flexible, flowing. When you feel fixated, you seem to get nowhere; you are uncomfortable and unable to function properly. Some people experience this state as aging, madness or boredom. Now, what can we do?

Vipassana Meditation will say, look at this state of being fixed and see how you block yourself. What is happening right now? If you go into the present completely, you will see the facts and the truth of what is. Then you move on. You dissolve the problem into the light of clarity, the light of awareness. When you have the means to deal with yourself, you become your own psychotherapist. You need not say, "Oh, I am a psychotherapist. I will look into myself." No, the label is not important, but the ability to look is, for this looking will bring about insight. Insight will peer into a situation, penetrate, and break it. The barriers are cleared away and we can flow on with life. There is joy and happiness; there is sorrow and pain. We accept them all. When we are too happy, we can be lost in the happiness and gain no wisdom. We should regard unpleasant or unfortunate situations in life as spiritual lessons for growth and maturity. They test us to see whether we are strong enough, whether we are free or not.[4]

Dhiravamsa teaches that insight develops in accordance with our journey into clearer consciousness. He believes that there are four levels of consciousness. The first level is the consciousness of good and bad in our ordinary waking lives. We feel desire or we are repelled, and even our most insignificant actions are usually directed by one or other of these forces. The cause of this consciousness of good and evil lies, Buddhists believe, in the very nature of the personality itself. The five constituents which, they say, make up the person—body sensations, feeling, perception, consciousness, and ideas—are the reason for the two poles of life between which we are perpetually circling; the positive ways of wisdom, compassion, sanity, and health, and the negative ways of hatred, self-pity, and destructive self-will. Our journey between these extremes is not a pleasant one. It is full of conflicts and contradictions' which cause us to lose balance, so that we feel uncertain and afraid.

The step toward freedom from this sensation of being helplessly bound to the turning wheel of life is the second level of consciousness, says Dhiravamsa, insight into duality. We must see for ourselves and not only through books, the whole relationship of mind and body, and the way in which duality springs up between them. Then we can go on to a new area of insight which

. . . opens our understanding of conditionality. By observing our thoughts and emotions, we are able to see that each of them is conditioned by something else. Thought is not a thing in itself. If you look superficially, you may say, "Oh, it is only a thought, a single, isolated event." No. Look again. Do not try to put on any interpretation or come to an easy conclusion. That is a kind of self-deception. Just look to see as clearly and deeply as possible. . . . Perhaps you may be able to see how the thought connects itself with other thoughts or with the very ground of thinking. Look deeper and deeper with this enquiring mind and be careful that it is not noisy. You must not try to frame the word. The enquiring mind must be silent, though it can use very precise questions about what you are observing. After putting a question the mind becomes quiet, looks very attentively, deeply and thereby gains clarity. This process clears away the cloud of unknowing, the cloud of accepted "knowledge" and fear. All barriers pass away and the deep understanding of insight into conditionality appears. So . . . your mind becomes very steady and clear. This inner stability shows in a new level of perception and awareness. Consciousness is wakeful and restful, yet it still has a sense of form.[5]

The deepening of insight brings one to the third level of consciousness, where there is "objective thought." Instead of regarding every thing as being in relationship to me, the central subject, I must step outside "me" and begin to "think from the object, from the situation." In an altogether different perspective to my usual one, I must lose my sense of "me" and instead gain an understanding of what is going on without "me." From this angle I can see my "self" as a continually changing pattern, both body and mind, one activity replacing another in rapid succession. I can notice at first hand that everything known by the senses is impermanent. Then, says Dhiravamsa, "the ego grows supple and loses its grip on any idea or emotion."[6] There is calmness, lightness of body and clearness of head. The personality has somehow faced the worst—the dissolution of the idea of self —and now begins to change towards a more profound and purified consciousness, and a more positive and creative existence in the world.

The fourth level of consciousness is called "awakened" or "enlightened"—

. . . where there is illumination, clarity and alertness—perfect alertness with nonverbal insight. This awakened consciousness gives a freedom that is not connected to any form of emotion or with like and dislike. Freedom is just being free. If you sit, you are free to sit; if you walk, you are free to walk. There is no uneasiness, no anxiety, no disturbance. When you wake up fully, you see everything clearly. You are not distracted because you see everything as it is. You are not concerned with any elements or images of what you see. Buddhism regards this true, luminous consciousness as intrinsic to every human being. The sense impressions that intrude upon us becloud it. If we do not establish awareness at the doors of the senses, we are left without a keeper, when destructive elements enter our consciousness making it impure and defiled. Our task is to cleanse it away through meditation. Then we can get into the creative aspect of living where we find energy, wakefulness and the treasures of our life.

Many people feel that they don't know how to begin to become aware. Dhiravamsa says, just begin.

It is a matter of seeing. But *how* can I see? We always look for the *how*; the *how* becomes the greatest problem. Perhaps if we just drop this problem of how and then look at everything with full attention, now at this moment, then things will become simpler, easier. When the mind demands "How?," it can never come to simplicity, and that is the problem again, the problem of living. We are not free from the techniques, the methods, the means by which we know, see. So look into ourselves now. . . .[7]

Perhaps it is true to say that the one thing we can always do is to start again. There is never a time when I am not given the opportunity to drop my present ideas and think again, to close my eyes and look again, to still my fears and trust again. My heart and my mind can open themselves ever again to what is—I am always in relationship, never outside it.

If we do not have relationship with human beings, we may have a relationship with the Buddha and Dhamma, his teaching. Some of those who meditate will have a relationship with meditation. We have relationships with one thing or another all the time. Perhaps when we come to the void, emptiness, we will have a relationship with that and to put it more precisely we may say that relationship is relationship with the whole, of the whole, so that there is no individual being to have relationship. Then we will say there is only relationship, the movement of life, the movement of being without becoming.[8]

Dhiravamsa speaks of being "alone." By this he means being beyond dependence on other people or on second-hand experience.

Perhaps there comes a moment for all of us when we realize the essential solitariness of personal experience. What happens to me can never be completely communicated to you. Beyond the level of communication I am alone. The awareness that I exist is also the awareness that I am isolated. All my feelings and thoughts are private and although I can tell you about them I cannot give you the experience of them.

This awareness that in all circumstances we are by ourselves sometimes comes to people facing death. Then it can be seen that death is not the only solitary experience we have but that, in fact, all of life is on just the same plane as death—it is an "I experience" state from beginning to end.

But this inescapable aloneness is only felt as a matter for fear and sorrow when it is thought that the "I" is something with a name and form. Fear drops away when the real nature of "I" is discovered—the nature of which cannot be described by name and form for these are its attributes but not itself. When the "I" is experienced as reality, there takes place a growing detachment from the world. But this noninvolvement does not mean a step in isolation, but the reverse. Because you or I need nothing from each other, we are free to accept each other, whatever our condition. Because I want nothing from you in return, there is no bar to my total acceptance of you—an acceptance which Dhiravamsa calls "a relationship with the wholeness":

> We can say we have relationship with the whole, not with the details. In complete aloneness there is relationship with the wholeness. There is no relationship between you and something else in particular, but there is completely objective relationship, which is the movement of life. There is joy, there is wisdom, there is freedom in that movement of life. Perhaps in other religions they may call it relationship with

God, the One Being, the Supreme Being, but we can say that we have relationship with the wholeness; then the words "you" or "me" do not exist, the image of individuality does not exist. In that aloneness there is holiness in the ordinary and perfection in the doing.[9]

References

Chogyam Trungpa

1   Chogyam Trungpa, *Born in Tibet*, (London: Allen and Unwin, New York: Penguin, New York: J. Harcourt Brace,) p. 56.
2   Ibid., p. 57.
3   Chogyam Trungpa, *Cutting Through Spiritual Materialism*, (London: Robinson and Watkins Books Ltd., Shambala Publications Inc.), p. 13.
4   Ibid., p. 15.
5   Ibid., p. 19.
6   Ibid., p. 26.
7   Ibid., p. 69.
8   Ibid., p. 102.
9   Ibid., p. 104.
10   Ibid., p. 108.
11   Ibid., p. 129.
12   Ibid., p. 130.
13   Ibid., p. 146.
14   Ibid., p. 160.
15   Ibid., p. 188.
16   Ibid., p. 189.
17   Ibid., p. 198.
18   *Garuda II*, p. 56.

Further Reading

Meditation in Action, Shambala Publications Inc.
Mudra, Shambala Publications Inc.

Dhiravamsa

1   Dhiravamsa, *The Real Way to Awakening* (Hindhead, England: Vipassana Centre), pp. 13-14.
2   Dhiravamsa, *The Middle Path of Life*, (No publisher), p. 92.
3   Ibid., p. 93.

4   Ibid., p. 33.
5   Ibid., p. 31.
6   Ibid., p. 32.
7   Ibid., p. 39.
8   Ibid., p. 45.
9   Ibid., p. 86.

Further Reading

Insight Meditation, Hindhead, England: Vipassana Centre
Beneficial Factors for Meditation. Hindhead, England:
    Vipassana Center
A New Approach to Buddhism. The Dawn Horse Press
(All under Dhiravamsa's former name of Chao Khun Sobhana
    Dhammasudhi)
The Way of Non-attachment, by Dhiravamsa,
    Turnstone Books, London

7

A Jewish Prophet

Martin Buber is one of the hardest mystics to summarize, even briefly, because his use of "I" seems, on the face of it, more complicated than anyone else's. In fact it is not really very complicated, but it does demand a prepared ground in the form of some preknowledge of mystical experience—at least to the extent of knowing the difference between our usual ego-ridden way of looking at the world, and the way of seeing the world as it is in itself, in its numinous nature. When seen in the latter way, the relationship between the individual and the world is called I-Thou, and whereas the Buddhists find no need for the feeling of "I" at all, Buber insists that it is a necessary sensation because, he says, without the "I" feeling there could be no relationships at all.

Buber's influence on religious thought has been great, but his teaching is not sufficiently straightforward for everyone to agree immediately on what he really means.

Many people have interpreted Buber and the following account should be regarded as a personal one and not necessarily agreeing with the others.

When reading this chapter, it is perhaps important to bear in mind that he believes the sacred can be found here and now, at this moment. The only God worth knowing is the one you cannot hold on to or talk about; God can't be discussed but he can be spoken to and he can be listened to. This is the only real relationship we can have at all—to speak to God and to be spoken to by him.

Martin Buber
1882–1965

The world is twofold for man in accordance with his
   twofold attitude.
The attitude of man is twofold in accordance with the two
   basic words he can speak.
The basic words are not single words but word pairs.
One basic word is the word pair I-You.
The other basic word is the word pair I-It; but this basic
   word is not changed when He or She takes the place of
   It.
Thus the I of man is also twofold.
For the I of the basic word I-You is different from that in the
   basic word I-It.   *I and Thou*[1]

The feeling of "I" comes about, says Buber, only in
relationship. The "I" cannot exist on its own. This seems
fairly obvious when one thinks about it, but where Buber
goes into a more complicated field is when he declares
that there are two forms of relationship for the "I" to have.

One is with It, which means with everything we can sense or think about or feel or remember. The other is with Thou (or, in Kaufman's translation, You). People often think that Buber simply means God when he says You, and in one sense he does. But he does not mean the personal God of the Old Testament. He means the unconditioned timeless ground of God, which is also the ground of all creatures, and which can be seen in every creature and object when all one's conditioned ideas and feelings about it are dropped. I relate to You, the transcendent, when I find You in a person, animal, or object. When I do not find You, or do not know You when I see You, I relate to It, which means I relate to the person, animal, or object by seeing them as "things" for my own experience and use. I am then putting that person, animal, or object into a familiar category in my mind, thinking about it from my own store of concepts, and judging it accordingly, instead of seeing it afresh, as itself. Relating to You means relating to the person or scene in front of me at this moment entirely anew, as though it has never been seen before.

Martin Buber saw, as did Alan Watts, Ramana Maharshi, and some other sages in this book, that man's personality, what he thinks of as "I," is not the isolated self-entity running by its own power, which he imagines it to be, but that the feeling of "I" exists as a "something" according to what it is identified with. When it is identified with the body and bodily feelings then it seems to be mortal, fragile and changing. When it is identified with the unconditioned, with the absolute Void, Self, Suchness, or God, it feels changeless and at one with all things.

Buber's real discovery was that it, the feeling of "I," must be identified with *something,* or we would not exist as the creatures we are. It is in the nature of human beings from the moment of birth, he said, to identify with what is there—first with the outside world and then later, in maturity, with the inner essence of God.

To watch a baby develop is to see the play of the real longings of man, for from its first moments the baby is seeking relationship, he said. The aimless movements of the hands, the unfocused glances, all are exploring the "other," looking for contact.

> . . . precisely these glances will eventually, after many trials, come to rest upon a red wallpaper arabesque and not leave it until the soul of red has opened up to them. Precisely this motion will gain its sensuous form and definiteness in contact with a shaggy toy bear and eventually apprehend lovingly and unforgettably a complete body. . . . Little inarticulate sounds still ring out senselessly and persistently into the nothing; but one day they will have turned imperceptibly into a conversation. . . .[2]

Buber believed, as did Teilhard de Chardin, that evolving man is heading towards a final identification and merging of himself with God. Historically, Buber saw the development of the feeling of "I" as beginning in primitive man. An animal is not conscious of itself as being separate from its surroundings, he said. A cat *is* its pounce on its victim, a dog *is* its love for its master—neither animal is capable of the reflective self-consciousness which says, "I am now going to pounce" or "I love this man." In the same way as animals, primitive man at first was identified with his actions—he did not think about the moon except as it affected him in the night. Fire was hot and bright and was not a word called *fire* but a process in which he took part. The experiencing subject had not detached itself from the experience and it was only when the force of self-preservation caused the beginning of language and knowledge, that the "I-acting-You" and "You-acting-I" were split and the "I" "emerged with the force of an element."[3]

As man ceased to *be* his action so he began to think of himself as a solitary subject and as the "doer" of his deeds—as, by habit, we think of ourselves now. It is only rarely during our hectic, scurrying lives that the feeling of being an active "I" disappears—overwhelmed, perhaps, by a greater reality in a moment of love or an instant of awestruck revelation.

The development of man's brain, says Buber, gave him the ability to imagine and to recall. From his memory of an event he could imaginatively infer a future event. And he could use his remembered knowledge of the way things behaved, such as water, to imaginatively construct and then materially execute a tool, such as a waterwheel.

Buber sees this development in man as a relationship between "I" and "It." Previously, when man had not been aware of himself, there could not be a relationship because all man's processes were in themselves relational. But with his new growth of self-consciousness, a relationship came into existence between himself and that which was not himself. For, says Buber, relationship is only possible when there are two—when there is an encounter between myself and something that I feel to be not me.

In our world of today, we mainly encounter other things as objects of experience and use, as did developing man. From our sensation of them, we create an It-world of known phenomena, of names and categories. We use this world for our own preservation and benefit. Our mastery over it reinforces the feeling of separation and the separate "I" becomes the ego, the demanding, insatiable occupant of our feelings and thoughts. And so the It-world comes to consist of "It and It and It, of He and He and She and She and It."[4] Even God, as long as he is He, is an object, a something to be experienced.

But this is not the whole of man's life, says Buber.

There is a dimension in which I do not have the experience of "something" as the goal of my activities. This dimension becomes present when I say "You."

What is the You relationship? I or you can have a You relationship with another person, or even with an animal or an object, when I withdraw from it all my projected ideas of it and my feelings about it, so that I see it *not* as an object of experience and use, but as itself, supremely real in its own right, clearly shining from its own light. Possessively, we usually regard anything new to us as an object to be judged according to our habitual conditioned attitudes. But when we observe that the world is not ours, that even the chair on which I am sitting and the paper spread out before me are, in their essence, *unknowable* by me, then we can become aware of the supreme and total mystery of existence, which is reality.

Buber believed that our birth into the world means an encounter with being. This encounter is not man's work, he does not create himself. Nor does he create the existence that he encounters and which, in its essence, is unknowable by him. But what *is* man's work is the relationship he forms with existence—whether he chooses I-You or I-It.

To show what he meant, Buber used the example of an encounter with a tree. When he contemplates a tree, he said, it might be in one of several ways. He might look at the tree as an artist would, seeing a composition of colors—splashes of green about the pillar of the trunk against a blue and silver background. Or, imaginatively, he might "feel" the tree in its own movement of veins flowing round the core, of roots sucking from the earth, of leaves breathing in the air, and the whole tree growing of itself in the darkness. Still in the world of It, he might observe it botanically as one of a named species. Or he might recognize it as an expression of universal natural laws, and dissolve it into a series of numbers. On each of these occasions the tree would be It, his object, and would have its own place and time span.

But if, "through will and grace," he was drawn into a relationship with the tree so that it no longer existed outside himself as a separate object—so that the duality of I-It ceased, and was replaced by a wholeness of being in which the feeling of separation vanished—then the tree would exist as You.

This would not mean that all the other It attitudes to the tree and descriptions of it were rendered useless:

> There is nothing that I must not see in order to see, and there is no knowledge that I must forget. Rather is everything, picture and movement, species and instance, law and number included and inseparably fused.[5]

All that belongs to the tree has been gathered into a wholeness in which it exists as its own reality, as "tree." It has become "bodied" and confronts him as itself. It is here, perhaps, that Buber's thought, so crystal clear as it leads up to the revelation of You, becomes a bit ambiguous about the I-You relationship when it is fully revealed. He seems to be describing what Trungpa terms the *isness* of things—seeing a tree in its own tree*ness*, as its own being, a state in which no shadow of self encroaches. The observer, the "I" who observes, is obliterated by the treeness of the tree, although this does not mean that I lose consciousness of my own existence. I am still here, I am still physically looking at the tree and would not see it if I closed my eyes. And yet, Trungpa might say, it is not the same I. It is as though I have been wholed, made one; and the myriad feelings and thoughts which usually fill my consciousness have dropped from me and are meaningless. In an unconditoned and infinite way, the tree is then seen by me as more itself than it can ever be seen when I am identified with my selfhood.

Alan Watts once wrote that while the finite is seen in the light "of the infinite Reality, the finite is *by comparison* nothing. As a relative reality it remains, but it has no more power to limit or conceal the infinite than nothing at all. Its effect upon the infinite is as if it were not."[6]

Buber, however, does not seem to go as far as this in his vision. He remains sturdily dualistic in his use of the term I-You. He seems to have an authentic realization of the unconditoned *isness* of life, but his "I" remains obstinately durable. Where other mystics, such as Ramana Maharshi, use the term I-I to describe the realization of nonduality, because the small I is seen as merging into the great I, Buber keeps the two firmly apart.

But he understands the nondualist realization. He knows that there is a transformation of the ordinary I, and he states clearly that none of the human attributes of I, such as reasoning and experiencing and understanding, can bring about the You-realization.

—What, then, does one experience of the You?
—Nothing at all. For one does not experience it.
—What, then, does one know of the You?
—Only everything. For one no longer knows particulars.[7]

The question remains: if "one does not experience it"—why is the term I-You habitually used? "I" surely must refer to an experiencer?

The answer may lie in Buber's religion of Judaism, which emphasizes the distance between man and God and is, perhaps, more dualistic than any other religion. Buber was a convinced Jew. His greatest inspirations came from the Hasidim, a mystical sect of Jews, some of whom lived near his father's estate in Bukovina in Northern Rumania, where, as a boy, he spent his summers. His father would sometimes take him to the nearby village of

Sadagora, the seat of a dynasty of Hasidic rabbis, and here the boy would watch the "rebbe" striding through the rows of the waiting and "the Hasidim dance with the Torah." Here he felt the strong relationship of community. It was the Hasidim to whom he came back in spirit as a young man, after a period of alienation from Judaism, and it was they he wrote about and their poems and legends he translated. He once summed up the teaching of the Hasidim, so much in accord with his own, as "God can be beheld in each thing and reached through each pure deed."[8]

However much it may be inwardly felt, it would be hard for a Jew to outwardly agree that surrender to God means becoming of the same substance as Him. This is perhaps why Buber chose the term I-You for the man-God relationship, seeing it essentially as *relationship* and not as *being*.

> The I of the basic word I-You is different from the basic word I-It.
> The I of the basic word I-It appears as an ego and becomes conscious of itself as a subject [of experience and use].
> The I of the basic word I-You appears as a person and becomes conscious of itself as subjectivity [without any dependent genitive].
> Egos appear by setting themselves apart from other egos.
> Persons appear by entering into relation to other persons.
> One is the spiritual form of natural differentiation, the other that of natural association.[9]

The word "person" to Buber was all-important and he distinguished it from ego. Egos belong to the It world, and their desire is to survive, to possess, to experience, and to use. But none of these desires occur in the I-You relationship, because the I becomes unconditioned and unlimited through its participation in this relationship. The I, he said, becomes *actualized,* and this establishes the person as distinct from the ego:

> The person says, "I am;" the ego says, "That is how I am."
> "Know thyself" means to the person: know yourself as being.
> To the ego it means: know your being-that-way. By setting
> himself apart from others, the ego moves away from being.[10]

There is nothing for the I to *have* in the I-You relationship, there is only the encounter, the recognition of the
other as infinitely other—no longer even he or she, but a
mysterious wholeness which includes he and she and yet
transcends all classification. The I-You encounter exists
in the present moment; whereas the I-It encounter cannot exist in the present because the It is seen through a
fog of ideas and concepts derived from past conditioning
and remembered events. The I-It encounter can become
an I-You encounter when conditioned memory is dropped
and no previous associations cloud the gaze of the I.

It is in this option of relationship that man has choice
and free will, and Buber saw the continual exchange of It
for You and You for It as constituting the nature of the
world. He did not believe (as Teilhard de Chardin did)
that the You world will eventually triumph over the It
world, in a sort of mystical conglomeration, leaving nothing of the old It behind. Rather, he saw that the You can
not be sustained without It—that there must be alternation:

> The It is the chrysalis, the You the butterfly. The You is
> constantly submerged into the It, the direct relationship de-
> generating into means, the ineffable captured in form. Even
> the noblest form loses its actuality, even love can only endure
> by the alternation of the actual and the potential—"The
> human being who but now was unique and devoid of qual-
> ities, not at hand but only present, not experienceable, only
> touchable, has again become a He or She, an aggregate of
> qualities, a quantum with a shape."[11]

> The individual You *must* become an It when the event of
> relation has run its course.

> The individual It *can* become a You by entering into the
> event of relation.[12]

From this alternation, he believed, there can emerge a
"faithful humanism," the "faculty innate in man to enter
into encounters with other beings." He believed that it
was man's duty to develop this faculty, and he himself
certainly seemed to embody it. He welcomed encounter.
He loved people. The passing stranger as well as the
close friend could be sure of Buber's full and warm attention. His home in Jerusalem, where he spent the last
twenty-seven years of his life, was a center of attraction
for young people who came from all over the world to
argue and discuss with him and to bring out their problems.

Buber differed from other, more orthodox, Jews in that
he did not try to interpret his discoveries in the way that
prophets have done in the past. For him it was enough to
recognize that there is in man an innate faculty for unselfish, loving encounter. He did not believe in prophecy or
revelation and, like the Buddha, he did not believe in
religious speculation:

> I do not believe in God's naming himself or in God's
> defining himself before man. The word of revelation is: I am
> there as whoever I am there. That which reveals is that which
> reveals. That which has being is there, nothing more. The
> eternal source of strength flows, the eternal touch is waiting,
> the eternal voice sounds, nothing more.[13]

Rather, he believed that answers come through
actions—but that nobody can be told how to act—

> ... even as the meaning itself cannot be transferred or
> expressed in a universally valid and generally acceptable

piece of knowledge, putting it to the proof in action cannot be handed on as a valid ought. . . . The meaning we receive can be put to the proof in action only by each person in the uniqueness of his being and in the uniqueness of his life. No prescription can lead us to the encounter and none leads from it.[14]

Buber's insights have penetrated deeply into modern Christianity and greatly affected such theologians as Dr. John Robinson, the author of *Honest to God*, Bishop Pike of California, and many others. In particular, it is the mysterious unfathomable encounter between I and You which has fired the imagination of some Christians and has helped to bring about such movements as the Death of God, spurred on by one of Buber's most famous books, *The Eclipse of God.*

For it is this encounter, the "space" between I and You, which Buber calls the spirit; and some of his most important teaching is about "distancing," the distance which comes into being when the I makes the effort of will to stop projecting ideas and feelings onto the world.

In the pragmatic It world, distancing emerged as part of man's development of conceptualized thought, Buber believed, for the ability to distance himself from an object and abstract the idea of it so that it could be reproduced again and again, has not been displayed by animals except in rare instances. To show what he means by this sort of distancing Buber uses the example of a monkey who swings a stick as a weapon, as against a man who gives the stick a separate existence in which it is known as a "weapon."

To be able to distance himself from objects in order that he can conceptualize them is man's unique, self-preserving gift. Unlike other creatures, he is by nature distanced over against the world. Just because of this and unlike other creatures, he can enter into relationship with it over and over again. Distancing is essential for self-survival and without distancing man would never have become the dominant species that he is. But the other side of the coin to domination is slavery, and man appears to have misused his unique gift enslaving himself to that which he dominates. He is enslaved by material objects and by power. His desires keep him bound to the material world of It, unable to recognize or respond to You.

And yet he *can* wake up from enslavement at any moment and turn toward the liberation of I-You. In all the world, he alone can distance himself from You, he alone can discover You in It, and can thus redeem It. Buber saw this act of redemption as man's true response to the challenge of life in this world. To him physical matter was never inert or dead as it seems to be to those who live exclusively in the It-world. Everything is always potentially You in all its concreteness. Not only do I find You, he said, in the ineffable wholeness, in the timeless You-ness of the It which I contemplate, but I must also look for You in all its particularities. I must never dismiss any aspect as unpleasant, distasteful, or irredeemable, thus consigning it to a frozen It-world. I must always be aware that You are never absent and that my whole purpose of living is to discover You in every It. Mere acceptance of You will not do, it must be an act of discovery and affirmation.

> . . . Whatever has thus been changed into It and frozen into a thing among things is still endowed with the meaning and the destiny to change back ever again. Ever again—that was the intention in that hour of the spirit when it bestowed itself upon man and begot the response in him—the object shall catch fire and become present, returning to the element from which it issued, to be beheld and lived by men as present.[15]

How do I consciously turn toward You? By opening myself to all that is real and actual. By having the courage

to move forward without knowing where I am going. By
sacrificing the "little will, which is unfree and ruled by
things and drives" for a greater will in which I no longer
interfere with or alter that which is, but attempt to embrace it. By listening "to that which grows, to the way of
Being in the world." By constant strength and courage,
for the world of You is characterized by unreliability—"it
appears always new to you and you cannot take it by its
word. It lacks density for everything in it permeates everything else. It lacks duration, for it comes even when
not called and vanishes even when you cling to it. . . . It
does not help you to survive; it only helps you to have
intimations of eternity.

> The It-world hangs together in space and time.
> The You-world does not hang together in space and time.
> What is essential is lived in the present, objects in the
>   past.[16]

Martin Buber's best-known book was called *I and Thou*
(recently translated as *I and You*). He wrote it when he
was still a young man, but changed very little in it as he
grew older. His main beliefs have helped to shape modern man's thinking in many ways. Let us briefly sum them
up.

Man's real nature and purpose is that of response to
You, and this response is itself the "spirit."

> Man speaks in many tongues—tongues of art, of language,
> of action—but the spirit is one; it is response to the You that
> appears from the mystery and addresses us from the
> mystery. . . . Spirit is not in the I but between I and You. It is
> not like the blood which circulates in you but like the air in
> which you breathe. Man lives in the spirit when he is able to
> respond to his You. He is able to do that when he enters into
> this relation with his whole being. It is solely by virtue of his
> power to relate that man is able to live in the spirit.[17]

Man can encounter You by transcending his understanding that is formed by his intellect, and his feelings formed from his desires. In this transcendence he can have a relationship with that which is other than himself, with You. But if he clings to his thoughts and ideas and beliefs, he will not see You properly, You will be his creation and not Yourself; You will be reduced to It, an object of his experience and use.

You are always there. In every situation he can turn to You and find You—but not if he keeps himself intact. You are not there if he merely looks for You as an object among other objects. To relate to You, he must commit himself to You, and do this so totally that his I is changed by the undifferentiated reality of You.

> The basic word I-You can only be spoken with one's whole being.

> The basic word I-It can never be spoken with one's whole being.[18]

That you need God more than anything, you know at all times in your heart. But don't you know also that God needs you—in the dullness of his eternity, you? How would man exist if God did not need him, and how would you exist? You need God in order to be, and God needs you—for that which is the meaning of your life. Teachings and poems try to say more, and say too much: how murky and presumptuous is the chatter of "the emerging God"—but the emergence of the living God we know unswervingly in our hearts. The world is not divine play, it is divine fate. That there are world, man, the human person, you and I, has divine meaning.[19]

230

References

1   Martin Buber, *I and Thou*, trans. Walter Kaufmann
         (Edinburgh: T. and T. Clark, New York: Charles
         Scribner's Sons), p. 52.
2   Ibid., p. 78.
3   Ibid., p. 73.
4   Ibid., p. 55.
5   Ibid., p. 58.
6   Alan Watts, *The Supreme Identity* (London: Wildwood
         House), p. 72.
7   Buber, *I and Thou*, p. 61.
8   Ibid., p. 111.
9   Ibid., p. 112.
10   Ibid., p. 113.
11   Ibid., p. 69.
12   Ibid., p. 84.
13   Ibid., p. 160.
14   Ibid., p. 159.
15   Ibid., p. 90.
16   Ibid., p. 84.
17   Ibid., p. 64.
18   Ibid., p. 89.
19   Ibid., p. 130.

Further Reading

Between Man and Man. London: Fontana; New York:
    Macmillan
Hasidism and Modern Man. New York: Harper and Row
Knowledge of Man. London: Allen and Unwin; New York:
    Harper and Row
Pointing the Way. London: Routledge Kegan Paul; New York:
    Harper and Row
Way of Man. London: Stuart and Watkins; New York: Citadel
    Press
Philosophy of Martin Buber. London: Cambridge University
    Press

8

The Occultists

At the root of much of Martin Buber's intuitive thinking lay the great Hebrew outline of the cosmos—the Qabalah—the mystical Tree of Life. The Qabalah, an inner Hebrew teaching that has been passed down through the ages, often secretly, was the vigorous and powerful spiritual way that inspired the Hassidim; and their stories, which Buber translated, reflect his own penetrating understanding of the Tree. In his book *Jewish Mysticism* he describes how the Qabalah suddenly rose up "purified and exalted" among the villages in Little Russia, and how it became the movement called Hassidism. "Mysticism became the possession of the people."

Buber's own aim was to make concrete the teachings of the Qabalah, and he would demonstrate it, without disclosing its origin, at every level. For instance, using the symbol of a shell, which represents in the Qabalah a level

231

of atrophy and separation from life, he would describe the everyday state of resistance to suffering which, he said, prompted people to grow a protective shell around themselves—a shell that could grow into a barrier keeping out any contact with real life.

With similar motives to Buber (although without his remarkable intellect and flair), the Englishwoman, Dion Fortune, spent much of her life teaching the Qabalah in practical form as "right-hand" or "white" magic. Perhaps because of its connections with fortune-telling through the misuse of its offspring, the Tarot, the Qabalah has suffered in Western eyes. But stripped of its false accretions, it is revealed as a giant among the religious ways; a great and superb outline of existence which, to be understood, must be *experienced*, level after level.

The methods used for ascending the Tree are what are known in the East as yogic ones, for they include meditation, concentration and contemplation, mantra and visualization. The way in which Dion Fortune translates what she terms the "Yoga of the Qabalah" into everyday language is her particular contribution to Western understanding, for she was convinced that Eastern practices, emerging from a vastly different cultural milieu, were not right for Westerners. She points out that a "direct" mystic follows what she calls "the way of illumination," the immediate path to the Unconditioned Ground or Godhead, and that those who follow this path often look askance at the occultist, seeing him as foolishly caught up in a number of mental states, none of which seem to come near the sublime certainty of true union. But Fortune makes out a convincing case for the occultist, and clarifies the issue for us:

> There are two paths to the Innermost: the way of the mystic, which is the way of devotion and meditation, a solitary and subjective path; and the way of the occultist, which

is the way of the intellect, of concentration, and of the trained will; upon this path the co-operation of fellow workers is required, firstly for the exchange of knowledge, and secondly because ritual magic plays an important part in this work, and for this the assistance of several is needed for most of the greater operations. The mystic derives his knowledge through the direct communion of his higher self with the Higher Powers; to him the wisdom of the occultist is foolishness, for his mind does not work in that way; but on the other hand, to a more intellectual and extrovert type, the method of the mystic is impossible until long training has enabled him to transcend the planes of form. We must therefore recognise these two distinct types among those who seek the Way of Initiation, and remember that there is a path for each.[1]

Such a clear comparison helps us to place ourselves and, if we happen to prefer the direct path, it helps us to look objectively at such emotive subjects as magic and ritual. Even further clarification can come from writers such as Evelyn Underhill, who was interested in the Qabalah, and who had this to say about magic:

... Real "magical initiation" is in essence a form of mental discipline, strengthening and focussing the will. This discipline, like that of the religious life, consists partly in physical austerities and a deliberate divorce from the world, partly in the cultivation of will-power: but largely in a yielding of the mind to the influence of suggestions which have been selected and accumulated in the course of ages because of their power over that imagination which Eliphas Levi calls "the eye of the soul." There is nothing supernatural about it. Like the more arduous, more disinterested self-training of the mystic, it is character-building with an object, conducted upon an heroic scale. In magic the "will to know" is the centre round which the personality is rearranged. As in mysticism, unconscious factors are dragged from the hiddenness to form part of that personality. The uprushes of thought, the abrupt intuitions which reach us from the subliminal region, are developed, ordered, and controlled by rhythms and symbols which have become traditional because the experience of centuries has proved, though it cannot explain, their efficacy: and powers of apprehension which normally lie below the threshold may thus be liberated and enabled to report their discoveries.[2]

And, with specific reference to the Qabalah, Underhill points out:

He [the mystic] has got to find God. Sometimes his temperament causes him to lay most stress on the length of the search; sometimes the abrupt rapture which brings it to a close makes him forget that preliminary pilgrimage in which the soul is "not outward bound, but rather on a journey to its centre." The habitations of the Interior Castle through which St. Theresa leads us to that hidden chamber which is the sanctuary of the indwelling God: the hierarchies of Dionysius, ascending from the selfless service of the angels, past the seraphs' burning love, to the God enthroned above time and space: the mystical paths of the Kabalistic Tree of Life, which lead from the material world of Malkuth through the universes of action and thought, by Mercy, Justice and Beauty, to the Supernal Crown; all these are different ways of describing this same pilgrimage.[3]

Rudolf Steiner's pilgrimage was mostly concerned with the hierarchies of creation, and thus he was a more materialistic occultist than Fortune, although they were friends and she consulted him several times. His terminology is also based on the Qabalah, although he borrowed freely from the Eastern religions and also from the Theosophists. His practical work is better known than his cosmology, which is detailed and covers the whole evolution of the world and of mankind. Because he was a clairvoyant, he could describe Beings and worlds which most of us don't see and this puts the ordinary reader at a disadvantage. Nevertheless, the movements in education and agriculture which he set in motion have proved to be of considerable value to modern life, and his general doctrines are very popular with the young, insofar as they are revealed in practice.

Dion Fortune
1891–1946

Dion Fortune's real name was Violet Mary Firth. When she was a young woman she joined the Golden Dawn —that turbulent group of spiritual searchers and practicing occultists that included such varied names as W. B. Yeats, MacGregor-Mathers, Alastair Crowley (who was thrown out), Evelyn Underhill, Charles Williams, and E. Nesbit. Violet Firth then took, as they all did, a Latin name and she chose Deo Non Fortuna (by God and not by luck). This title became shortened to Dion Fortune when she began to write novels.

The history of the Golden Dawn is one which includes a large amount of credulity and over-excited imagination. People quarrelled over intiations, gradings, and interpretations, and Evelyn Underhill, for one, got out of it fairly quickly. But underneath all the fuss and commotion of astral journeys and mediumistic messages ran a stream of real understanding that inspired much of Yeats's poetry

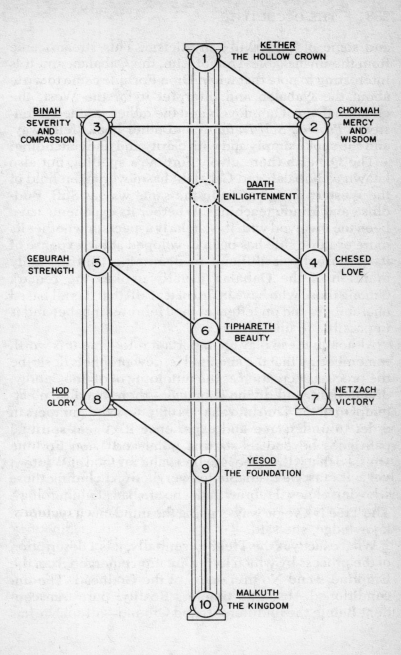

KETHER
THE HOLLOW CROWN

BINAH
SEVERITY
AND
COMPASSION

CHOKMAH
MERCY
AND
WISDOM

DAATH
ENLIGHTENMENT

GEBURAH
STRENGTH

CHESED
LOVE

TIPHARETH
BEAUTY

HOD
GLORY

NETZACH
VICTORY

YESOD
THE FOUNDATION

MALKUTH
THE KINGDOM

and some of Underhill's mysticism. This stream came from the unshakable Tree of Life, the Qabalah, and it is interesting to note that when Dion Fortune came to write about the Qabalah and interpret it for the West, the emotionalism of her novels and the rather strained intensity of *Psychic Self-Defense* and other books fell away, and she spoke simply and with clarity and understanding.

The Qabalah (here given Fortune's spelling but also known as Kabalah and Cabalah) has never taken hold of the Western imagination in the same way as Sufi, Buddhist, and Hindu teachings. Whether its exponents have been too involved with its scholarly aspects or whether its more esoteric side has been developed at the expense of its philosophy is difficult to determine. But certainly mention of the Qabalah usually evokes the remark (among those who have heard of it at all) that it is all based on numbers and on letters of the Hebrew alphabet and is impossible to understand.

Although these play an important role—and it is worth remembering that the ancient Hebrew prophets describe the process of creation as the unfolding of divine energy, divine light, and divine *language*—there need be no attempt to fit the Tree into a series of letters and numbers in order to understand and experience it. A real spiritual path goes beyond its starting point and Dion Fortune stressed that if the Tree is to be a valid method of Western yoga, it must be available to everybody, including those who don't know Hebrew and who are bad at numerology. The Tree is a yogic way of using the mind, not a system of knowledge, she said.

What exactly is the Tree? Essentially, it is a description of the process by which living creation emerged from the Emptiness and No-thing-ness of the Godhead. The unconditioned Absolute; timeless Reality; pure transcendent Being; the undifferentiated Ground—all such terms try to convey what no description can ever give—the THAT which transcends man utterly. In the Qabalah it is termed Ain, the Ultimate Void.

Through Ain Soph, which is one stage nearer to creation and is apprehended as limitlessness—the timeless without which time could not exist and the emptiness without which forms could not be or move—the realm of Ain Soph Aur, Limitless Light, comes into being. Out of Ain Soph Aur, God emerges from the unknowable and ineffable region of his own Being to manifest himself as creation. God, the Beginning of the world, stands at the top of the Tree of Life as Kether, the Hollow Crown, through which the Uncreated flows and becomes manifest. Kether is the living dynamic force of life, the "I AM" of existence, the source of all the universes and of every creature.

Behind Kether is the ineffable stillness and emptiness of the Godhead, about which man can know and say nothing. In front of Kether is the world about us, the world of appearances.

The Qabalah sees the world as symbol—everything that can be known symbolizes the eternal Reality that is its source—and it has condensed the myriad aspects of manifestation into ten basic categories, each of which is called a sephirah and together constitute the sephiroth. The sephiroth make up the Tree, with Kether at the top and Malkuth, the physical earth, at the bottom (see diagram).

But the importance of the Tree is not just its penetration into the ways of the manifest Spirit (in which case it would be only a system of knowledge) but the Tree is also one's own self, for the sephiroth that mark the descent and particularization of God also form the rungs of the ladder up which man can ascend and become unified. Each sephirah symbolizes divine energy at a different level.

Dion Fortune shows us the Tree as consisting of three pillars. The sephiroth of the left-hand pillar are negative and female; and of the right-hand pillar, positive and male. Two vital stages of realization are centered in the middle pillar, which is based on the earth and topped by the gateway to heaven. The sephiroth are connected by a zigzagging lightning flash—or flash of enlightenment —and the two central processes of realization are known as Tiphareth, or Beauty (in which Kether is first seen), and Daath, or Divine Knowledge (although Daath is a rare rather than a regular stage and is not regarded as a definite sephirah).

Many readers will see a strong resemblance between the pillars of the Qabalah and the Taoist philosophy of Yin and Yang, the dual aspects of all life that show themselves as darkness and light, female and male, etc. The Tao, the Way, is of the same nature as the Middle Way of Buddhism and the central pillar of the Qabalah.

Although all the sephiroth make up the ladder that must be climbed by man, the bottom rungs are of no less value than the top. The earth of physical matter is also the Kingdom where God is manifested at his most dense and concrete. Thus one need not feel ashamed if one is at a low rung of the ladder rather than a high one. This freedom from strain (a strain which, by contrast, is the hallmark of some religions) is an essential feature of Tantric Yoga, which looks upon physical life as a holy arena, a uniquely equipped laboratory for the transmutation of matter into spirit; and the meditations and visualizations of the Qabalists are as much a Tantric path as are Tibetan mandalas and Hindu yantras.

The Tree of Life, when it is properly accepted as a ladder, seems to contain a flowing, creative force that impels one forward without risk. The symbols of the different sephiroth appear in the mind quite concretely as signposts, and contain no hidden dangers that might give rise to mental unbalance. Everything is serenely revealed as one goes along insofar as one applies exercises for strengthening the will and focusing the attention, and for yielding the mind to the influence of symbols that, through the ages, have become imbued with creative strength.

It was through her understanding of the symbols of the sephiroth and her practice of meditation to bring about their realization, that Dion Fortune herself acquired balance and sanity. She came to the Tree first of all by way of the deeply occult—the strata that seems most confusing of all to the real mystic—the spirit-world of mediums and astral planes. "Pickled in Spirit" was how Alan Watts described it and Fortune, later on, might have agreed.

She was an orphan, related to the "Stainless Steel" Firth family and brought up in Yorkshire in a household where Christian Science was rigorously practiced. She did not fit in and was often so unhappy that she retreated from the world into prolonged bouts of daydreaming, which became intensified into perception of auras and development of mediumistic powers. This alarmed her guardians and caused some stir in her small home town.

Then, when she was twenty, she had the misfortune to serve as a schoolteacher under a viciously neurotic headmistress who had lived in India and learned hypnosis, which she used as a weapon. Fortune was soon asked to support this headmistress, called the Warden, in a lawsuit against a former employee, and she describes how she was persuaded to do this. "Her method of collecting my evidence was to look into my eyes with a concentrated gaze and say, 'Such and such things happened.'"[1]

The same thing occurred again when the Warden

wanted to fire another of her staff and asked Fortune to
back her up. After several more incidents, Fortune herself got on the wrong side of the Warden. When, her case
packed, she went to tell the Warden she was leaving
(having decided on flight as the best course open to her) a
terrible scene took place, one that was to have an effect on
her for years afterwards. For four hours the Warden made
her repeat two statements, one that she was incompetent
and another that she had no self-confidence. Like a rabbit
before a snake, Fortune tells us that she was incapable of
leaving the room but was able to resist admitting the two
accusations until at last she saw that her only hope of
sanity lay in pretending to be beaten. When she reached
her own room she went into a stupor for thirty hours.
Eventually a colleague discovered her state and sent for
her family, who took her away. But from this experience
she suffered a breakdown in health that was only cured
some years later by a combination of Freudian psycho-
analysis and study of the Qabalah.

In 1918, having attended courses at London University, she became a lay psychotherapist at the East London
Clinic. Certain psychosomatic cases seemed to her to
bear a close resemblance to the states described in Tantric Yoga. She came to the conclusion that the Western
attitude to women was fundamentally wrong because it
was based on the idea that the femininity of women is the
passive, receptive counterpart to man's dynamic action.
But Fortune felt strongly that the female is the positive
creative force that awakens man and brings alive his mas-
culine energy in much the same way that Shakti, the
feminine power of Tantric Yoga, is said to ascend the
spine of man as Kundalini, the serpent power, awakening
man's whole being as she does so until he and she unite
in his head.

With all this in mind, Fortune began to write novels

portraying the union of male and female principles. In 1919, she joined the Golden Dawn and came under the tutelage of J. W. Brodie-Innes, whom she greatly respected. He taught her the rituals of "magic" which she later adapted to her own teaching of the Qabalah.

In 1920, she joined a London Lodge of the Golden Dawn (Brodie-Innes's was a Scottish Order) and came directly under a very powerful and rather destructive force—Moina Mathers, the sister of the philosopher Henri Bergson and the widow of S. Liddell Mac-Gregor-Mathers, who was one of the founders of the Golden Dawn and an authority on the Qabalah. Moina Mathers was beautiful, temperamental, and clairvoyant. W. B. Yeats and others had a high respect for her clairvoyant powers and were swayed by her beauty.

There is no doubt that she was considerably put out by the critical attitude of the much younger Dion Fortune to the way the Lodge, called the Alpha and Omega, was run. Fortune thought that the Lodge consisted "mainly of widows and grey-bearded ancients" and that the quality of the teaching "was conspicuous by its absence." She felt that the whole Lodge needed an injection of vitality and her idea was to form an organized outer society with open lectures and a magazine, etc., through which the public would be filtered into the Golden Dawn.

Mrs. Mathers, rather surprisingly, agreed to this —secrecy had been considered essential up till then —and, in 1922, the Fraternity of the Inner Light was born; although for a time it bore the title of the "Christian Mystic Lodge of the Theosophical Society," which Fortune had joined early on.

Fairly soon it became apparent that Mrs. Mathers's country was being threatened by a rival queen and any amicability between the two ended. Mrs. Mathers tried to expel Fortune from the Golden Dawn, but Fortune continued a friendship with many of its members and also persisted in using its system. She then established her own Temple, declaring it to be part of the Golden Dawn Order. Mrs. Mathers retaliated with a psychic attack —according to Fortune—which resulted in Fortune's body being "scored with scratches as if I had been clawed by a gigantic cat."

Fortune lost no time in accusing Moina Mather of "astral murder"! A young woman, an ex-pupil of Mrs. Mathers', had gone to Iona to meditate. One day she disappeared and later her nude body was discovered lying over a cross which she had carved in the heather. She had died of heart failure, according to newspaper reports, but Fortune discovered that scratches had been seen on her body that were similar to those on her own, and this left her in no doubt as to who had produced them.

In time, however, both Fortune and the Fraternity of the Inner Light prospered. She married a doctor called Henry Evans, who was keenly interested in her work, and between them they treated cases of schizophrenics and other mental patients, sometimes curing seemingly hopeless cases.

The bulk of her work was concerned with "magic," the practical application of esoteric principles to daily life. One of the chief practices she taught was meditation on the various symbols of the sephiroth.

The word "symbol" is an emotive one, for the direct mystic is usually rather blind to symbolism and regards the whole subject as an unnecessary diversion from reality—this is particularly so in the Zen school of Buddhism. But to the followers of the Tantric way, symbols are the paths *to* reality. They stand for something of which the pupil is as yet unconscious, something that cannot be known in any other way but through itself. A symbol is a means of recognition and therefore of understanding and knowledge. In Tibetan Tantrism for instance, the various gods who adorn the tankas are the approaches by which we are drawn towards the Emptiness beyond form. Each god is a force, and his individual quality is expressed in gesture and color. One such as Ratnasambhava is golden-yellow in color because the golden light of the equality of all beings shines through him. He represents the principle of Feeling, which, through him, becomes love and compassion for all that lives; and he is seated on a horse for speed and energy. Meditation on him fills the mind with the quality of compassionate love, because the symbol not only represents this state but is believed actually to call it forth into the meditator's consciousness. In a yet more concrete example, Dion Fortune takes a coat of arms:

The initiates of the Ancient Wisdom made no bones about their philosophy; they took each factor in Nature and personified it, gave it a name, and built up a symbolic figure to represent it, just as British artists have by their collective efforts produced a standard Britannia, a female figure with shield charged with the Union Jack, a lion at her feet, a trident in her hand, a helmet on her head, and the sea in the background. Analysing this figure as we would a Qabalistic symbol, we realise that these individual symbols in the complex glyph [hieroglyph] have each a significance. The various crosses which make up the Union Jack refer to the four races united in the United Kingdom. The helmet is that of Minerva, the trident is that of Neptune; the lion would need a chapter to himself to elucidate his symbolism. In fact, an occult glyph is more akin to a coat of arms than anything else, and the person who builds up a glyph goes to work in the same way as a herald designing a coat of arms. For in heraldry every symbol has its exact meaning, and these are combined into the coat of arms that represent the family and affiliations of the man who bears it, and tells us his station in life. A magical figure is the coat of arms of the force it represents.[2]

In exactly this way, the sephiroth of the Tree symbolize the qualities of God. When they are taken all together, they reveal the Whole as it flows. For no one sephirah is a closed, complete state—all open into each other, each pouring its quality into the next in a continuous moving spiral.

When she came to teach meditation on the Qabalah, Fortune stressed the great importance of beginning with the very top—Kether. Students are usually taught, she said, that the three top sephiroth belong to the realm of Pure Spirit and cannot be realized while we are still in bodily form. But to start elsewhere would not be in harmony with cosmic law.

... The affirmation of pure being, eternal, unchanging, without attributes or activities, underlying, maintaining, and conditioning all, is the primary formula of all magical working. It is only when the mind is imbued with the realisation of this endless unchanging being of the utmost concentration and intensity that it can have any realisation of limitless power. Energy derived from any other source is a limited and partial energy. In Kether alone is the pure source of all energy. The operations of the magician that aim at the concentration of energy [and what operations do not?] must always start with Kether, because here we touch the upwelling force arising from the Great Unmanifest, the reservoir of limitless power.

The human mind, knowing no other mode of existence than that of form and activity, has the greatest difficulty in obtaining any adequate concept of an entirely formless state of passivity which is nevertheless most distinctly not non-being. Yet this effort must be made if we are to understand cosmic philosophy in its fundamentals. We must not draw the veils of negative existence in front of Kether or we shall condemn ourselves to a perpetual unresolved duality; God and the Devil will for ever war in our cosmos, and there can be no finality to their conflict. We must train the mind to conceive the state of pure being without attributes or activities; we may think of it as the blinding white light, undifferentiated into rays by the prism of form; or we may think of it as the darkness of interstellar space, which is nothing, yet contains the potentialities of all things. These symbols, dwelt upon by the inner eye, are a greater aid to the understanding of Kether than any amount of exact philosophical definitions. We cannot define Kether; we can only indicate it.[3]

To help the student bring realization to a conscious level, the image of Kether is that of an ancient bearded king in profile. Only the right side of him can be seen, the unmanifest side is hidden because it can never be comprehended by human consciousness. As a king, Kether conditions all things and all things evolve from him and thus share in his Unmanifest nature.

The two sephiroth that top the outside pillars and form the first triangle with Kether are the principles of male and female (Adam and Eve, Shiva and Shakti, Yang and Yin). Chokmah, the male source, is also the Supreme and Merciful Father.

"In order to contact Chokmah," says Fortune,

we must experience the rush of the divine cosmic energy in its pure form; an energy so tremendous that mortal man is fused into disruption by it. . . . But although the sight of the Divine Father blasts mortals as with fire, the Divine Son comes familiarly among them and can be invoked by the appropriate rites—Bacchanalia in the case of the Son of Zeus and the Eucharist in the case of the Son of Jehovah. Thus we see that there is a lower form of manifestation, which "shows us the Father," but that this rite owes its validity solely to the fact that it derives its Illuminating Intelligence, its Inner Robe of Glory, from the Father, Chokmah.[4]

Binah, heading the opposite pillar and representing at the same time the other side of Chokmah, is termed "Severity" by Fortune although other interpretations give her as "Understanding." She is, however, the Mother who, like Nature itself, is capable of both storm and tranquility, of death and life. She can be compared to Shakti, whose destructive side is Kali wearing a garland of severed heads about her neck, and who embodies the great truth that we must not cling to creation nor shrink from what seems to be destruction. Binah receives the force of Chokmah, while she herself is the creator of form.

Fortune knew where she stood in regard to symbolic sex. She knew that the interlocked figures of the Hindu Shiva and Shakti are sacramental representations of the pure union of wisdom and compassion, and gave excellent practical advice.

Chokmah and Binah, then, represent essential maleness and femaleness in their creative aspects. They are not phallic images as such, but in them is the root of all life-force. We shall never understand the deeper aspects of esotericism unless we realise what phallicism really means. It most emphatically does not mean the orgies in the temples of Aphrodite that disgraced the decadence of the pagan faiths of the ancients and brought about their downfall; it means that everything rests upon the principle of the stimulation of the inert yet all-potential by the dynamic principle which derives its energy direct from the source of all energy. In this concept lie tremendous keys of knowledge; it is one of the most important points in the Mysteries. It is obvious that sex represents one aspect of this factor; it is equally obvious that there are many other applications of it which are not sexual. We must not allow any preconceived concept of what constitutes sex, or a conventional attitude towards this great and vital subject, to frighten us away from the great principle of the stimulation or fecundation of the inert all-potential by the active principle. Whosoever is thus inhibited is unfit for the Mysteries, over whose portal was written the words, "Know thyself."

Such knowledge does not lead to impurity, for impurity implies a loss of control that permits forces to override the bounds that Nature has set them. Whoso has no control of his own instincts and passions is no more fitted for the Mysteries than he who inhibits and dissociates them. Let it be clearly realised, however, that the Mysteries do not teach asceticism or celibacy as a requirement of achievement, because they do not regard spirit and matter as an unreconcilable pair of antinomies, but rather as different levels of the same thing. Purity does not consist in emasculation, but in keeping the different forces to their proper levels and in their proper place, and not allowing one to invade another. It teaches that frigidity and impotence are just as much imperfections, and therefore pathologies of sex, as is uncontrolled lust that destroys its object and debases itself.[5]

The other sephiroth of the Tree are defined at length in Dion Fortune's book, *The Mystical Qabalah*. But before leaving the Tree itself, undoubtedly Fortune would want mention made of the two strange and interesting stages in the middle pillar—Tiphareth and Daath. Perhaps this is the moment to follow Fortune's advice and insert ourselves backward into the Tree so that the middle pillar becomes the spine. The two stages are then states of our own consciousness.

Tiphareth is Beauty—the extraordinary clarity and luminosity of the first sight of God. It is the reflected radiance of Enlightenment and it marks the turning point of one's life. It is also the center of equilibrium of the whole Tree, as it is in the middle of the central pillar. According to the Qabalah it is the point where force is transmuted into form.

Because of its unique properties and position, the ancient Qabalists called the six sephiroth around it Adam Kadmon, the archetypal man; Tiphareth, the first moment of realization, is the king of these six.

In her description of Tiphareth, Fortune tells us:

The four Sephiroth below Tiphareth represent the personality or lower self; the four Sephiroth above Tiphareth are the Individuality, or higher self, and Kether is the Divine Spark, or nucleus of manifestation.

Tiphareth, therefore, must never be regarded as an isolated factor, but as a link, a focussing-point, a centre of transition or transmutation. The central pillar is always concerned with consciousness. The two side pillars with the different modes of the operation of force on the different levels.[6]

The other, even higher, stage of realization is Daath, pure Knowledge. Daath is not so much a definite branch of the Tree, as an impression of the Tree taken as a whole. It is unique Knowledge, of which Tiphareth is the reflection. Fortune says little about Daath. She points out to students of Kundalini, however, that Kether, Daath, and Tiphareth are in line in the middle pillar, or spine of man, and that Kundalini is coiled in Yesod, immediately below them in the middle pillar.

As Dion Fortune grew older, her style of life showed some eccentricity. Her house in Bayswater contained a number of rooms dedicated to particular aspects of the esoteric Mysteries and her Fraternity had a Lodge in Glastonbury, a place that she regarded as a center of energy. She herself, according to Kenneth Grant,

. . . wore rich jewels beneath a flowing cloak, and, on the rare occasions when she went out, a black broad brimmed hat from which her sun-glinting hair sometimes strayed and fluffed about her head like a golden nimbus. Her personality contained more than a streak of exhibitionism, strongly reminiscent of Crowley, and towards the end of her life she collected about her an odd assortment of talismans and magical impedimenta; she burned strange perfumes in curiously chased basins of glittering metals. Her afternoon stroll in Hyde Park was undertaken in the voluminous cloak which recalled the advertisement for Sandeman's Port. She describes the heroine of *Moon Magic* [one of her novels] as similarly dressed as she paces the misty Thames embankment . . . she imagined that she passed unnoticed on these casual strolls![7]

But when the war came in 1939, Fortune's personality altered and she threw herself into organizations of all sorts and seemed to relish contacts of the most humdrum kind with ordinary people. Her death in 1946 from a severe illness came when she was still a relatively young and vigorous woman.

Since then her teachings have gained impetus and she now has a large following, particularly among the young. Whatever secrets her advice contained within her Fraternity, her books are open, lively, and pungent, and treat magic with both respect and common sense.

Her counsel was always practical. On Qabalistic meditation, for instance, she said:

There are some psychologists who will tell us that the Angels of the Qabalists and the Gods and Manus of other systems are our own repressed complexes; there are others with less limited outlook who will tell us that these Divine beings are the latent capacities of our own higher selves. To the devotional mystic this is not a point of any great moment; he gets his results, and that is all he cares about; but the philosophical mystic, in other words the occultist, thinks the matter out and arrives at certain conclusions. These conclusions, however, can only be understood when we know what we mean by reality and have a clear line of demarcation between the subjective and the objective. Anyone who is trained in philosophical method knows that this is asking for a good deal.

The Indian systems of metaphysics have most elaborate and intricate systems of philosophy which attempt to define these ideas and render them thinkable; and though generations of seers have given their lives to the task, the concepts still remain so abstract that it is only after a long course of discipline, called Yoga in the East, that the mind is able to apprehend them at all.[8]

Although Indian philosophy *is* hard to grasp, Fortune is somewhat unfair to the Yoga of the Hindus from which she herself took many ideas—particularly that of the *chakras,* the zones of psychic energy within the body, which she related to the endocrine system of man's anatomy. She goes on to say, however, that the Qabalist goes to work in a different way from the Hindu.

He does not attempt to make the mind rise up on the wings of metaphysics into the rarefied air of abstract reality; he formulates a concrete system that the eye can see, and lets it represent the abstract reality that no untrained human mind can grasp.

There are a great many symbols which are used as objects of meditation; the Cross in Christendom; the God-forms in the Egyptian system; phallic symbols in other faiths. These symbols are used by the uninitiated as a means of concentrating the mind and introducing into it certain thoughts, calling up certain associated ideas, and stimulating certain feelings. The initiate, however, uses a symbol-system differently; he uses it as an algebra by means of which he will read the secrets of unknown potencies; in other words, he uses the symbol as a means of guiding thought out into the Unseen and Incomprehensible.

And how does he do this? He does it by using a composite symbol; a symbol that is an unattached unit would not serve his purpose. In contemplating such a composite symbol as the Tree of Life he observes that there are definite relations between its parts. There are some parts of which he knows something; there are others of which he can intuit something, or, more crudely, make a guess, reasoning from first principles. The mind leaps from one known to another known and in so doing traverses certain distances, metaphorically speaking; it is like a traveller in the desert who knows the situation of two oases and makes a forced march between them. He would never have dared to push out into the desert from the first oasis if he had not known the location of the second; but at the end of his journey he not only knows much more about the characteristics of the second oasis, but he has also observed the country lying between them. Thus, making forced marches from oasis to oasis, backwards and forwards across the desert, he gradually explores it; nevertheless, the desert is incapable of supporting life.

So it is with the Qabalistic system of notation. The things it renders are unthinkable—and yet the mind, tracking from symbol to symbol, manages to think about them; and although we have to be content to see in a glass darkly, yet we have every reason to hope that ultimately we shall see face to face and know even as we are known; for the human mind grows by exercise, and that which was at first as unthinkable as mathematics to the child who cannot manage his sums, finally comes within the range of our realisation. By thinking about a thing, we build concepts of it.[9]

Fortune was very keen to impress on her students that *every* situation in life is a learning situation. If one thinks about this, it becomes apparent that life, seen in this way, is endlessly rewarding and invigorating. It gives back its own newness to the routine-stale mind, reminding one of the fact that we can only guess and can never actually know what the next minute will contain.

But although Fortune encouraged her students in every form of new thinking, at the same time she cautioned them sharply against psychic quackery:

... Indiscriminate dabbling in seances, fortune-telling, psychism, and suchlike is classified as grey under our definition, because it takes no account of anything save personal desires, and never asks itself what may be the spiritual quality of what it is doing. No obvious evil being immediately forthcoming, and in fact a plentiful amount of specious piousness being very much in evidence—a form of piousness wherein God is called upon to bless what is being done, but is never asked whether it is according to His will—it is taken for granted that what is afoot is a harmless entertainment, or even actively edifying as tending to raise the mind above materialism, thus reinforcing faith; the after-effects are not considered, and experience shows that the after-effects are far-reaching, and though they may not necessarily involve moral deterioration in persons of naturally wholesome character—and we must acquit them of that charge so often brought—they do cause a marked deterioration in the quality of the mind, and especially of the capacity for logic and judgement. Any form of promiscuous psychic or supernormal dabbling is definitely undesirable, in my opinion, and unfits the person who indulges in it for serious work.[10]

Use of the Tarot divination cards was not included in this warning, for Fortune had a profound respect for the Tarot representations. Once more, an unprejudiced mind is a great help when it comes to taking a proper look at what is regarded by many people as sheer superstition. The Tarot cards, in fact, do seem to represent the symbols of the Tree and their use is certainly of some help in visualizing the sephiroth. As for their fortune-telling aspect, properly studied they seem to have much the same relation to prophecy as the hexagrams of the I Ching—a book of divination edited by Confucius. The great merit of the I Ching is that it does not so much forecast the future as give advice on the right way to behave in the present. The Tarot cards, too, give one the sense of advice along noble lines when they are studied properly.

Fortune's use of the Tarot was fundamental to her understanding of the Tree, and equaled her total belief in astrology.

The Tree of Life, astrology, and the Tarot are not three mystical systems, but three aspects of one and the same system, and each is unintelligible without the others. It is only when we study astrology on the basis of the Tree that we have a philosophical system; equally does this apply to the Tarot system of divination, and the Tarot itself, with its comprehensive interpretations, gives the key to the Tree as applied to human life.

All systems of divination and all systems of practical magic find their principles and philosophy based upon the Tree; whoever tries to use them without this key is like the foolhardy person who has a pharmacopia of patent medicines and doses himself and his friends according to the descriptions given in the advertisements, wherein backache includes every disease which does not cause pain in front. The initiate who knows his Tree is like the scientific physician who understands the principles of physiology and the chemistry of drugs, and prescribes accordingly.[11]

Fortune died convinced that the Qabalah would become the true Yoga of the West. She saw that a religion that is all theory and welfare and that lacks the essential practices of yoga and meditation is impoverished and limited. She constantly stressed the need for yoga in Christianity, correctly foreseeing that without its enriching life, more and more people would take up Eastern methods.

As yet the Qabalah has not been accepted to the same extent as Eastern yoga, which is in the very midst of undergoing its transplant now. But there can surely be no doubt that for those who follow the occult path the Tree offers a unique key to understanding *all* yogas, and is itself a way for many to follow.

Rudolf Steiner
1861–1925

When Rudolf Steiner was a boy, growing up in a remote region of the Carpathian mountains, he became strangely aware of the presence of living beings who seemed invisible to the eyes of others. Some solitary children do develop an inner world of fantasy but Steiner's world seems to have been one of direct perception rather than of imagination, for he was a realistic boy, gifted with an exact sense of order and a talent for mathematics.

To a child who is sensitive to natural beauty and who has the luck to be brought up in country surroundings, the heart and the mind are constantly spoken to by such events as sunlight filtering through great forest trees, by the wind setting everything in motion, by soft grass and clear moonlight. Such a child becomes deeply aware of stillness and movement, of silence and sound, of light and darkness in a way that the child who lives with street lights and constant traffic can never be.

An intense inner life may develop in the country child. He may feel, more profoundly than he can ever describe, a sense of wonder and awe; of being in touch with the *essence* of things, which is infinitely greater than the objects which confront his eye. Oddly enough, this is not the high-road to fantasy and unreality—this particular way of awareness of things in their thing*ness* usually leads to a good grasp of practical issues, for intuitive awareness develops the capacity to be at one with what exists. To sense things in their beingness (Buddhists call it Suchness) is the mark of the mystic.

Steiner both was and was not such a mystic. On the one hand he was profoundly aware of and awed by the beauty around him: on the other, his intuitions assumed concrete form and he *saw*, with what he terms "clairvoyant perception," the spiritual beings at work creating this beauty.

Like many of us, Steiner had to lead a double life. He found himself divided between the spiritual world of creation and harmony on the one hand, and the everyday world of hard work and deprivations on the other. He was the eldest child of a stationmaster employed by the South Austrian railway. The family was above the poverty line, but not much. As well as walking several miles to school every day, the young Rudolf was expected to help in all sorts of ways with the household. From the age of fifteen, he supported himself at school by giving lessons to other pupils. This left little time for imaginative fantasy to rule and Steiner would assert that it never did. He always averred that what he saw were facts about life that other people did not see, but that they could were they to develop the right organs of perception.

One of the advantages of a railway background was that from an early age Steiner was fascinated by technology. He pored over timetables, learned about steam engines, and became wholly absorbed in the way machines worked. As well, when he was eight, he was allowed to borrow a geometry book from school and this opened a new door in his mind. For weeks at a time, his thoughts would be filled with shapes and the similarities between them. Again and again he stretched his mind over the question of where parallel lines actually meet. When he looked back at his childhood, Steiner believed that it was in geometry that he first experienced the conscious satisfaction of living entirely from the mind, envisaging the problems without impressions on the external eye.

This pleasure in geometry eventually brought him to realize that

> the objects and occurrences which the senses perceive are in space. But, just as this space is outside of man, so there exists also within man a sort of soul-space which is the arena of spiritual realities and occurrences.[1]

In his thoughts, he could see not only the straightforward representations or mind-pictures that we use all the time, but he also saw that the concepts man arrives at derived from these mind-pictures form a different level of thought altogether. He explains this with the example of a cow. If asked to think of a cow, each one of us will visualize a different cow based on our individual experience. But if asked to explain the concept, cow—what a cow is—we will all give the same explanation. The concept is what we all hold in common and it is an area in the mind that Steiner saw as unique to man and as having knowledge in it that leads beyond man.

He came to believe that all concepts have their origins in spiritual Beings. He took the view, first stated in slightly different form by Plato, that each quality—love, goodness, mercy, etc.—has its archetype (its pure original) in a world beyond man, a world from which man has severed himself through "the Fall." Steiner saw the archetypes as actual Beings radiating their qualities to earth, of which man catches the shadow as the concept in his mind.

This is the key to Steiner's thought. The world is spiritual and everything has arisen from a spiritual source. For example, it is not the brain that creates thinking, but Thinking that creates the brain.

It was through the realization that "here one is permitted to know something which the mind alone, through its own power, experiences"[2] that Steiner was able, even as a child, to reconcile the two worlds in which he lived —the ordinary outer world and the inner world of spiritual Beings who seemed to be creating his own thoughts. But he spoke to nobody about his inner world although the sense of it grew stronger as he grew up until at last he realized he *must* speak about it.

By the time he actually came to do so, he had spent some twenty years in ardent study and investigation in order to build the bridge between spirit and matter, between his inner experiences and the world of ordinary physical senses. His researches had taken him, among other investigations, to the mysterious Emerald Tablet of Hermes Trismegistus. References to this tablet, which is said to have been engraved by Hermes with Phoenician characters and discovered in his dead hand by Alexander the Great in a cave-tomb, abound throughout esoteric Western history. Societies, such as the Rosicrucians, of which Steiner was an active member, look upon the Emerald or Hermetic Tablet as the key to the transformation of man's knowledge of natural laws into the supersensible knowledge of the spiritual laws of the universe, because the opening sentence of the Emerald Tablet reads: "That which is above is like that which is below and that which is below is like that which is above, in order to achieve the wonders of the one thing." In later life, Steiner was to see this statement as the basis of alchemy, and to link it with the work of other alchemical philosophers, such as Jacob Boehme.

During the years of this inner search, Steiner's outer life progressed, but only by dint of hard work and struggle. First he worked his way through the Technical University in Vienna, always financially dependent on his own efforts at teaching. Then, when he had graduated in mathematics and science, a great opportunity came to him. He was asked to edit the scientific writings of Goethe for the new Kürschner edition. He had already seen in Goethe a mind that was deeply akin to his own, and now he was able to immerse himself in the two worlds that Goethe, too, had discovered. For Goethe had spent years in setting down very exact observations of natural phenomena, such as plants and birds, clouds and colors. From all this, Goethe also had drawn forth the Platonic vision already referred to, that behind every natural object is an archetype—an "Idea" of it—existing in a higher world.

This corresponded very closely to Steiner's own perceptions. It may have needed the encouragement of Goethe's thought to bring forth from Steiner his own outline of the universe, but at last the time came when he was able to produce it in all its aspects. He called it Spiritual Science, or Anthroposophy (a name taken from two Greek words meaning *man* and *wisdom*).

His first publication in 1894, *The Philosophy of Freedom* (now translated as *The Philosophy of Spiritual Activity*), stands out from all his other works. Without reference to his own clairvoyant perceptions, it seeks to define, entirely on its own merit, the relationship between the natural world about us, the inner world of thoughts, and the activity of "thinking" or reflection that brings the first two together in our consciousness as an actual experience. It is this activity that leads to freedom, he said, and it is the one activity that we fail to notice. We notice the idea that results from the action and we appropriate it as our own. Thus we seem to have our own "world of thoughts" and we fail to realize that thoughts are the products of an activity that precedes them. It is this activity that links the perception and the concept, and without it we would never see relationships between things. Steiner regards thinking as the road to freedom because it is the only objective instrument of knowledge we have. Before any ideas can be formed at all, the thinking process must be there. If we start from any assumption, even one such as "this is difficult to understand," for instance, we have already gone past the thinking stage and reached its product, the thought. Thinking comes even before the distinction between subject and object, and this led Steiner to point out that thinking actually produces the ideas of inner and outer, I and you, just as it produces all other concepts.

So for Steiner, the real starting point for knowledge and understanding was not the idea but the process of recognition and thinking by which the idea arrives. He believed that this process is the vehicle by which higher powers work within us and that if we can bring the mind back to that state of pure thinking before the concept is formed, we will develop in ourselves a freedom to see the real nature of existence (Freedom from the known is one of Krishnamurti's great themes too, and, although his conclusions are very different, he too believes it is essential to be able to drop the world of concepts—the world called *maya* by the Hindus).

The audience that received Steiner's speculations was not an entirely sympathetic one. Years in Weimar working at the Goethe archives had given him a wide circle of friends among philosophers, artists, and writers, for

Weimar was, at the turn of the century, a vital center for modern thought. But *The Philosophy of Freedom* was written just after Steiner's Weimar period was over, when he was editing a literary magazine in Berlin, and the great thinkers of the day failed to respond to the book.

Steiner's main supporters came from the Theosophical Society, of which he was a highly respected member. A very brief outline of their beliefs is given on page 63, and when he became head of the German branch of the Theosophists in 1902, Steiner added his own cosmology to theirs. There was some suggestion at this point that he hoped to take over the Theosophical Society. It is a fact that he adopted the curious policy of joining another society in 1906, The Order of the Temple of the Orient, which was known to practice sexual magic, and he even went as far as running one of its lodges, called Mysteria Mystica Aeterna, while saying all the time that he never intended to work in the spirit of such a society.

Despite his critics, for several years, however, his reputation remained high among Theosophists, especially with the publication of his book, *Theosophy*, which was followed later by *Knowledge of Higher Worlds and Its Attainment* and then by *Occult Science*. This last contains his whole message based on his clairvoyant observation.

Man, he believed, is comprised of three bodies or sheaths that have been developing since time began, for man is not the youngest species on earth but the oldest —the whole of evolution has contained evolving man in all his myriad forms. Only the rocks, the mineral element, has not contained any aspect of man's growth. But man as fish was succeeded by man as vertebrate animal and so on up to the present. In each aspect of man's existence, there was an increase in consciousness, a growing away from the plant world towards the spiritual. As for the multitude of fish and animals who stayed as they were and are with us today, they failed to evolve into man because they could not detach themselves from their fishy or animal nature. They became bogged down in fishiness or animalness (as it must be admitted we see many humans often immersed in an opaque sort of humanity).

Given the conundrum of man as he is, and the fact that *he can reflect upon his own consciousness*—an ability which nothing in nature seems to demand—such a theory of psychological evolution is not without a plausible appeal. Steiner sees two forces perpetually at work in all evolution: the force that holds back, prevents, and ultimately destroys, and which comes from the earth itself; and a force from *outside the earth* that lifts the mind towards higher and higher consciousness and freedom, and which is reflected in actual physiological processes. He worked out the origin of these two forces from his clairvoyant observations and the very precise details are contained in the books already mentioned.

Thus man has arrived and is as he is because of an immensely long evolution. Traces of this remain within him—the fetus that passes through the stages of evolution in the womb, for instance—and the mind, which Steiner believes bears memory traces from other eons. For in his philosophy, each man is not newly minted on the day he was born. He has reincarnated as a spiritual entity in all the ages of evolution. Death is not the final end of man but a time for rest, just as a day ends in sleep.

The three bodies or sheaths in which man reincarnates are of vital importance to Steiner's theories. The idea of them does not originate with him but it is he who has worked out in tremendous detail and with the help of technology, how they interact and what roles they play.

The first is the physical, earthly body, about which a

good deal has been discovered by modern science. In Steiner's terms it is the material vehicle for the others.

The second is the etheric body. It is here that we begin to pull back a bit, if we are honest. For nobody except a clairvoyant has actually seen an etheric body. What is it? Steiner says it is the force of life that keeps the organism together and on its feet, as it were. None of our organs or limbs have a life of their own. Yet they remain together as a compact body and perform actions. When the etheric force leaves the body, the body dies and disintegrates. The words *etheric body* are perhaps misleading but in a sense it can be thought of as something semiphysical, like gas or atmosphere that surrounds the physical body as a cloud.

"To the investigator of spiritual life," says Steiner,

> . . . this matter presents itself in the following manner. The ether-body is for him not merely a product of the materials and forces of the physical body, but a real independent entity which first calls forth these physical materials and forces into life. . . . In order to see this body, to perceive it in another being, one requires the awakened "spiritual eye." Without this, its existence can be accepted as a fact on logical grounds; but one can see it with the spiritual eye as one sees color with the physical eye.[3]

People who speak of etheric bodies have often been laughed at but the most modern research is beginning to reveal much evidence pointing to just this condition. Steiner and his pupils often described it as an aura surrounding the physical body, which assumed precise colors according to the health of the individual. Now, Russian research has revealed that man's physical body does send out electromagnetic waves that *might* be seen with the naked eye. Most people's eyesight stops just short of these wavelengths but a Cambridge biologist, who made an eye sensitizer out of goggles with hollow lenses that he filled with a particular transparent dye, saw auras clearly. He reported that they are not blown about by air, but that they do respond to a magnet held close to the skin. They are composed of two layers, the outer one misty and the inner one bright, and they extend farthest from bodily projections such as fingers and nose.

But a Russian scientist, Kirlian, has gone even further and produced not only a machine that generates high-frequency electrical fields, but also an optical viewer which makes it possible to use the eye directly without film or dye. The result, although still controversial, is that anything living put within the high-frequency discharge, glows and sparkles with light and color. But most significant of all, the patterns and color (revealed, for instance, in a finger) change according to the mood and health of the subject. Lyall Watson, who reports the whole experiment in *Supernature*, says that "a freshly picked leaf shines with an internal light that streams out through its pores in beams that gradually flick out one by one as it dies. Leaves taken from plants of the same species show similar jewelled patterns, but if one of the plants is diseased, the pattern in its leaf is entirely different."

So it is possible that when Steiner "saw" the etheric bodies of people, he did so with his ordinary eye, for, as Lyall Watson points out,

... the range of human sensitivity is quite wide; some people hear sounds that to others are supersonic, and some people see wavelengths that to others are invisible. Those who claim to be able to see an aura surrounding living things could be supersensitive at the infra-red end of the spectrum. Waves of this length are beyond the capability of the cone-shaped cells in our retina, which appreciate visible colors, but they may be within the range of the rod-shaped cells that are more sensitive to low light intensities.[4]

But no activity of the ordinary senses can see the third of Steiner's bodies or sheaths, which is man's astral body. All members of living creation, including plants, have an etheric body or they would disintegrate, but only animals and man have an astral body, which is the inner life of consciousness, said Steiner. Thinking, feeling, and willing are the activities of the astral body and it is here that there is a qualitative difference from the other two. The physical and etheric bodies are essentially connected with matter. The etheric brings the physical body alive, Steiner thought, because it is drawn upwards and outwards by spiritual influences working from the circumference of the universe. But when we get to the astral "thinking" plane of a person's organism, those spiritual influences are revealed as Beings:

> When we go on to speak of the "astral world," we advance, according to the perceptions of Inspired Consciousness, from the influences from the World-Circumference to the spiritual Beings who reveal themselves in these influences—just as the materials of the Earth reveal their nature in the forces that go outward from the Earth. We speak of definite spiritual Beings working from the universal spaces, just as we speak of the stars and constellations when with the eyes of sense we look into the Heavens at night-time.[5]

Since we all seem to be able to think, we can go along with Steiner when he includes consciousness and all its functions as part of the human organism, and perhaps it helps us to realize how we are made up when it is given a particular name—"astral"—and singled out for special attention. But it is a step further to "see" the Beings of whom our thoughts are reflections, or shadows, and not everybody will agree that it is a step towards enlightenment.

Fourthly, Steiner includes the organizer and harmonizer of the three bodies, the essential "I" or "Ego." In the pure feeling of "I," Steiner sees the spirit and in his definitions he calls the astral body the Soul and the "I" the Spirit. Other sages in this book, particularly Ramana Maharshi, have believed in the great spiritual importance of attention to the feeling of "I."

Perhaps Steiner's universe-analysis can be better understood if it is turned round. Instead of building up from the mineral body to spiritual outer-space Beings, as he always tends to do in his books, it may be easier to start from those Beings and work downward, because really the basis for all his thought was the Whole that becomes particularized. If we bear in mind that Steiner is inclined to attribute spiritual bodies to *everything* as he works out his hierarchy, we will begin to understand how it happens that his universe is so populated by Beings and Entities and Folk-Souls, etc., rather than by planes of experience.

It must not be thought that Steiner wanted to be considered in any way unique because he was able to "see" what others couldn't. All the accounts of his life bear witness to a genuine sincerity and a desire to help others discover what he had found out through occult powers. He devised a whole series of graded exercises for helping a clairvoyant eye to open and he was emphatic that before any esoteric work took place at all there should be a groundwork of moral preparation—three steps of moral progress for every step of spiritual progress.

Exercises to develop thought, will, equanimity, positiveness, and open-mindedness abound in his book, *Occult Science*—most of them very sensible indeed, their origin lying in the Buddha's Eightfold Path. One exercise in particular—at the end of the day reliving one's activities as though watching somebody else doing them —is such an eye-opener that perhaps it should become standard practice. He also emphasized that one should *never* judge other people's progress (the opposite to Gurdjieff who used to ask for reports) or indeed judge people at all, but should always look for their potential best and attune oneself in a sympathetic way towards this.

The more esoteric exercises to do with the unfolding of the *chakras* (a Hindu term meaning psychic centers in the body) are given by teachers at the Steiner centers. So, too, are other exercises designed to bring alive the memory of past existences. It is in this sort of connection that Steiner could certainly be accused of romantic fantasy by his critics. For he wrote about and encouraged belief in the lost continents of Atlantis and Lemuria, and many people were under the impression that they remembered incarnations in these mythical places.

Occult waters can become very muddy indeed, but although one may look impatiently at some of Steiner's more splashy plunges into occult "fact," there is no doubt that within his own character he had plenty of integrity and independence. Too much of the latter, in fact, for some of the leaders of the Theosophical Society who were not very happy about the way the German branch was developing. In return, Steiner, who was deeply Christ-centered, did not think much of the adoption by Annie Besant of Krishnamurti as the new Christ. Various other differences occurred—one in particular was connected with Marie von Sivers, a Baltic Russian whom Steiner married and who had a very strong influence on his life. An impassioned actress, intensely involved with speech and drama, she encouraged Steiner to set forth his ideas in dramatic form, and in fact to translate his beliefs into art in all its expressions. Thus, when the more influential members of the Theosophical Society arrived in Berlin one year for their annual congress, they were taken aback to find the lecture halls bedecked in vivid paintings and the subject matter containing poetry and drama

(Marie von Sivers was playing Demeter) instead of the program of lectures they were more used to. A rift arose immediately and, in 1912, Steiner disassociated himself from Theosophy.

Under his own flag of Anthroposophy Steiner was now free to put into practice everything that he believed in. He gave lecture courses and began to attract professionals from a number of fields—medicine, ecology, and physics, and also from the arts and education. By 1920, the need for a center for all his work had brought into being the Goetheanum at Dornach in Switzerland, a remarkable building designed architecturally to embody the spiritual secrets of the universe and made of the same combination of woods as violins so that it would vibrate with all the arts. Steiner related each of the arts to man's bodies— i.e., architecture reflects the physical body, sculpture the etheric body, painting the astral body, music the Ego or Spirit, poetry a further body, the Spirit-Self, and Eurhythmy (a particular art of movement developed by Marie von Sivers) yet a higher body, the Life-Spirit.

Alas, the beautiful Goetheanum was set on fire and burned to the ground by Steiner's enemies—among whom were theologians and scientists, politicians and trade-union officials. People were afraid of "Jewish-Bolshevik" movements at that time and any occult group was regarded with great suspicion in case it harbored political rebels. As well, Steiner himself was regarded as a suspect character, for not only was he known to be sympathetic to Jews but he was also accused of having weakened Germany's chances during the war by mesmerizing General von Moltke, who occupied a high position, and rendering him militarily incompetent. Steiner vigorously denied this but the accusation stuck.

A concrete Goetheanum was built to replace the wooden one and activities went on as before. But two years later, Steiner was taken seriously ill and shortly afterward, in March, 1925, he died.

Many of Steiner's discoveries, so scorned by the conventional of his day, are now coming into fashion in the light of new understanding. His followers, who have patiently worked to promote his ideas, are now seeing results. In such fields for instance, as biodynamic soil cultivation, homeopathic medicine, and education for both the normal and the mentally retarded, Steiner's ideas are now receiving real consideration, although others may have developed the techniques.

His work in the field of organic farming, for instance, involved an immense study of plants and their properties and he opened up new areas for the unprejudiced to explore with his belief that the great polarities of earth beneath our feet and cosmos above and about us are the factors behind all growth. He saw the forces of the earth (gravity and electricity) as pulling the seed into the earth itself, while the spiritual forces of the cosmos pull the seed outwards towards the sky. Thus it is these two influences of earth and heaven that create the metamorphosis of change, the process of growth. This, perhaps, may not be news to any of us, but the way in which Steiner worked out the intricate details of the relationship between earth and heaven may be.

Suppose that we wish to hold back in the root-nature of a plant that which would otherwise tend upward through the stem and leaf. No doubt this is not so important in our present earthly epoch, for through various conditions we have already fixed the different species of plants. In former epochs—notably in primeval epochs—it was different. At that time it was still possible quite easily to transform one plant into another; hence it was very important to know these things. Today, too, it is important if we wish to find what conditions are favorable to one plant or another.

What do we then need to consider? How must we look at a plant when we desire the cosmic forces not to shoot upward into the blossoming and fruiting process but to remain below? Suppose we want the stem and leaf-formation to be held back in the root. What must we then do? We must put such a plant into a sandy soil, for in silicious soil the cosmic is held back; it is actually "caught." Take the potato, for example. With the potato this end must be attained. The blossoming process must be kept below. For the potato is a stem-and-leaf-formation down in the region of the root. The leaf and stem-forming process is held back, retained in the potato itself. The potato is not a root, it is a stem-formation held back. We must therefore bring it into a sandy soil. Otherwise we shall not succeed in having the cosmic force retained in the potato.

This, therefore, is the ABC for our judgement of plant-growth. We must always be able to say, what in the plant is cosmic, and what is terrestrial or earthly. How can we adapt the soil of the earth, by its special consistency, as it were to densify the cosmic and thereby hold it back more in the root and leaf? Or again, how can we thin it out so that it is drawn upward in a dilute condition, right up into the flowers, giving them color—or into the fruit-forming process, permeating the fruit with a fine and delicate taste? For if you have apricots or plums with a fine taste—this taste, just like the color of the fruits, is the cosmic quality which has been carried upward, right into the fruit. In the apple you are eating Jupiter, in the plum you are actually eating Saturn.[6]

Steiner believed that the earth, after its evolvement through planetary phases, was still closely linked to certain planets. In particular, the moon, he thought, had a powerful effect on conditions and such a process as seeding should be done by the light of the full moon:

With the Moon's rays the whole reflected Cosmos comes on to Earth. All influences that pour on to the Moon are rayed back again. Thus the whole starry Heavens—though we may not be able to prove it by the customary physical methods of today—are in a sense rayed back on to the Earth by the Moon. It is indeed a strong and powerfully organising cosmic force which the Moon rays down into the plant, so that the seeding process of the plant may also be assisted; so that the force of *growth* may be *enhanced* into the force of *reproduction*.[7]

But biodynamic farming is most famous for the humus with which the crops are manured. Special preparations were put into the compost heap according to time and season. They were made from certain plants that were enveloped in a covering of animal organs (bladder and intestines) for these were thought to lift the forces of the growing crops to a higher and more etheric activity. Another preparation, made from cow manure and quartz crystals packed and matured in a cow horn, was believed to help the crop plant to become "a citizen of the earth" and in time to find its true place in the sphere of the sun.

In medicine, as in ecology, Steiner related every aspect to the polarity of earth and cosmos, of earthly gravitation and the levitating force of the spiritual cosmos that is expressed in upright carriage and in the circulation of the blood. Each group of organs, he believed, has its own balance to maintain between material and spiritual. For instance, if the kidneys, organs of excretion and therefore closely connected with the earth, are dominated too powerfully by the astral body an inflammation (disproportionate amounts of astral and ego tend to bring about inflammation) such as nephritis may develop.

So as well as a physical diagnosis there must be a spiritual one. When it is made, the cure must then reflect it. As well as a homeopathic medicine, the patient must be helped psychologically to overcome the imbalance in his system. This two-way treatment of illness fits in very well with modern medicine, which nowadays is beginning to admit the links between mind and body.

Important as this work is, perhaps Steiner is best known to most of us for his excellent understanding of the educational needs of children. When he was a very young man and was first in Vienna, he earned a living by teaching. One boy in particular, who was thought by his parents to be mentally deficient, was so helped by Steiner that he was able to go to school and to a university. Years of close contact with this boy and with his other pupils helped Steiner become conscious of the way children develop, and one of his greatest projects was the founding of schools for both normal and mentally handicapped children where their natural growth could take place.

Now, over 40,000 normal pupils attend the Waldorf schools all over the world. The schools are coeducational and unstreamed and their methods are based on Steiner's "spiritual research." He believed that each one of us is an eternal spirit that incarnates from time to time in a body and the whole process of childhood is the gradual assuming of this body. First the child grows into the digestive and metabolic functions; then, after the change of teeth, he grows into the rhythms of the heart and lungs; finally he grows into the nerves and the senses. Thus Steiner saw childhood as three seven-year stages that approximate to the three functions of the astral body—willing, feeling, and thinking—and he carefully planned his curriculum accordingly.

The atmosphere of a Steiner school is one of trust and devotion. The personal relationship between teacher and child is thought to be all-important and young children stay with one teacher for several years. Through gentleness and idealism, the teachers are able to bring alive in their pupils a sense of wonder and of fascination with the world, and a love of science and the arts.

There is a reaction today, particularly among the

young, against a tailoring of life to fit formal patterns, against domination by machines, and against the dehumanizing effects of living in large cities. Rudolf Steiner's work appeals strongly to those who want to live organically from within outward, and to live in harmony with the natural world.

He appeals as well to those to whom it is important to be part of a spiritual plan, to whom memories of past incarnations bring a heightened sense of living, and to whom messages received through supersensible means are of great significance.

But a direct mystic parts company with an occultist such as Rudolf Steiner. The Chinese speak of the world as "the ten thousand things." Steiner has added at least another ten thousand when one takes into account all the gnome-spirits and fairy-spirits at work in and on the earth as well as the Beings in the universe. But to the mystic, it is really the *un*manifest, that which has no entity and is beyond name and form which concerns him, and which, strangely, Steiner was silent about. Nevertheless, the human occupants of this world, mystics and all, owe a considerable debt of gratitude to a man who took so much trouble to promote the good of mankind and who cared so intensely about its spiritual welfare.

276

References

1   Dion Fortune, *The Esoteric Orders and their Work* (London: Rider & Co.), p. 77.
2   Evelyn Underhill, *Mysticism* (London: Methuen & Co. Ltd.), p. 157.
3   Ibid., p. 103.

Dion Fortune

1   Dion Fortune, *Psychic Self-Defense* (London: The Aquarian Press), p. 12.
2   Dion Fortune, *The Mystical Qabalah* (London: Ernest Benn Ltd.), pp. 67-68.
3   Ibid., pp. 111-114.
4   Ibid., p. 129.
5   Ibid., p. 149.
6   Ibid., p. 190.
7   Kenneth Grant, *The Magical Revival* (London: Frederick Muller Ltd.), p. 178.
8   Fortune, *The Mystical Qabalah*, p. 73.
9   Ibid., pp. 14, 16.
10   Dion Fortune, *Applied Magic* (London: The Aquarian Press), pp. 52-53.
11   Fortune, *The Mystical Qabalah*, p. 73.

Further Reading

Fortune, Dion, *Practical Occultism in Daily Life*, London: The Aquarian Press.

Fortune, Dion, *Through the Gates of Death*, London: The Aquarian Press.

Fortune, Dion, *The Cosmic Doctrine*, Helios Book Service Ltd.

Fortune, Dion, *The Secrets of Dr. Taverner*, Llewellyn Publications.

Fortune, Dion, *Sane Occultism*.

Rudolf Steiner

1 Rudolf Steiner, *The Course of My Life* (London and New York: Rudolf Steiner Press), p. 11.
2 Ibid., p. 12.
3 Rudolf Steiner, *Theosophy: An Introduction to the Supersensible Knowledge of the World and the Destinations of Man* (London and New York: Rudolf Steiner Press), p. 27.
4 Rudolf Steiner and Ita Wegman, *Fundamentals of Therapy: An Extension of the Art of Healing through Spiritual Knowledge* (London and New York: Rudolf Steiner Press), p. 18.
5 Lyall Watson, *Supernature* (Coronet Books, Hodder Paperbacks Ltd.), p. 143.
6 Rudolf Steiner, *Agriculture* (London: Bio-Dynamic Agricultural Association), p. 38.
7 Ibid., p. 109.

Further Reading

Steiner, Rudolf, *Knowldege of the Higher Worlds, How Is It Achieved?* London and New York: Rudolf Steiner Press.

Steiner, Rudolf, *Occult Science—An Outline*. London and New York: Rudolf Steiner Press.

Steiner, Rudolf, *The Case for Anthroposophy*. London and New York: Rudolf Steiner Press.

Steiner, Rudolf, *Spiritual Science and Medicine*. London and New York: Rudolf Steiner Press.

Steiner, Rudolf, *The Education of the Child in the Light of Anthroposophy*. London and New York: Rudolf Steiner Press.

9

The Seers

Douglas Harding works on the assumption that usually we think of ourselves as a "thing" located within our body wherever that happens to be at the moment, and particularly located within the head where we look out of eyes and speak out of mouths. But, says Harding, where is the actual firsthand evidence that this is so? In a secondhand way, we see other people behaving like this, but firsthand, do we? I cannot see my own head, says Harding, thus for all working purposes I do not have one. What takes the place of all that lives above my shirt buttons is everything that I actually *do* see—the scene around me. That scene, whatever it is, has replaced my head and taken away my feeling of being a confined and limited "I." Instead of my head there are just things as they are, and there is no "I" there to think about them or to judge them. That is liberation, insists Harding, for when my head is gone I am clear and empty of myself.

Seeing who you really are (not your head, but the scene around you) is his great theme, and he has devised many techniques to help people to perform this "simple" act. It is, in fact, simple but difficult and, when done, has rather the same effect as those eye and brain teasers—the pair of figures that alternate as one looks at them, one moment being two profiles, and the next, a vase. In Harding's seeing, however, the implications are far more profound.

Don Juan's seeing has some similarities to Harding's, for he notices that when he "stops the world" he is no longer identified with it and *sees* it without self-projection. That is not the way he puts it, for his language is remarkably vivid, fresh, and stimulating. "When a man learns to *see*," he says, "not a single thing he knows prevails."

Castaneda, who went to him originally for instruction in plant lore, was taught by him to *see*. Don Juan's techniques included getting Castaneda to *notice* things, first of all. Castaneda, like many of us, was so wrapped up in self-inspired dreams that he took the outside world for granted and paid it little real attention. By being made to notice it (by being told to talk to plants, for instance) he began to put his attention outside himself, and this caused the feeling of self to loosen up. The next step was to give up the concentrated attention on the object and to *see* it *without knowledge of it*. This was the real *seeing*, when all intellectual content of imagination and concept was dropped.

Don Juan is lovable, moving, and wise. Although his seeing bears some resemblance to Harding's, it is not talked about to the exclusion of everything else, and his techniques are laced with such practical wisdom that his seeing is only one of many good facets of his whole understanding.

Douglas Harding
1909–

Douglas Harding was born at Lowestoft in Suffolk, England, of parents who belonged to the Exclusive sect of the Plymouth Brethren—an ultrafundamentalist Christian body that, puritan and intolerant and scrupulous to a degree, forbids all unnecessary contact with the "world." Gradually he came to doubt, to question and explore, until, at twenty-one, while studying architecture at University College, London, he finally broke away from the Brethren. Disowned by his parents and relatives, he found himself alone, penniless, and jobless in the London of the slump.

His upbringing, though indeed narrow and bigoted (no newspapers, no novels, no theater or cinema, no music or art, no friends outside the Brethren's meetings, little laughter and much sense of sin) had nevertheless been loving and in its own odd way truly spiritual, and it left an ineradicable impression for which Harding remains

grateful. After some youthful tribulations and waverings, the whole effort of his subsequent life has been to regain, at quite another level and in quite another way, the religious certainty he lost when he lost the faith he had been brought up in. Though he qualified as an architect and practiced successfully in England and India (where he lived for eight years) he says that he never gave his mind to his profession. His concern instead has been to answer, without any reliance on outside authority —whether teachers or books or institutions—the great questions: "What or Who am I?" "What am I up to here?" "What is my true relation to others, to the world, and to God?" His book, *On Having No Head*, describes how, at the age of thirty-four, he came to "see clearly into his own Nature," thereby finding his own answer to all such questions. Only gradually did he discover that his "seeing" had much in common with the mystics, and in particular, he thinks, with Zen and Sufi masters. Encouraged by their writings, he has spent the second half of his life working out the implications and applications of his original insight and presenting his discoveries in writing and speech and—recently—in group work, involving a growing repertoire of nonverbal "games" or "workshop exercises."

For long he was entirely unsuccessful—alone once more, and quite unable to convey his message. After twenty years of talking and writing about "having no head," people still thought he was somewhat crazy or else speaking in riddles (many still do). They couldn't believe he meant exactly what he said. It was not until the early 1960s that he found himself actually sharing his experience with a few friends, whom he had encouraged to see for themselves what it's like being "first-person singular, present tense." Since then there has been a growth of "headlessness," particularly among young people, on both sides of the Atlantic. For the condition is catching, he says; anyone who sees it can *at once* show others quite independently of Harding (who took twenty years about it) and his work. The appeal is to the enquirer's own, direct, first-hand experience, for he is the sole authority on 'how it is where he is.' Accordingly, Harding has set up no sect or organization, and says he doesn't regard himself as any sort of guru. He and his friends claim that the in-seeing they enjoy and practice is, in any case, perfectly natural and nothing new. They say it is (though the language differs) central to all the great mystical traditions, where it has, however, been overlaid and often overlooked. But now, stripped bare of accumulated irrelevancies, they believe it has at last become so obvious and so accessible that it can be trusted to make its own way on its own merits, unburdened by personalities or mystification. Initiation into "headlessness" or "no-thingness" is free and immediate, and there are no strings attached to it.

Harding spends most of his time at Nacton in Suffolk, where he keeps open house for interested visitors. For a few weeks in the year, he travels in America and Europe conducting workshops and giving informal talks. He speaks, he insists, only for himself as 1st-person, because he is in no position to speak for you or me. Whether, when we look into ourselves, we find what he suggests, is for each of us to settle as honestly as we can. But when reading his own words, a phrase such as "only I am in a position to say what it's like here" refers to head only and not to the whole body, head included.

"What matters is attention," he told me.

Normally, I am more-or-less attentive to the world around me—to objects ranging from stars and sun and moon, clouds and hills and trees, houses and streets and cars and people, to my own arms and legs and trunk. But at this point, so near Home, my attention is suddenly turned off. I don't wish to know what—if anything—lies at the very Centre of this many-layered, onion-like universe of mine. I seem afraid of the Spot I occupy, determined to overlook it. Much worse than this, I read things into it that aren't there at all. Having no confidence in my own findings, I let everyone out there tell me what it's like right here; and they inform me that, exactly where I am, is a solid, opaque, colored, limited, complicated lump of stuff, a kind of meatball, and that I am peeping out of two little holes in it. With one voice they have been telling me this since my earliest childhood—so many people, so big and clever and assured and consistent, that it's not surprising I took their word for it, and rejected my own. On the subject of my Nature I was outvoted—millions to one.

But this is absurd. Only I am in a position to say what it's like here. All they can tell me is how I strike them. Out there, some feet off, they are indeed well placed to report on my manifold appearances, but quite unqualified to report on this central Reality from which all my appearances stem. Nobody has peeped in, much less occupied, this Place but me. I am the sole authority here; I alone have inside information. And when at last I dare to attend, to look at what I'm looking out of, to see what I make of myself at 0 feet instead of imagining what others make of me at (say) 6 feet, why then I find here no shape, no color, no opacity, no limits, nothing at all. In all respects my story is the opposite of theirs.

But it certainly isn't a *mere* nothing. First, I am aware: this Emptiness here is fully awake to itself as empty: it enjoys itself as speckless Clarity. Second, and precisely because it is nothing, it is everything. It is Capacity, Room for the world to happen in. I am space, but filled space, in which are displayed this trunk, these arms and legs, these people and cars and houses, and so on, with all the thoughts and feelings that they evoke. Empty of myself, I am filled with everything else. As 3rd person I am in the world; as 1st person it is in me. To see this, to live from this simple truth, is to be Who I am. And this is sufficient. It is the meaning of my life and the radical answer to my problems.

Such is Harding's message. The two main states of human experience, he believes, are what he terms 1st-personhood and 3rd-personhood. In the 1st-person state, the person is not identified with the *contents* of his consciousness (his body and mind and the world around him) but with the source of it all—actual Consciousness itself. In the 3rd-person state (what for most people is ordinary existence) the person feels himself to be made up of parts (the contents of consciousness) such as shape, color, name, and place. The teaching about these two states and the ways to the first of them can be found in Vedanta (Advaita) Hinduism, particularly in Jnana Yoga, but where Harding's originality lies is in his techniques for the actual discovery of 1st-personhood. For he believes that to grasp the truth intellectually, even to feel it deeply from time to time, is of very little value. You have actually *to see* the absence of everything that had been—or could ever be—imagined here, where the head is. Books and lectures, thinking and meditation, are at least as likely to divert you from the Spot you occupy as direct you to it, he says. For instance, these printed pages are about twelve inches from the Point—namely, the One who is now reading them. He urges the reader to turn his attention around 180 degrees and carry out a very few simple experiments—attending to the Attender—of which the following are a typical selection. Harding insists that there's no alternative to *doing* these experiments, and that a minute of active discovery is worth years of reading: indeed, he says, it takes no time at all to see, beyond the possibility of doubt, Who you really are. All you have to do is answer the following questions *on present evidence,* on what you find given at this moment, instead of what people have been telling you:

a) Point to your feet, legs, belly, chest, then to what's above that. Go on looking at what your finger's now pointing to.

Looking at what?

b) How many eyes are you looking out of? See what happens when you put your glasses on, slowly. Outline with your hands the extent of your "Eye." What's behind it?

c) See if you can get face-to-face with anyone. To reduce distractions, take a paper bag about 12" square, cut the bottom off, and get a friend to fit his face into one end while you fit yours into the other. What's at your end of the bag?

d) Observe where you keep your face. Is it where you are? Or is it over there in your mirror, and where your friend is in receipt of it (and can therefore tell you all about it) and where he holds his camera (which can therefore record it)?

e) By stroking and pinching and pummeling, try to build up on your shoulders a pink, opaque, complex, bounded thing. Try to get inside and describe its contents. Aren't you still at large, unboxed? Look at your trunk. Are you in it, or is it in you?

f) Get your friend to check your faceless emptiness (at 0 feet) by coming right up to you with his camera (a viewfinder-hole in a sheet of paper will do). Doesn't he start at a place (say 6 feet away) where he finds you to be a man, then come to where (at, say, 3 feet) he finds half a man, then a head, then an eye, then a mere blur? [Supposing he had the right equipment, wouldn't the blur read as, say, an eyelash, then as cells, then as one cell, then as particles of descending order, and in the end as practically empty space—featureless, transparent, colorless?] Isn't it true that the closer he gets to you the closer he gets to your own view of yourself as No-thing whatever?

g) Close your eyes and be still. How many toes . . . legs . . . arms . . . heads . . . do you have? Try to find and follow your boundaries. What age are you, what sex, what species? Are you anything at all but the limitless space in which these sounds and smells, these thoughts and feelings and sensations, are coming and going? But are you any the less able, now that you are neither this nor that—now you are nothing at all—to say I AM? (It's best to get a friend to read these questions out to you, so that you don't have to keep opening your eyes.)

When you have completed these exercises, Harding assumes that you will see your absence clearly.

"The two points at issue," he explains:

are my identity, and what to do about it. Now I find I'm not even remotely like what people told me I was, I can hardly pretend it makes no difference, and go on living in the same old fashion—as if I were a small, local, perishable *thing*. Here, dishonesty is fatal. If, suppressing the most obvious and accessible of all facts—my No-thingness—I am so utterly wrong about what lies at the very Centre of my universe, am I likely to be at all right about the rest of it? Is a life-style built upon such a lie at all likely to make sense, to prove a natural and efficient design for living? If it's important for me to know what tool I happen to be using (whether a hammer or a saw or a cut-throat razor) surely it's still more important to know Who happens to be using it—for safety's sake, let alone good work. Not to mention ordinary curiosity! Is it *uninteresting* to inquire Who one is? To have occurred, actually to be, yet to look no further into the matter—how unenterprising, how feeble: yes, how shameful!

And all the more so because the difficulties are quite imaginary. According to Harding, it is the easiest and simplest thing in the world to see its missing nucleus —yourself. To continue to see it, on the other hand, steadily, throughout all the diversions and pressures of everyday life, isn't at all easy. Practice is essential, if this seeing is to go on naturally and without interruption and bear its proper fruits.

This practice is the conscious enjoyment of 1st-personhood. It is also, says Harding, meditation—of a most radical sort, and different in many respects from meditation as usually taught. Harding describes it thus:

First, and above all, it is a *two-way attending*, a simultaneous looking in and out, which loses itself neither in the Emptiness nor in what fills it, but holds both together in one glance. [Outside the paper bag, (see exercise c) as inside, you see the total distinction between that face and this no-face, thus overcoming all the feeling of separation caused by believing that there are two different faces]. Accordingly, it works at least as well in the marketplace as in the meditation hall, when you are talking or walking or driving no less than when you are sitting still with closed eyes. So far from requiring or inducing a somewhat trancelike state and temporary retirement from the busy world, it sharpens your appreciation of what's going on. You are *more* alive. It's not when you look at, but when you overlook, the See-er that the seen grows dim and distorted. Not only the "outer" world, but also your "inner" world of psychological states, is obscured when you ignore the Inmost which covers and underlies them all.

Not everybody would agree that meditation necessarily leads to a trancelike state. Also, Harding's "Inmost" may seem to some an unnecessarily complicated image, sounding rather like what Watts might call Cosmic Jello. For surely, to find oneself gloriously empty is the aim of most mystics, and enough, and it seems a pity to start qualifying that Emptiness with descriptions, such as Inmost.

Oddly enough, this particular point lights up the essential difference between the Hindu and the Buddhist, particularly Mahayana, positions. Harding takes the part of the Hindu—he believes in a total distinction between Subject and object, Self and self, 1st- and 3rd-person, No-face and face. But when Consciousness and its contents are seen as distinct from each other in this way, it is very easy to fill Consciousness, or Emptiness, with imaginary qualities, such as Inmost. Buddhists, on the other hand, and Zen Buddhists most of all, believe that No-face and face exist as one. There are no distinctions. The

Emptiness is not filled with the world, because it *is* the world. Because Consciousness and its contents are seen to be one and the same, imagination cannot find a chink to creep in and qualify Consciousness.

Once seen, says Harding, the Absence here can be reseen, any time, *at will*. Unlike ideas and feelings, you can have it when you need it most, as when you are agitated or worried. In fact, he believes that there are no occasions when this meditation is inappropriate, no times when you may safely wander from the 1st-person position. In the end, he says, you stay at Home where it goes on unbroken, though at times very unobtrusively, like the bass accompaniment in music.

This does not mean that there is any improvement—or deterioration—in the actual seeing. *While it lasts*, says Harding, this is an all-or-nothing meditation which can't be done badly. You can't see half your Absence, nor can you half-see it. Either you are looking at what is central to you, or you are overlooking it. One welcome consequence is, he says, that among those who consistently practice this meditation there can be no hierarchy or pecking order, no gurus or chelas, no spiritual one-upmanship or intimidation. Nothing is achieved, but only discovered. And What's discovered is totally humbling: your Nothingness when actually seen can't be doubted. This alone carries conviction. Here is the one Spot where you are real and have no appearance, the one Spot that is plainly free from egotism and everything else—in a word, free.

It is free from all content. This meditation, says Harding, is not a mystical or even a religious experience, not euphoric, not a sudden expansion into universal love or cosmic consciousness, nor any kind of thought or feeling whatever. Quite the contrary, it is absolutely featureless, colorless, neutral. It is gazing into the pure, still cool, transparent Fountainhead, and simultaneously out from it at the streaming, turbulent world—without being carried away into that world. You can ensure your full share of experiences, not by going downstream after them, but by noticing that you are forever upstream of them all, and they can only be enjoyed there from their Source in you.

Because of its featurelessness, says Harding, there is nothing special about the meditation he is describing. It is secular, simple, natural, he believes. There's nothing to be learned and therefore no expert guidance is needed, no meditation manuals and masters, no agonizing choice between their conflicting systems, no hunting for the infallible teacher—seeing that He lives within. This meditation is safe because it can't be bungled, he says; because it avoids dependence on others, and because it is uncontrived. There's nothing arbitrary or fanciful about it, nothing to strain credulity, nothing to go wrong, nothing to set us apart from ordinary people. It is safe because it is finding out how matters stand, not trying to manipulate them. What could be less dangerous than being honest about the Place we are always at, or more dangerous than being dishonest about it?

How inconsistent and hard to please we are! We would like, says Harding, a meditation that detaches us from all creatures yet unites us with them, that reduces us absolutely yet exalts us absolutely, that leaves us wholly present and self-aware yet wholly absent and self-forgetful, that gives peace yet inspires action, that calms yet energizes, that is aimless yet purposeful, that leaves us nothing to do seeing that we are already at the Goal yet everything to do seeing that we are still at the beginning. What's wanted, in short, is a meditation that reconciles all our built-in contradictions.

Our whole trouble, he claims, is that we lack the courage of our own Seeing and rely upon outside authority, which—because it is outside—is no authority. On this subject, no one but this Subject—the 1st-person—is qualified to pronounce. Here, the scriptures are for testing by our experience, not our experience by the scriptures. In fact, they pass the test. At the heart of each of the great mystical traditions lies simple, direct Liberation or Awakening to who and what we really are.

Harding quotes many scriptures to support his case. According to the Advaita of Hinduism, he says, there is one See-er—one Consciousness, one Being—in all things, as their Essence or Reality, and It is empty of all attributes: Liberation is seeing that you are neither the body nor the mind, but This alone. Enlightenment for Hui Neng, one of the founders of Zen, was seeing his "Original Face"—which, interprets Harding, is your No-face. And, he adds, many of the koans or puzzles used in Zen are for getting us to see our Original Face. Jesus taught that we shall find the Kingdom within (not blood and brains and bones, adds Harding). And, says Harding, Rumi, the great Sufi poet, celebrates "headlessness" in much of his poetry.

None of this proves anything, he says, but it does provide so many more reasons—if any were needed—for examining the Place the masters are pointing to.

The "normal" human condition is pathological, Harding declares (once more unfortunately emphasizing the theistic belief that the human condition is separate from its Source and is "bad" in comparison with that Source itself, which can then be thought of as "good").

Here is a derangement immeasurably more profound than any other sort of madness, underlying them all. For the difference between my believing I am one kind of thing rather than another (say, Napoleon or a teapot instead of Douglas Harding) is negligible compared with the difference between my believing I am a *thing* and my seeing I am *No-thing*.

It isn't that the 1st person and the 3rd are unlike, but that they can't be compared. Whatever is true of the one is untrue of the other. That is why their confusion is so damaging.

Tracing the development of this "pathological" state, Harding continues:

> Like any animal, the new-born infant is faceless and at large, unseparate from his world, 1st-person without knowing it. The young child is becoming briefly and intermittently *aware* of himself-as-he-is-for-himself. Yet he's also becoming increasingly aware of himself-as-he-is-for-others—a very human and special 3rd person complete with head and face. Both views of himself are valid, necessary and sane. So far, so good.

> But as the child grows up his acquired view of himself-from-outside comes to overshadow, and in the end to obliterate, his native view of himself-from-inside. In fact, he grows *down*. Infected and intimidated by all around, he is 1st-person no longer. Shrunk from being the Whole into being this contemptible part, he grows greedy, hating, fearful, closed in, and tired. Greedy, as he tries to regain at whatever cost a little of his lost empire; hating, as he revenges himself on a society that has cruelly cut him down to size; fearful, as he sees himself to be a mere thing threatened by all other things; closed in, because it is the nature of a thing to shut others out; tired, because so much energy is wasted in keeping up appearances, instead of letting them go where they belong—in other people. And all this trouble arises from his basic identity-delusion—his daydream that he is what he looks like. He suffers because he is beside himself.

His cure, says Harding, is to wake up and come to his senses, to himself; the seven exercises described on pages 285–87 enable him to do this and are first-aid treatment. From then on the person must go on seeing his true Identity, as and when he can, till the seeing is quite natural and unbroken. For it is operative only in so far as it is practiced. The results—freedom from greed, hate, fear, and all their brood—are assured only while one is attending to one's freedom right here (as 1st-person singular, present tense) from anything whatever.

Does Harding place too much emphasis on cures, treatments, and first-aid to free one from the human condition (which certainly includes "greed, hate, fear, and all their brood" but also includes love, happiness and beauty)? In an earlier statement, he said "It [headlessness] is the meaning of my life and the radical answer to my problems," but in the long run he seems more concerned with problems than with meaning. This may be a drawback to his whole teaching, for a technique that is used only to serve the ends of men is likely to attract only those who wish to escape their problems. To exaggerate man's "pathological" condition in order to spotlight the benefits of "headlessness" is to turn that perfectly authentic insight into a magic panacea, an instant cure-all, on the level of a course for improving the personality.

Like Maharaj Ji's, Harding's audience is mainly among the young. Within his own circle, he holds forth lengthily, ardently, and often quite brilliantly on his own subject, and he will travel anywhere and speak to anyone about it.

Is his advice valid? For some people, it certainly is. It has helped a small but growing number of people to realize that they are Consciousness and to identify themselves with the See-er rather than with the seen; it has helped them to disentangle themselves from invading feelings and thoughts and to see these as outside or "downstream" from Empty Consciousness itself.

Beyond this, Harding does not go. He does not take the further step of bringing Consciousness and its contents together again. Thus there may be some danger that Harding's followers may think of their first insight as the final one, and that "headlessness" will become an end in itself instead of a way.

But reflections of this sort need not affect the straightforward benefit to be found in Harding's techniques. Once the obvious but usually unnoticed fact becomes clear from direct perception that people see everything else *but* their heads, then the head need no longer be imagined as the place where "I" live. For if, when I look, I find the world about me has replaced me, then I have disappeared, become one with the world, and need no longer experience myself as apart from it.

Castaneda's "Don Juan"
1900–

Don Juan Matus, a Yaqui Indian from Mexico, is one of the real masters in this book. No doubt he would be highly amused by this statement were he to be told of it. For he has a sublime indifference to the opinions of the world, and does not consider that he has a personal history any longer. As for books—when Carlos Castaneda, his biographer, proudly brought a first copy of *The Teachings of Don Juan* to show him, he treated the book as though it were a deck of cards and flipped through the pages, although he admired the green of the dust jacket. Having felt the cover and turned the book round twice, he handed it back. Castaneda asked him to keep it. But, laughing, don Juan refused, saying that he had better not, and adding, "You know what we do with paper in Mexico."[1]

The relationship between Carlos Castaneda, a young anthropologist, and the old Indian whom Castaneda al-

ways called don Juan, resembles that of Boswell and Dr.
Johnson, of Ouspensky and Gurdjieff. On the one hand,
there is the earnest disciple, inclined to take the master's
words too literally, but nevertheless gamely willing to be
made a fool of and to be constantly, if affectionately,
laughed at for his clumsiness, his run-of-the-mill thinking, and his limitations. And on the other hand, there is
the swift and unpredictable master, deceptively simple
in his skillful teaching, constantly undermining the
long-cherished suppositions of his follower, inserting a
new idea here and then there, revealing unknown worlds
and roaring with laughter at their effect.

When he first met don Juan in 1960, Castaneda was a
postgraduate anthropology student from South America,
attending the University of California in Los Angeles. He
was doing research on the effects of medicinal plants
used by the Indians of the Southwest and had no idea
whatever that he was to become a sorcerer's apprentice.
While waiting for a bus to take him away from a town on
the Arizona-Mexico border, his friend-helper suddenly
noticed don Juan at the bus stop, a white-haired Yaqui
Indian from Sonora in Mexico, who was known to be very
learned about plants, especially the hallucinogenic plant,
peyote.

They talked to don Juan, who was helpful and friendly.
Castaneda spoke Spanish as a native language and don
Juan also spoke it fluently and well. Castaneda said he
wanted information about plants, especially peyote, and
pretended to know more about plants than he did in order
to impress don Juan. Castaneda talked compulsively but
don Juan said very little. However, his eyes seemed to
shine with a special light of their own. He seemed to
know that Castaneda was making things up, but nevertheless invited Castaneda to visit him at his house. Then his
bus arrived and he left.

The shine in don Juan's eyes aroused a great curiosity in Castaneda because he had never seen such a look before. He wanted to know what lay behind it and the desire to find that out became an obsession with him. He thought about the shine endlessly and all the time it seemed to become more and more unusual.

He returned to visit don Juan and saw him constantly for a year. He found his manner to be reassuring and his sense of fun always in evidence. Not only that but his actions all seemed to have an underlying consistency that was strangely puzzling to Castaneda. For he found that the mere company of don Juan was forcing him to reassess all his values. He felt a delight in don Juan's presence but also a discomfort, for don Juan seemed to live by other and better values than Castaneda himself.

Don Juan, apparently to his own surprise, took Castaneda as his pupil, as the one he had been waiting for and to whom he could pass on his knowledge of sorcery (of medicinal plants, and of strange and secret powers). He did this almost against his better judgment, for he obviously thought little of Castaneda's abilities in that direction, especially as he was not even an Indian and seemed to don Juan "a very strange plugged-up fool." But an extraordinary omen impelled don Juan to take Castaneda seriously, for he believed that "Mescalito," a personalized form of peyote who appeared when peyote was taken, had pointed Castaneda out to him. Mescalito was to don Juan a benevolent protector and teacher of men, who taught "the right way to live." When Castaneda, under the influence of peyote for the first time, played in an unusual way with a dog and even began to bark like a dog, don Juan was certain that the dog was really Mescalito; and as he rarely played with a man this must mean that he favored Castaneda as don Juan's successor.

So he began to impart his understanding to Castaneda

but after five years of frequent visits Castaneda withdrew from the apprenticeship. His twentieth-century world, the world of Western intellectual man, was too threatened by don Juan's teaching and he felt his personality was at stake, for the teachings were shaking the foundations of his confidence in normal, everyday life. He felt his sanity and understanding were being snapped and he became uncertain about everything.

One senses in Castaneda an oversuggestible credulity, perhaps a too-easy emotionalism ("You indulge too much," said don Juan, when Castaneda, weeping on his shoulder, gave up his apprenticeship). Castaneda himself tells us that his nature is overdramatic and perhaps this accounts for his eager acceptance and then rejection of don Juan's teaching, for nothing that don Juan says is really harder to accept than the teachings of some Zen masters, or the words of other sages in this book. At any rate, Castaneda had second thoughts. After an interval of three years he returned to don Juan, was warmly welcomed by him, and began a second term of apprenticeship that was different in kind and turned out to be better. He no longer felt acute fear and don Juan was more relaxed, often clowning at crucial moments and helping Castaneda to accept more lightly and easily the knowledge he was being taught.

"The reason you got scared and quit is because you felt too damn important, . . . " he said. "Feeling important makes one heavy, clumsy and vain. To be a man of knowledge one needs to be light and fluid."[2]

Even then it took Castaneda another five years to realize that all don Juan's ministrations of psychotropic plants and all his detailed lessons in sorcery were not essential to understanding life at all, but were aids to help Castaneda let go his frantic grasp of the known world. After he appreciated the relative unimportance of the sorcerer's "tricks," he began to see what don Juan was really getting at, and in his second book, *A Separate Reality*, and his third book, *Journey to Ixtlan*, he relays to the reader some of don Juan's excellent teachings, which, although Castaneda had not realized it at the time, had been given to him at the beginning of their association as lessons in techniques for "stopping the world."

Thus Castaneda's first book about don Juan, *The Teachings of Don Juan: A Yaqui Way of Knowledge*, is to some extent written under a misapprehension. He thought that hallucinogenic trips were essential to the teaching and he takes the reader through a dense forest of fascinating facts about the plants themselves, the way they are gathered and used, and their effects. He worked conscientiously from field notes, and this book has a genuine sense of being on the edge of great discoveries. He has wonderful and terrifying experiences on his trips into the desert with don Juan, and with peyote and other plants, but the discoveries themselves came later. What were they?

The most important is undoubtedly *seeing*, and it is an action similar to Douglas Harding's seeing, although explained in a different way and with different side effects.

Like Harding, don Juan points out that seeing is a way of regarding the world with the eyes, but it is different to looking. A man who does not see, looks at the world and believes in its reality. Looking then becomes the same as interpretation—he interprets to himself as he looks. Looking is thus never a clear and pure seeing without the confines of interpretation; rather, it is a process of thought in which the actual seeing of an object becomes less important than the ideas thought about it.

It is the individual ego or self who looks and interprets and has ideas. When seeing takes place, the feeling of individual self goes because it is replaced by the object purely seen. This results in a marvelous freedom from the burden of value judgments—the object exists as itself only, it is unique and beyond all interpretation or comment ("there is really nothing to say about them," said don Juan when asked about plants). No interference with the perception of the object can be brought about by the ordinary thinking mind because somehow all thoughts are equally clear and void of self.

This is not to say that memory has disappeared. Not a bit. The name for the object I am seeing is still mountain or rose or tree. "There is nothing that I must not see in order to see, and there is no knowledge that I must forget," says Buber. But name belongs to a mode of looking that has become irrelevant and unimportant. The whole world we look at is merely description, according to don Juan. If I drop this mode of descriptive looking and begin to see, then I see it, the object, transcending all names in its utter clarity that is yet mystery; its numinous beingness about which there is nothing to be said.

So profound is this mystery in which there is nothing of myself, that personal hopes and desires and plans seem as meaningless as colored confetti when the bride has left. Don Juan told Castaneda that he no longer felt he had any personal history.

Castaneda, confused by this statement, suggested that don Juan surely knew who he was. But don Juan denied any knowledge of himself and laughed so much at Castaneda's astonishment that he rolled on the floor. How could he know who he was, he said, when he was all that—and he indicated the surroundings with a gesture.

Another point of confusion to Castaneda was the way his thinking mind compared one thing with another and found inequalities. But when *seen*, each object is perfect in itself and therefore comparisons are pointless—every object can be said to be equally important or equally unimportant.

Don Juan explained to him that first we learn to think about everything and then we teach our eyes to see those things as we think they are. For instance, we like to think of ourselves as important, and then we have to feel we are! But when a man learns to *see*, he finds that there is no need to think about things and so his thoughts are no longer attached to them. Then they all seem equally unimportant.

Castaneda was disturbed by the prospect of nothing being more important than anything else. He then felt that the whole of life must be unimportant and therefore worthless, but don Juan told him that this was because of his habit of thinking as he looked at things and also thinking as he thought of them.

"Thinking," to don Juan, meant the constant flow of ideas that we form about everything. The habit of thinking, instead of seeing, could be broken by the act of seeing. He pointed out that Castaneda should know by that time how a man of action lives—that he lives by acting and not by thinking about his acts, or by imagining what he would think when he stopped acting. A man who can act without thought is a man of knowledge, he said, and such a man will choose a path that has heart and follow it. He is aware that his life will not last forever; that there is nowhere for him or anyone else to go; and that nothing is more important than anything else. Such a man of knowledge can drop his feelings about honor, dignity, family name, and country, because he knows that the only point of being alive is to live. He simply laughs and rejoices in things as they are. He behaves outwardly as other men behave because he can control his "folly," his life, and so he seems to be just like an ordinary man, struggling and sweating and puffing. He is so much in control that he can choose to do anything and seem to do it as though it really mattered to him, but he knows that it is not important and does not matter. So when his actions are done he is able to go away in peace and be unconcerned as to their results.

Still dissatisfied, Castaneda recounted to don Juan the story of a wealthy, politically minded American lawyer, a conservative who fought against many innovations, such as the New Deal. He was defeated and, filled with bitterness and self-pity, retired. At last, at age eighty-four, he had told Castaneda that he realized he had wasted forty years of his life. What is the difference, asked Castaneda, between the emptiness of that old man and don Juan's feeling that nothing really mattered? Would not don Juan end up in no better position than the lawyer?

Don Juan replied that Castaneda's friend was lonely because he would not *see* before he died. He must have felt that he had thrown away his life because he was determined on victories and found only defeats. He would never know that his victories and defeats were of equal importance. But the way in which nothing mattered to him any more was quite different to don Juan's state. For don Juan, victories and defeats had no meaning, for his life was filled to the brim, everything in it was equal, and he felt that all his struggle had been worthwhile:

> In order to become a man of knowledge one must be a warrior, not a whimpering child. One must strive without giving up, without a complaint, without flinching, until one *sees*, only to realize then that nothing matters.[3]

Don Juan undoubtedly *sees* in the way that Douglas Harding does, but there is a further effect of seeing for don Juan that Harding would be unlikely to accept. For whereas the seen world is, for Harding, "empty," for don Juan it all becomes, in some way, shining. Men are composed, when *seen*, of luminous fibers which project from the navel and are long or short according to their state of enlightenment. Don Genaro, a friend of don Juan's, was observed by Castaneda to scale a sheer rock face and somersault across a waterfall with complete ease. He could do this, said don Juan, because he was attaching his fibers like ropes to any projections.

It is this particular aspect of "seeing" that casts doubt on don Juan's stature as a master revealing eternal truths, and makes one wonder how much he was also a shaman, conditioned by his culture, a specifically local culture that has little to say to most of mankind. How much, too, did the continual ingestion of peyote and the smoking of two other plants (jimson weed or *Datura inoxia* and a mushroom of the genus *Psylocebe*) affect his ability to apprehend actuality?

The part that peyote played in don Juan's life is not clear at all. This is not the fault of Castaneda, who has noted down all that seemed to take place and all that was said. But one cannot read between these lines to discover how much don Juan regarded peyote as a means and how much as an end. He instructed Castaneda to smoke the plants as much as possible as they were "an indispensable prerequisite" to *seeing*. Only the smoke, he said, could give Castaneda the quickness and agility to catch a glimpse of that elusive world.

But whether he felt they were indispensable to himself remains in doubt. He gave them to Castaneda avowedly to crack the young man's two-dimensional (place and time) idea of the world. "You are too real to yourself," he said. And he accused Castaneda of being too available and obvious, his life such a routine that he was predictable. He advised Castaneda to be inaccessible, like a hunter.

When a man is a hunter, he said, his contact with the world is sparing and economical. Instead of eating five quail, he eats one. He doesn't hurt and destroy plants in order to dig a barbecue pit; nor does he expose himself to the elements unnecessarily. Most of all, he does not manipulate and use people for his own ends, especially those he loves.

A hunter feels confident in what he is doing and therefore he does not worry. When a man worries he becomes vulnerable and accessible, and once he begins to worry he will grasp at whatever he can get hold of. Then he will either wear himself out or wear out the person or thing he is clinging to.

A hunter feels a protective tenderness towards all the things in the world and so he uses them carefully and sparingly. He feels intimately at home in the world, but it cannot get hold of him. He is not accessible because he does not have to cling to it with a life-destroying grip. He touches it lightly, leaves it when he is ready, and puts barely a mark on it.

Through peyote, don Juan tried to shake Castaneda free from his habitual thought-patterns by introducing him to other ways of experiencing the world—ways that seemed to show that the objective world itself and the laws that govern it could be altered. This was when Castaneda became too scared, and left, but returned after some years.

It is easy to dismiss don Juan's different worlds as peyote-inspired hallucinations. But to do so is to ignore a fact that is rarely spoken of. This fact is the realization, revealed to us by both science and ordinary perception, that our common, everyday world of shapes and colors appears as it does only to the eyes of the beholder. The objective world, as we know it, only appears to us because we are equipped with senses that apprehend it. If I were a cat, I would not see clouds or mountaintops; the shape of my objective world would not be merely limited by a lesser sense capacity, it would be entirely different. From the way cats behave, it is possible that they see many things that we do not. Do such things exist? For cats, yes: for people, no. Our worlds do not coincide at this point. And seen through the eyes of a beetle or an ant, again the world is not just our world on a minute scale—it is *a different world.*

Is it possible to know even the world of my neighbor? Never. We may agree on a large number of descriptions of it, on the sort of attributes that human organs can perceive, but we can never ultimately *know* another person's world. The only real evidence for an objective world that we have to go on is our own.

"The world is a construct of our sensations, perceptions, memories," says Dr. Erwin Schrödinger, an eminent physicist. "It is convenient to regard it as existing objectively on its own. But it certainly does not become manifest by its mere existence. Its becoming manifest is conditional on very special goings-on in very special parts of this very world, namely on certain events that happen in a brain."[4]

Don Juan declared that he knew other worlds. Whether one considers these worlds to be merely new aspects of the same world discovered through hallucinogenic plants, or to be altogether different worlds is, finally, unimportant because their effect is that of being "other," in the same way that a dream scene can be entirely different in place and time from our normal surroundings.

Don Juan introduced Castaneda to these other worlds in order to crack his rigid grip on "normality," on Castaneda's everyday "too real" world. Don Juan did not quite succeed but neither did he fail. Castaneda *saw* only fleetingly and not at will. But he did become pliant and open, and was able to experience moving moments of insight. On one such occasion he had been sent to the desert by don Juan and after some days, found himself uneasy and depressed. He was sitting on a high plateau when a large black beetle came towards him, pushing a ball of dung. At the same time he became aware that a shadow had flickered somewhere to his left—traditionally the vulnerable side. He thought it might be the shadow of death watching both him and the beetle. Suddenly he realized that he and the beetle were not different after all, and he had a great moment of elation, so overwhelmingly happy that he wept. He saw that don Juan had always been right and that he was indeed, as we all are, living in a strange and mysterious world. He saw that he himself was an unknowable being and yet of no more importance than a beetle.

Did don Juan regard sorcery as indispensable to seeing? He once told Castaneda that seeing was a process independent of sorcery, for sorcery served only to manipulate other people whereas seeing had no effect on people at all. Why then did he involve Castaneda in so much sorcery? Throughout the three books one is aware that there are two don Juans. One is the master, simple, compassionate, serene, and detached from results. The other is the sorcerer, sewing together a lizard's eyelids in order to make it reveal the answer to a question, powdering a devil's root for vigor, attributing the power of life and death to a clay pipe, frightening Castaneda badly with tales of a witch flapping around as a blackbird. And there is even a third don Juan, a Gurdjieff who uses sorcery to place Castaneda in such circumstances that his own personality traits will bring him to the verge of defeat; who doubles up with laughter at Castaneda's reactions; who mesmerizes Castaneda, hoodwinks him, and plays startling jokes on him.

It is don Juan, the master, who urges Castaneda to become a warrior. When Castaneda was feeling queasy after a meal in a small Mexican cafe and fearful that the food was bad, don Juan reproached him and told him very sternly that once he decided to visit Mexico he should forget about his fears. Such fears and worries should have been dealt with before he set out and then forgotten, for many other situations would arise to demand his attention. To face fears at the beginning and then put them aside was the way of a warrior.

A warrior, he said, knows that death is the only factor that can bar his way and he should always remember death when things became muddled or distorted. He should also learn to be free of the fear of death, so that the knowledge that it was always awaiting him would be a spur to his actions rather than a brake.

In this way, he said, a man who wants to be a warrior must always be sharply conscious of the presence of death. But to keep thinking about death would focus all his attention on himself and would immobilize him. So he must be keenly aware of it but also indifferent to it.

Ramana Maharshi once said something similar:

> . . . No man takes seriously the fact of death. He may see death around him, but he still does not believe that *he* will die. He believes, or rather, feels in some strange way, that death is not *for him*. Only when the body is threatened does he fall a victim to the fear of death. Every man believes himself to be eternal, and this is actually the truth. . . .[5]

The result of being a warrior and of *seeing*, is to discover that one's actions amount only to "controlled folly." Don Juan used this term to express his understanding of the ultimate lack of importance of any one act as compared to any other that we do. Doing is not important, he said; what is important is "not-doing." By this he did not mean that we should never act, but that we should only act from clarity within, from an area of not-doing. Then the doing emerges with the crystal clearness of the not-doing. This is "controlled" folly as distinct from the ordinary folly of most people's muddle-motivated acts.

First we must realize, he said, that our acts are useless, and then we must take no notice of this understanding and go on living as though we didn't know it.

Castaneda was puzzled by the idea of controlled folly and asked don Juan more about it.

Don Juan said he was delighted actually to be asked after all the years Castaneda had known him, although if Castaneda had never asked he wouldn't have minded. However, he had chosen to be pleased as if he cared whether Castaneda asked him or not—and as if it mattered whether he cared! And that, he said, was an example of controlled folly.

Did he exercise controlled folly with everybody, Castaneda asked. When told yes, he then asked if don Juan was never sincere but was always acting?

In one of his most profound replies, don Juan said, "My acts are sincere, but they are only acts of an actor."[6]

He seems to imply by this that to be human at all is necessarily to be an actor. The very structure of the organism demands a mask. Only consciousness is formless; all that consciousness *perceives* is clothed in one shaped and colored mask or another. Each shape acts out the role it has been given, plants and animals unconsciously doing so—a tree behaves like a tree and a cow like a cow—and human beings self-consciously doing so. When the role-playing is at last seen through, the actor carries on with the play—sincerely, but with the knowledge that it *is* a play—and this is a difference between the enlightened and the unenlightened man. To the unenlightened, the play is real. To the enlightened, the play is real as a play but no more real than that.

"I am aware of something in myself *whose shine is my reason*," said an unknown mystic. The *something* is what is real for the enlightened man, and he recognizes it as the source of himself; whereas the content of the world outside, he perceives as merely the external appearance, or "description," of That which shines. To regard the *content* of the world as ultimately real is to be taken in by the actors of the play. "Once a man learns to *see* he finds himself alone in the world with nothing but folly,"[7] says don Juan.

That was don Juan, the master.

Don Juan, the sorcerer *sees* people as illuminated egg-shaped bunches of fibers and the way in which he manipulates them is by "not-doing"—not in the sublime sense of deep stillness from which springs actionless action, but in a shaman's sense of magic.

After teasing Castaneda and some other young men by repeatedly going behind a rock and then emerging as a seemingly different person each time (and different to each member of the group as well) don Juan explained how he could do this. When each one of us is born, he said, we enter the world with a little circle of power. Almost immediately it is put to use. So everyone, from birth onwards, is caught up in the organization of the world about them and their circle of power joins on to everyone else's. In this way each individual helps to make the recognized world. This is the *"doing"* of the world, according to don Juan, and for each person it is effective from the moment when he hooks on, with his own circle of power, to other people's *doing*.

Don Juan startled Castaneda by saying that at that very moment his circle of power and also Castaneda's were hooked to the *doing* of the room about them. The room was being brought into existence by their spinning circles of power.

Castaneda protested that the room was there by itself, he wasn't creating it. But don Juan calmly insisted that the room was brought into existence and kept in place by everybody's ring of power. But a man of knowledge, he said, develops another kind of power-ring, the ring of "not-doing" and with that ring he can spin other worlds. When he had stepped from behind the rock and had appeared differently to each observer, he had accomplished this by hooking his not-doing ring of power to their doing rings. They had then done the rest.

Castaneda found this hard to comprehend.

Over and over again in these books, one has the impression that don Juan is teaching Castaneda a sorcerer's lore because he believes that this will bring about a freedom of mind in Castaneda, whereas it is the words of the master that really strike home to Castaneda rather than the sort of episode on dark and desolate mountaintops when an "ally," a sorcerer's "vehicle," as violent and harmful as it can be helpful, appears in various guises, all of which Castaneda accepts as literally real; or the peyote visions that nearly send Castaneda over the edge of madness. Perhaps the constant practice of sorcery had brought don Juan to misjudge one who really needed a master. Or perhaps he simply took Castaneda literally when he said, at the beginning of their acquaintanceship, that he wanted to learn about plants. Whatever his motives, they remain undisclosed to us, but in all four books his teaching is both that of a sage and a sorcerer, and it finally leaps into sorcery at the end of the last book.

In this last book, *Tales of Power*, Castaneda is helped by don Juan to understand the "totality" of himself. Don Juan uses the Mexican terms *tonal* (pronounced toh-na'hl) and *nagual* (pronounced nah-wa'hl) to teach him this. These terms approximate roughly to man's ego or feeling of himself (tonal) and to Harding's Emptiness (nagual), for don Juan believes that the nagual contains the tonal, as

Harding believes the Emptiness contains all that is manifest.

In order to know his totality, says don Juan, man must know himself as two halves of a bubble. One half of him, the tonal, is centered around his reason, and is based on his perception of the world. His reason organizes this perception into his personal view of the world, which will be to him a coherent and understandable description of it. The tonal, then, is everything that man understands himself to be. The companion of man's reason is talking, says don Juan, and anything man has a word for is the tonal. Thus it is all that he can describe.

The nagual is the indescribable. It is the real creator of the world, whereas the tonal is merely the witness or describer of it. The nagual is the half of man for which there is no name or description, no feeling or knowledge. It can only be discovered when man's internal talking ceases and his tonal is emptied of reasoned beliefs. In the emptiness, his nagual can then become apparent to his tonal.

In an extraordinary account of flying down ravines with the help of the nagual, Castaneda discovers that his intrinsic nature is made up of a cluster of "me's"—feelings, thoughts, and bodily sensations. This Gurdjieff-like conclusion is affirmed by don Juan, who says that all the multitude of possible feelings and "me's" float peacefully before birth in the nagual-like barges. Then, in the prebirth stage, some of them adhere together, bound by what he calls "the glue of life." A being is created by this means, but as soon as he is born he loses his sense of the nagual and adopts the ideas and values of the tonal. When he dies, he disintegrates again, and all the parts of him sink back into the unchanging nagual.

We may think that an eternal, unchanging, and peaceful nagual out of which emerges a conglomeration of parts called a person, could seem a feasible explanation of birth and death; and undoubtedly it has features in common with Hinduism. But whereas the Hindu THAT is held to be beyond man's comprehension altogether and yet intimately himself, the nagual seems a peculiar force because it can be *used* by sorcerers! It is certainly incomprehensible, but not in the sublime way of the Uncreated and Unconditioned, or of Harding's Emptiness. The nagual is anything but sublime. It can appear as a magic moth or as a fierce animal or as a terrifying sound. When used "properly," it can carry a man through the air, up mountains and down ravines, and even to other worlds in outer space, according to don Juan.

In fact, space travel seems its greatest accomplishment, and this final confirmation that don Juan is a sorcerer rather than a sage may disappoint many people. It will at least disappoint those to whom the perfection of man's outward powers is of less importance than the discovery of his real inner meaning. For, as Zen Buddhism says, why bother to cross the water miraculously if you can get to the other side by boat? If one of the major discoveries of four books and a great deal of teaching is to see the floor of a ravine by flying rather than by climbing down, it seems a great amount of effort for very little.

It is the journey inward, rather than to outer space, that concerns many people; because instinctively we know that it is a journey towards real wisdom and real compassion. Don Juan, too, seemed to believe this and he conveyed these qualities in his teaching. However baffling his conclusions, and however physically superpowered his pupils turn out to be, we can remember the clear-seeing and lovable Indian who emerges from Castaneda's writing; the far-seeing sage who could, in Krishnamurti's style, point out how men delude themselves when they attach names to the world and then expect the world to conform to their descriptions of it—how they act and then believe that their actions *are* the world. Don Juan saw to the root of man's ignorance.

"The world is incomprehensible," he said, "we won't ever understand it; we won't ever unravel its secrets. Thus we must treat it as it is, a sheer mystery!"

The ordinary man, he went on, never does treat the world as a mystery and when he becomes old he thinks he has discovered it all. Really he has only discovered the actions of men, but in his ignorance he believes that he has exhausted all the secrets and that there is nothing left to live for.

"A warrior," he said,

is aware of this confusion and learns to treat things properly. The things that people do cannot under any conditions be more important than the world. And thus a warrior treats the world as an endless mystery and what people do as an endless folly.[8]

314

References

Douglas Harding

Further Reading

Douglas Harding, *The Hierarchy of Heaven and Earth: A New Diagram of Man in the Universe*. London: Faber and Faber).

Douglas Harding, *The Science of the 1st Person*. Suffolk: Shollond Publications.

Douglas Harding, *On Having No Head: A Contribution to Zen in the West*. London: The Buddhist Society, New York: Harper and Row.

Harding, *The Science of the 1st Person*.

Douglas Harding, *Religions of the World*
London: Heinemann Educational
Books.

Don Juan

1 Carlos Castaneda, *A Separate Reality* (London: The Bodley Head; University of California Press), p. 25.
2 Ibid., p. 13.
3 Ibid., p. 94.
4 Erwin Schrödinger, *Mind and Matter* (London: Cambridge University Press; New York: Cambridge University Press), p. 1.
5 Mercedes de Acosta, *Here Lies the Heart* (New York: Reynal and Co.), p. 295.
6 Castenada, *A Separate Reality*, p. 84.
7 Ibid., p. 86.
8 Ibid., p. 226.

Further Reading

Castaneda, Carlos, *The Teachings of Don Juan*. London: Penguin; University of California Press.

Castaneda, Carlos, *Journey to Ixtlan*. New York: Simon and Schuster.

Castaneda, Carlos, *Tales of Power*. New York: Simon and Schuster.

10

Mystic and Mother

Mother Theresa is a practical mystic who needs no introduction, for her life illuminates both her insight and her teaching.

Mother Theresa
1910–

Make us worthy, Lord, to serve our fellow men throughout the world who live and die in poverty and hunger.

Give them, through our hands, this day their daily bread; and by our understanding love, give peace and joy.

Lord, make me a channel of Thy peace that, where there is hatred, I may bring love; that, where there is wrong, I may bring the spirit of forgiveness; that, where there is discord, I may bring harmony; that, where there is error, I may bring truth; that, where there is doubt, I may bring faith; that, where there is despair, I may bring hope; that, where there are shadows, I may bring light; that where there is sadness, I may bring joy.

Lord, grant that I may seek rather to comfort than to be comforted, to understand than to be understood; to love than to be loved; for it is by forgetting self that one finds; it is by forgiving that one is forgiven; it is by dying that one awakens to eternal life.

Amen.[1]

(A prayer used daily by Mother Theresa and the Missionaries of Charity)

Total charity—the giving up of one's body, mind, and heart to God as He appears in the tramp muttering to himself on the park bench, or the drunken man retching on the street corner—is not always the practice of mystics and sages. Of all the mystics in this book, Mother Theresa, ignoring explanations completely, lives and acts by giving all of herself to God all of the time. What impels her to do this?

Her answer is quite clear. It is Jesus, eternally alive in the heart of man, whom she and her Sisters serve; and the keynote of her teaching and her work has always been: "Inasmuch as you did it to the least of my brethren, you did it unto me." Every person, to her, is Jesus. Every derelict or abandoned child or leper-rotted carcass is the Divine Presence—He to whom she has given herself:

Actually we are touching His body. It is the hungry Christ that we are feeding, it is the naked Christ that we are clothing, it is the homeless Christ that we are giving shelter and it is not just hunger for bread, and nakedness for clothes and homelessness for a house made of bricks but Christ today is hungry in our poor people, and even in the rich, for being cared for, for being wanted, for having someone to call their own.

Today, like before, when Jesus comes among his own, his own don't know him. He comes in the rotten bodies of our poor, he comes even in the rich, who are being suffocated by their riches, in the loneliness of their hearts, and there is no one to love them. And here Jesus comes to you and me. And often, very, very often, we pass Him by.

Very often I ask people to come to our home for the dying. We have a big place in Calcutta and in the twenty-one years we have picked up over twenty-seven thousand people from the streets. And I ask the people not to come and give things—things I can get for the asking—but I want their presence, just to touch them, just to smile at them, just to be present with them, it means such a lot for our people.[2]

A sense of vocation began in Mother Theresa when she was a very young girl. Her name was Agnes Gonxha Bojaxhiu and she was the daughter of an Albanian grocer in Skopje, Yugoslavia. The family atmosphere was warm and loving and she spent a happy childhood, but even in this carefree period an unusual *awareness* of God began to define itself, and by the time she was twelve she knew that somehow she must devote her life to God in the form of service to the poor. But she did not want to be a nun. Between the ages of twelve and eighteen she rebelled wholeheartedly against commitment to this particular religious path. But when she was eighteen she decided that she must leave her beloved home and join an order of missionaries, the Loreto nuns. From then on she had no doubts.

After a stay in Dublin, she began her novitiate in India. She took her first vows in Loreto in 1931 and for twenty years, between 1929 and 1948, she taught geography at St. Mary's High School in Calcutta. During this time she became the principal of the school, and she was also put in charge of the Daughters of St. Anne, and Indian religious order attached to the Loreto Sisters. She was very happy. She loved teaching and she also loved the whole atmosphere of the high school, of which she was undoubtedly an ideal Headmistress.

But one day, no longer a young woman, she put it all behind her and left the school to take up a totally different life.

While on her way to Darjeeling for her annual retreat she had received, in the train, a "call" to give up her work and her position at the school and to follow Jesus into the slums, to serve him through the poorest of the poor. This "call" came with utter clarity and certainty and she had no second thoughts about obeying it.

She wrote personally to Pope Pius XII and by return

post had his reply, which gave her permission to go out of the convent and become an unenclosed nun. So she went first to the Loreto Sisters in Patna to have some medical training. Then, four months later, she returned to Calcutta with no money at all except five rupees. A family in the slums gave her their compound to use as a school and she began to bring in children from the streets. Gradually word got about and people came with food and money and presents. Other Sisters, and girls she had taught at St. Mary's, arrived to join her, and then doctors and nurses offered voluntary help. In 1952, she opened the first home for the dying, called "The Home for Dying Destitutes."

Calcutta is a city in which there is unbelievable poverty. Death from starvation and disease is widespread and the streets in the poorer parts contain many who are abandoned and dying and dead. The first woman Mother Theresa picked up, she recounts, had been eaten by rats and ants but was still alive. Mother Theresa took her to the hospital where they only accepted her because Mother Theresa refused to leave unless they did.

She begged the municipality to give her a place where she could take the dying. She was offered an empty temple that had been devoted to the Hindu goddess, Kali —who symbolizes the Mother of the Universe, the Giver of Life and Death. No sectarian scruples inhibited Mother Theresa from immediately and delightedly accepting the Kali temple; in fact she was especially pleased that it had been used as a place of worship. Within twenty-four hours she had filled it with patients, all destitute and most of them dying. Of the many thousands of people picked up by the Sisters since that first day, about fifty percent have died.

It would be wrong to put Mother Theresa in the category only of an immensely active do-gooder. She is not concerned with the conventional do-gooding that we connect with social welfare and that often stems from the belief that material well-being is more important than anything else. Indeed some enthusiastic welfare workers might be shocked by Mother Theresa's attitude, for although the Sisters do what they can medically, Mother Theresa does not try to prolong life at any cost. She is not equipped to do so. Her only aim is to give loving comfort to the poor as they die so that they will know they are not forgotten but are wanted and cared for.

Even more than that, Mother Theresa wants them to know that they are close to God and that this is a joyous state. If the work of the Sisters is just useful but gives no happiness to people, she says, then these people would never be able to rise to the acceptance of God that she asks of them. They must *see* the contentment and happiness of the Sisters, they must *feel* that they are loved by the Sisters for themselves, and that this love comes from God. Then they may die with acceptance and dignity.

In some ways, Mother Theresa has the same feeling for humanity as don Juan, the Yaqui Indian seer. When he was seven, his parents were killed by Mexicans in front of his eyes, he told Castaneda. But it was not their terrible deaths that saddened him so much as the fact that they had died as humble Indians—"They lived like Indians and died like Indians and never knew that they were, before anything else, men."

In her own way, Mother Theresa understands that attitude. She knows the closeness of God to man, and that the knowledge of God's presence makes a man human so that he no longer thinks of himself as merely unwanted and destitute:

One day a man was brought in screaming and yelling. He didn't want to die. His backbone was broken in three places, and he had many terrible ulcers. His pain was intense. He didn't want to see the Sisters. He didn't want to die.

He was given morphine and love in generous doses, and he was told of the sufferings of One who loved him very much.

Gradually he began to listen and to accept love. On his last day, he refused the morphine because he wanted to be united to the One who saved him.[3]

Being unwanted, says Mother Theresa, is the worst state of all. For most diseases there are medicines nowadays. But only love can cure the terrible illness of being unwanted and abandoned. In Calcutta, Mother Theresa saves the discarded babies, as well as the dying. Some the Sisters bring from hospitals, some from jails, some are brought by the police. So far they have never refused a child. Each one is beloved to them. Each one is the embodiment of Christ, from the children swollen with malnutrition to the tiny, premature semicorpses found on the rubbish heap:

> I don't know the future but to me, today, when a life comes into my hands, all my love and energy goes to support that life, to help that life to grow to its fullness, because this person has been created in the image of God. We have no right to destroy that life.[4]

The terrible disease of leprosy takes its toll of the rich as well as the poor. If it is caught in time, it can these days be cured, and the Sisters have been specially trained for this work. But it takes time, up to two years for an easy cure, and many Indians in the meantime lose their jobs and are sometimes disowned by their families. If they are poor, nobody wants to know them except the Sisters. They now look after some ten thousand lepers in Calcutta alone, and in a place called Shanti Nagar the Indian Government has given them thirty-four acres to build a rehabilitation center, a "town of peace," where lepers can be trained to work in their own homes so that they won't have to go begging.

There are 47,000 lepers in India and elsewhere that the Sisters touch in love, and serve. These are the people who are not wanted. Leprosy is a terrible disease; it disfigures people. It makes them look so terrible. Yet, they are very lovable people.

We have mobile clinics and we go to them. We do not ask them to come to us, they are scorned and rejected, sometimes they are unable to walk. When they see the young Sisters coming with a smile, taking care of them, singing for them, they feel there is someone in all this world who cares. We cannot heal their disease, but we can make them feel that they are wanted.[5]

What sustains Mother Theresa? And what sustains her Sisters, many of whom are young girls from high-caste Indan families performing unheard-of menial jobs for those they were brought up to despise? The vows they take are simple but hard, and every candidate must have certain qualities that are listed on a chart:

Health of body and mind
Ability to acquire knowledge
Common sense in abundance
Cheerful dispositions
Poverty, chastity and obedience. Obedience means
    freedom.

It is that final sentence that gives the clue to the source of the spirit that upholds and nourishes them. *Real* obedience does mean freedom. Not the freedom to go about getting what one wants, which is not really freedom at all but slavery, but a different freedom in which the heart is singularly clear and open because it is filled with the sense of oneness with something greater than itself.

The isolated sensation of having to carve out of life all that one can for oneself by oneself is replaced by a certainty that this is not the purpose one was born for: that life itself is so incredible and so wonderful that to exploit it for one's own ends is to lose the point of it entirely, and that the way to *find* the point is to obey life at the cost of all self-interest—to listen to what one is given to hear, to look at what one is shown, to understand what one is being taught, and to accept what one is presented with. To *obey* is to give oneself up to God's will—to whatever occurs in life—without ego-judgment.

We must "taste God as the sole good," says the 17th century mystic, Jean Pierre de Caussade, with whom Mother Theresa could be said to have many links. "We have to arrive at the point at which the whole created universe no longer exists for us, and God is everything.... Creatures by themselves are (then) without power or efficacy and the heart lacks any tendency or inclination towards them because the majesty of God fills all its capacity."[6]

The God-filled heart, he continues, is moved towards creatures when they are seen as part of God's design. It is exactly this mystical understanding that the inner and the outer world are one that gives spiritual strength to Mother Theresa and the Sisters of Charity. Their strict rule of poverty applies to their egos as well as to their bodies. When they lack "any tendency or inclination" to dominate the world for their own purposes, then the world itself becomes nothing—without self-nature. It no longer holds power over them. This gives them the freedom and strength to serve and cherish it, for as the manifestation of God's design it is infinitely marvelous and dear to them. The Designer and His design cannot be separated. The incoherent, filthy leper in the streets is as much Christ as He to whom they surrender their hearts.

Without this surrender there is insufficient strength, and, as a practical mystic, Mother Theresa knows well the dangers attached to serving the poor—that a Sister might do it just for its own limited sake because she thinks it is social work that needs to be done—or that a Sister might regard it as a way of perfecting herself and thus turn the work into a way of boosting her ego.

The real safeguard against wrong motive, she says, is to remember to love. To remember that not only is the work done *for* Christ but also that it is done *by* him—that in herself a Sister is nothing. When a Sister understands this, she sees that the perfection of "self" is meaningless.

Mother Theresa meditates for several hours early every morning. She then attends Mass, profoundly empty of herself. Without the morning Mass, she says, and the strength that comes from it, the whole work would be too difficult. But when she and the Sisters go out into the streets they are happy and buoyant, stripped of self-interest, and finding genuine delight in all the tasks they do. For where the ordinary self-motivated person would see only degradation facing him in the streets and would shrink from it in horror, the Sisters know that they are meeting Christ and that the most embittered, ugly, or horrific face will seem to them singularly beautiful and lovable.

"For me each one is an individual," Mother Theresa says, "I can give my whole heart to that person for that moment in an exchange of love. It is not social work. We must love each other. It involves emotional involvement, making people feel they are wanted."[7]

The Sisters are given intensive spiritual training during their novitiate (which lasts nine years), and nobody is accepted without a "calling." The vow of poverty is especially strict, and there is an extra vow of giving wholehearted free service to the poor. This means that they are not allowed to work for the rich, nor to accept any money for the work they do. Few Sisters ever leave. Their emotional equilibrium must be unstrained and constant so that they are genuinely unperturbed by the sights they see and feel no need to talk about what they are doing.

Touching disease-ridden people is important and the Sisters learn to express love in their touch. As well, they learn to sense intuitively what are the real needs of those they serve—not always what one might expect. Among all the small, unhappy children to be looked after, for instance, Mother Theresa saw one who wasn't eating because his mother had died. She found a Sister "who looked exactly like a mother" and told her to do nothing but play with the child. The child recovered.

It is easy to accuse missionaries who are doing good in other countries of ignoring the poor on their doorstep, but this does not apply to Mother Theresa. Although India (and particularly 54a Lower Circular Road, Calcutta) has become her home and she feels happier among the poor there than anywhere else, yet she goes wherever she feels needed in the world. There are now her Sisters—the Missionaries of Charity—in Venezuela, Rome, Tanzania, Australia, Jordan, Mauritius, Bangladesh, the Yemen, Peru, New York, London, and Belfast. To all these places Mother Theresa flies, her wrinkled, Albanian face alight with love. She still works as hard at menial tasks as any of the Sisters, wherever she goes.

"Do you ever take a holiday?" she was asked.

"No!" she replied, "Every day is a holiday."

328

References

1 Daily Prayer
2 Templeton Prize for Progress in Religion,
    (Mother Theresa's reply to Prince Philip)
3 Sister Sue Mosteller, *My Brother, My Sister,* (Toronto:
    Griffin Press Ltd.), p. 65.
4 Ibid., p. 81.
5 Ibid., p. 105.
6 Jean-Pierre de Caussade, *Self-Abandonment to Divine
    Providence* (London: Burns and Oates Ltd.,
    Templegate), p. 58.
7 Mosteller, *My Brother, My Sister,* p. 84.

Further Reading

Muggeridge, Malcolm, *Something Beautiful for God.* London:
    Collins.

11

In Search of Identity

The general message of this book is that we should wake up to the immediate here and now of the natural world in all its wonder. We should see things whole, washed clear of personal feelings. Man's spirit thirsts, the sages say, for the clarity and luminosity of mind in which the feeling of "me" and "mine" loses its importance; for the self-detachment in which the world is accepted without judgment, seen without shadow of need to grasp or possess it; for the stillness and silence of mind in which the numinous and transcendental nature of life is revealed.

But, we may ask, does this mean that man must lose his personality, extinguish himself as a human being? Will he be negated, a person with no proper identity at all? Each mystic makes a different answer to this question but each seems to agree that a man finds himself rather than loses himself when he discovers his true nature and that of the world about him.

Why does he not know it already? Why does he have to make this journey to discover something that was intrinsic to him all the time—like the prince in a story who traveled the world in search of a jewel that he had never noticed to be on his forehead. It is because he is deluded, say most of the mystics, and his basic delusion lies not in himself but in his *image of himself*. When he can stop identifying with this image he can become truly human, a real person, at one with himself.

It certainly seems true that a man's intrinsic identity is often hidden, even to himself, because of the dependence he places on other people's opinion of him. Certainly to Gurdjieff, man is no better than a walking machine until he stops identifying himself with every incident, every reaction, and every thought. Man's true personality begins, he believed, when a man sees himself as having been hitherto unreal, and perhaps the greatest value of Gurdjieff's teaching lies in the emphasis he places on the need to stop behaving like a rat in a cage, jumping at every shadow.

Just as Gurdjieff would say that a man does not even exist in a human way at all until he begins to crystallize his essential nature by withdrawing his dependence on the world about him, so don Juan, too, spoke of unhooking one's projected thoughts and feelings from all that lies outside of oneself. In fact, there is general agreement among the mystics and sages that man must look at both himself and the world afresh if he is to experience reality. Where they differ from each other is in their methods for helping man to accomplish this.

There is an area of agreement between Alan Watts, Krishnamurti, Ramana Maharshi, Martin Buber, and don Juan. In general, they say that man is conditioned from birth to understand himself and the world in certain ways. But really the world is like a Rorschach blot—humans turn it into whatever suits them and this may have little relationship to what it really is. We describe to ourselves what is going on rather than really experiencing it, we know *about* instead of *knowing,* and so we come to live in a dreamworld of ideas and words rather than of reality. Both Alan Watts and Krishnamurti are very clear on this point, but neither give any real ways for breaking through the word barrier, although Alan Watts certainly practiced and advocated various traditional techniques, such as sitting in silent meditation, and chanting mantras. Krishnamurti advocates choiceless awareness so that we can see for ourselves that it is the monkeylike mind with its endless chatter and ideas that is responsible for our delusions—but he does not tell us what we should do when we *do* begin to realize this. Perhaps the best harvest to be gleaned from both is in the stimulation they give to our thoughts and feelings by the lively and lucidly clear understanding of life itself that they convey.

Ramana Maharshi, Buber, don Juan, Merton, and Harding tackle the same problem of man's conditioning from a different angle—that of man's relationship to God (or the Self, or the *nagual,* or the Inmost). Here there is a general agreement that man errs in his estimate of himself—he thinks that he is autonomous and self-powered—whereas, they say, he must find out that he is really neither and that his Unconditioned nature is infinitely greater than his individual self.

Ramana Maharshi offers a difficult but rewarding exercise of following the "I"-thought to its end, when it will be found to be the Infinite Self. "Who am I?" is perhaps the most basic question of all but it is also the one whose answers hold most pitfalls, and some sort of guru seems necessary for his teaching.

Buber employs statements without methods for understanding them, and thus he is not easy to comprehend unless one has already reached his own level of realization. Nevertheless, his statements, although seemingly simple, are so profound as to carry his reader, if willing, a long way toward the truth of his own identity.

Merton, too, offers us more of mysticism than of practical teaching, for his "contemplation" seems to depend on a monk's routine. His great value for us lies in the clarity with which he sees the man-God relationship and the simple but powerful language in which he describes the fruits of contemplation ("the intuitive awakening in which our free and personal reality becomes fully alive to its own existential depths, which open out into the mystery of God").

Harding's method for seeing the difference between man and his Source-Emptiness-Inmost, is an unusual and original technique of literally looking inward and noticing that one can see nothing there. His inference that the nothing is No-thing is his own, but undoubtedly his technique gives a feeling of liberation.

Teilhard de Chardin is less concerned with individual man and his attempts to discover his true identity than with humanity's overall development and future. He does not go in for methods of self-realization. But his observations on man's condition are of great general interest.

Nor does Aldous Huxley really have any methods he can advise us to follow (unless we include mescaline and LSD). He, like most of us, was an explorer and it is just his failures as well as his discoveries which endear him to the reader and also help the fellow explorer to see his own mistakes.

This is where Pak Subuh, Meher Baba, and Maharaj Ji are of less help to us. For Pak Subuh and Maharaj Ji insist that an outside force must enter one before any work can begin, and Meher Baba demands surrender to himself.

There is a great truth about the idea of surrender, particularly the surrender of the latihan, where submission to the will of God begins to order one's life. But one can't help feeling that the act of surrender and its consequent reward should be *earned*; that without the experience of falling and picking himself up, man is not ready to walk. It all seems a bit too easy and slightly unreal. But Pak Subuh's analysis of the structure of man is clear, and very much in accord with other mystics, particularly with Gurdjieff, for he shows man's nature as wholly conditioned except for one thing—his ability to wish to submit to God.

For many people the Maharishi's mantra system demands just about the right amount of effort they can spare from a busy life. He does not set high spiritual targets and, perhaps because of this, there are thousands of people who use his mantra as a therapy. But the healing relaxation may lead on to a deepening of understanding and in some ways the Maharishi may have a better quick answer to man's spiritual problems and needs than many of the other mystics. For, as he points out, it is possible with his mantra to begin to see how thoughts arise and thus to explore the area of one's own identity. His technique is based on tradition but it does not carry the full traditional philosophy which the Buddhists expound. Therefore, it too, like Krishnamurti's choiceless awareness, may leave one on a plateau.

Neither of the Buddhists could be said to do that. They explore the central search for identity with full traditional knowledge behind them, and they assert that man's feeling of himself as a separate entity is erroneous. There is no separation, they say. Form is emptiness and Emptiness is form. Thus form, in all its Suchness, is the way in which we should experience the world. This is a difficult doctrine (although in the end perhaps the most satisfying of all) for most of us to realize. For we are conditioned to the dualistic idea of God and man being separate, even if we don't call him God anymore. But the Buddhists offer us help to understand their point of view in the form of a large number of methods and techniques.

The two occultists, Dion Fortune and Rudolf Steiner, also make use of Buddhist as well as of Hindu techniques, but with very different ends in view. The aim of the great religions is to transcend the ego; to turn man's consciousness towards That which is its Source; and to unite man with the world so sublimely that he sees all things in their wholeness, he is at one with what is, in a way that totally transcends yet also includes every aspect of the "ten thousand things." The aim of occultism at its purest is to learn about and intellectually to understand the great unknown planes of existence beyond man's ordinary consciousness—such as his life before and after death —in order that through this supersensible knowledge he can live an ideal life upon the earth.

The techniques of Hindu and Buddhist Yoga lend themselves to occult practice because they develop the heart and the mind. But the danger of the occult way is that the desire to know rather than to be, to conquer rather than to surrender the self, leads to strange malpractices and to highly inflated egos. The two occultists in this book, however, both had safeguards against the cruder and sillier extremes of magic and have not noticeably fallen into these traps. In fact, Dion Fortune's study of the Qabalah and practice of its ways to mystical realization nearly takes her out of the category of occultism altogether, for the Qabalah itself is a genuinely religious path and any practitioner of it must eventually come to that point of surrender that is the fulcrum of the religious mystic. But she was an ardent believer in the stage-by-stage ascent of the occultist where every symbol can be verified by research and cross-reference, and every condition of the mind can be classified: thus her initial approach was entirely different from that of the mystic.

Rudolf Steiner's safeguard was his love of humanity and his great desire to serve it through the cultivation of his own powers. The final transcendent union of the mystic was of less importance to him than establishing a right understanding of this world, which basically meant seeing its relationship to other, higher worlds. He foresaw a glorious ascension of man's evolving thought and feeling in rather the same way as Teilhard de Chardin envisaged it, and the reader may notice a number of parallels between these two thinkers on the subject of evolution. Steiner, like Fortune, made use of Tantric methods, but his aim was to bring about realization of the many conditions through which the eternal soul of man progresses, rather than to attain union with the Source of all souls.

Mother Theresa, although profoundly Christian, perhaps comes close to Buddhism in her complete adoration of whatever she encounters. She has surrendered herself to God and sees God in all things. Theologically she is far apart from the Buddhists, for to Mother Theresa, God is *in* things whereas to Buddhists he (or Suchness) *is* things. But in practice they are close and the highest Christian and Bodhisattva ideals are very concordant.

Within all the different messages of these sages and mystics lies the injunction to arouse ourselves, to discover who we are, to look at the world around us as though for the first time, and to come into contact with reality. We must break the chains of our conditioned minds and step out into freedom—now. For these chains resemble spider's webs that look as though made of shining steel but break at a touch. The more we hesitate, the thicker the web grows around us. The spider resembles the belief that each one of us is separate from the rest of the world, complete and final within this small self. Nirvana, Heaven, Being-Awareness-Bliss, Liberation, lies in finding out that this is not so.

Index

ARKANA – NEW-AGE BOOKS FOR MIND, BODY AND SPIRIT

With over 150 titles currently in print, Arkana is the leading name in quality new-age books for mind, body and spirit. Arkana encompasses the spirituality of both East and West, ancient and new, in fiction and non-fiction. A vast range of interests is covered, including Psychology and Transformation, Health, Science and Mysticism, Women's Spirituality and Astrology.

If you would like a catalogue of Arkana books, please write to:

Arkana Marketing Department
Penguin Books Ltd
27 Wright's Lane
London W8 5TZ

ARKANA – NEW-AGE BOOKS FOR MIND, BODY AND SPIRIT

A selection of titles already published or in preparation

The Networking Book: People Connecting with People
Jessica Lipnack and Jeffrey Stamps

Networking – forming human connections to link ideas and resources – is the natural form of organization for an era based on information technology. Principally concerned with those networks whose goal is a peaceful yet dynamic future for the world, *The Networking Book* – written by two world-famous experts – profiles hundreds of such organizations worldwide, operating at every level from global telecommunications to word of mouth.

Chinese Massage Therapy: A Handbook of Therapeutic Massage Compiled at the Anhui Medical School Hospital, China
Translated by Hor Ming Lee and Gregory Whincup

There is a growing movement among medical practitioners in China today to mine the treasures of traditional Chinese medicine – acupuncture, herbal medicine and massage therapy. Directly translated from a manual in use in Chinese hospitals, *Chinese Massage Therapy* offers a fresh understanding of this time-tested medical alternative.

Dialogues with Scientists and Sages: The Search for Unity
Renée Weber

In their own words, contemporary scientists and mystics – from the Dalai Lama to Stephen Hawking – share with us their richly diverse views on space, time, matter, energy, life, consciousness, creation and our place in the scheme of things. Through the immediacy of verbatim dialogue, we encounter scientists who endorse mysticism, and those who oppose it; mystics who dismiss science, and those who embrace it.

Zen and the Art of Calligraphy
Omōri Sōgen and Terayama Katsujo

Exploring every element of the relationship between Zen thought and the artistic expression of calligraphy, two long-time practitioners of Zen, calligraphy and swordsmanship show how Zen training provides a proper balance of body and mind, enabling the calligrapher to write more profoundly, freed from distraction or hesitation.

ARKANA – NEW-AGE BOOKS FOR MIND, BODY AND SPIRIT

A selection of titles already published or in preparation

Being Intimate: A Guide to Successful Relationships
John and Kris Amodeo

This invaluable guide aims to enrich one of the most important – yet often problematic – aspects of our lives: intimate relationships and friendships.

'A clear and practical guide to the realization and communication of authentic feelings, and thus an excellent pathway towards lasting intimacy and love' – George Leonard

The Brain Book   Peter Russell

The essential handbook for brain users.

'A fascinating book – for everyone who is able to appreciate the human brain, which, as Russell says, is the most complex and most powerful information processor known to man. It is especially relevant for those who are called upon to read a great deal when time is limited, or who attend lectures or seminars and need to take notes' – *Nursing Times*

The Act of Creation   Arthur Koestler

This second book in Koestler's classic trio of works on the human mind (which opened with *The Sleepwalkers* and concludes with *The Ghost in the Machine*) advances the theory that all creative activities – the conscious and unconscious processes underlying artistic originality, scientific discovery and comic inspiration – share a basic pattern, which Koestler expounds and explores with all his usual clarity and brilliance.

A Psychology With a Soul: Psychosynthesis in Evolutionary Context   Jean Hardy

Psychosynthesis was developed between 1910 and the 1950s by Roberto Assagioli – an Italian psychiatrist who, like Jung, diverged from Freud in search of a more spiritually based understanding of human nature. Jean Hardy's account of this comprehensive approach to self-realization will be of great value to everyone concerned with personal integration and spiritual growth.

ARKANA – NEW-AGE BOOKS FOR MIND, BODY AND SPIRIT

A selection of titles already published or in preparation

Head Off Stress: Beyond the Bottom Line D. E. Harding

Learning to head off stress takes no time at all and is impossible to forget – all it requires is that we dare take a fresh look at ourselves. This infallible and revolutionary guide from the author of *On Having No Head* – whose work C. S. Lewis described as 'highest genius' – shows how.

Shiatzu: Japanese Finger Pressure for Energy, Sexual Vitality and Relief from Tension and Pain
Yukiko Irwin with James Wagenvoord

The product of 4000 years of Oriental medicine and philosophy, Shiatzu is a Japanese variant of the Chinese practice of acupuncture. Fingers, thumbs and palms are applied to the 657 pressure points that the Chinese penetrate with gold and silver needles, aiming to maintain health, increase vitality and promote well-being.

The Magus of Strovolos: The Extraordinary World of a Spiritual Healer Kyriacos C. Markides

This vivid account introduces us to the rich and intricate world of Daskalos, the Magus of Strovolos – a true healer who draws upon a seemingly limitless mixture of esoteric teachings, psychology, reincarnation, demonology, cosmology and mysticism, from both East and West.

'This is a really marvellous book . . . one of the most extraordinary accounts of a "magical" personality since Ouspensky's account of Gurdjieff' – Colin Wilson

Meetings With Remarkable Men G. I. Gurdjieff

All that we know of the early life of Gurdjieff – one of the great spiritual masters of this century – is contained within these colourful and profound tales of adventure. The men who influenced his formative years had no claim to fame in the conventional sense; what made them remarkable was the consuming desire they all shared to understand the deepest mysteries of life.

ARKANA – NEW-AGE BOOKS FOR MIND, BODY AND SPIRIT

A selection of titles already published or in preparation

Weavers of Wisdom: Women Mystics of the Twentieth Century   Anne Bancroft

Throughout history women have sought answers to eternal questions about existence and beyond – yet most gurus, philosophers and religious leaders have been men. Through exploring the teachings of fifteen women mystics – each with her own approach to what she calls 'the truth that goes beyond the ordinary' – Anne Bancroft gives a rare, cohesive and fascinating insight into the diversity of female approaches to mysticism.

Dynamics of the Unconscious: Seminars in Psychological Astrology Volume II   Liz Greene and Howard Sasportas

The authors of *The Development of the Personality* team up again to show how the dynamics of depth psychology interact with your birth chart. They shed new light on the psychology and astrology of aggression and depression – the darker elements of the adult personality that we must confront if we are to grow to find the wisdom within.

The Myth of Eternal Return: Cosmos and History   Mircea Eliade

'A luminous, profound, and extremely stimulating work . . . Eliade's thesis is that ancient man envisaged events not as constituting a linear, progressive history, but simply as so many creative repetitions of primordial archetypes . . . This is an essay which everyone interested in the history of religion and in the mentality of ancient man will have to read. It is difficult to speak too highly of it' – Theodore H. Gaster in *Review of Religion*.

Karma and Destiny in the I Ching   Guy Damian-Knight

This entirely original approach to the *I Ching*, achieved through mathematical rearrangement of the hexagrams, offers a new, more precise tool for self-understanding. Simple to use and yet profound, it gives the ancient Chinese classic a thoroughly contemporary relevance.